Re-engineering and Redefining University Libraries in the Context of Modern Information and Communication Technologies

Re-engineering and Redefining University Libraries in the Context of Modern Information and Communication Technologies

A.T. Francis

Ess Ess Publications
New Delhi

Re-engineering and Redefining University Libraries in the Context of Modern Information and Communication Technologies

ISBN: 978-81-7000-659-6

Rs.1150/-

First Published 2012

Published by:
Ess Ess Publications
4831/24, Ansari Road,
Darya Ganj,
New Delhi-110 002.
INDIA
Phones: 23260807, 41563444
Fax: 41563334
E-mail: info@essessreference.com
www.essessreference.com

Cover Design by *Patch Creative Unit*

Printed and bound in India at Salasar Imaging Systems.

Preface

Information and communication technologies are the tools that underpin the emerging "Knowledge Society". Information being a key component of economic growth and world control, individuals and societies are formulating policies and adopting strategies to implement them for maximizing benefit. Exchange of information or knowledge between people and through networks of people has always taken place. But the ICT has radically changed the magnitude of this exchange, and thus factors such as timeliness of information and information dissemination patterns have become more important than ever.

During the recent several decades, Library and Information Service sector in India is witnessing rapid changes due to various factors such as knowledge explosion and consequent information explosion, developments in computer and communication technologies, Internet and other web related advancements, etc. The three advancements, that is, the processing speed of the computers, digital storage technologies and satellite/ optical fibre based transmission technologies, have totally revolutionized the entire information management scenario.

As information and knowledge are so vital, libraries and institutions that manage these resources are indeed invaluable. So, the Library and Information Centres have a key role in the acquisition, processing, preservation and dissemination of information and knowledge. In order to cope up with this situation, drastic measures were taken by the university libraries also. Website being a powerful instrument that can be deployed for providing information services universally, libraries are taking all efforts to utilize this technology effectively.

Modern libraries are providing services based on different types of documents such as manuscripts, printed, digital, etc. At the same time, acquisition, access, process, service etc. of these resources have become complicated now than ever before. The ICT made instrumental to extend libraries beyond the physical walls of a building and providing assistance in navigating and analyzing tremendous amounts of knowledge with a variety of digital tools. Thus, modern libraries are increasingly being re-defined as places to get unrestricted access to information in many formats and from many sources.

A study on the management and ICT application of university libraries identified that even though the information resources are flooding world over and several technologies have emerged to manage the situation for providing effective services to its clientele, most of the university libraries were unable to exploit these technologies at maximum level. Though the libraries have automated many of their functions, wide gap prevails between the possible services and provided services. There are many good examples world over in the application of ICTs in libraries for the maximization of services and many such libraries have adopted the principles of re-engineering and re-defining as a management strategy. This book provides a detailed account on how effectively the University Libraries in India adopted the modern ICTs.

All the libraries could exploit only a very few

possibilities of modern ICTs and hence they could not achieve effective Universal Bibliographic Control and desired efficiency and effectiveness in services. Functional effectiveness in acquisition, access and process of information resources in various formats, development and maintenance of OPAC and WebOPAC, digital document delivery to remote users, Web based clearing of library counter services and resources, development of full-text databases, digital libraries and institutional repositories, consortia based operations for e-journals and databases, user education and information literacy, professional development with stress on ICTs, network administration and website maintenance, marketing of information, etc. are major areas need special attention to improve the situation. Finance, knowledge level on ICTs among library staff, professional dynamism and leadership, vision and support of the administrators and policy makers, prevailing educational set up and social environment, etc. are some of the major hurdles in reaping the maximum possibilities of ICTs by the university libraries. The suitability of the principles of Business Process Re-engineering to re-structure and re-define the operations and service system of the libraries is discussed. As most of the conventional departments or divisions prevailing in the university libraries are functioning as watertight compartments and their existing management system are more rigid to adopt the principles of change management, a thorough re-structuring of the divisions is essential. Consortia based activities and pooling and sharing of information resources is also needed to meet the varied needs of the users in the main campuses and off campuses of the universities, affiliated colleges and remote stations. A uniform staff policy similar to that prevailing in research organizations in India is required for the entire country. The need for restructuring of LIS education, integrated and planned development of the school, college, research and public library systems, etc. are also discussed as a means for reaping maximum benefits of the modern ICTs.

A.T. Francis

Acknowledgements

With immense pleasure, I take this opportunity to place on record my heartfelt gratitude and indebtedness to Dr. S. Humayoon Kabir, Associate Professor, Department of Library and Information Science, University of Kerala and former Assistant Librarian, Cochin University of Science and Technology for his scholarly guidance, continuous inspiration and wholehearted support for the successful completion of this book.

I wish to place my deep sense of gratitude to Dr. V.P.N. Nampoori, Dean Faculty of Technology and Dr. K.V. Pramod, Head, Department of Computer Applciations, Cochin University of Science and Technology for their fervent interest, valuable suggestions and necessary support to enrich this work.

The encouragement and direction received from Dr. A.M. Michael and Dr. K.V. Peter, former Vice Chancellors of KAU, Dr. R. Raman Nair, Mrs. M.C. Lalitha and Mr. C. Abdul Razak, former University Librarians of KAU and my former colleague scientists in the Library of the Naval Physical and Oceanographic Laboratory (NPOL), DRDO, Kochi are hereby gratefully remembered.

I owe my heartfelt thanks and gratitude to my wife,

family members and friends for their inspiration, encouragement and co-operation all through the completion of this book. Above all, I dedicate the entire book to my mother who is now in heaven.

A.T. Francis

Contents

List of Abbreviations

AACR	Anglo American Cataloguing Rules
AAIM	Association for Automatic Identification and Mobility
AASL	American Association of School Librarians
AASLAECT	American Association of School Librarians and Association for Educational Communications and Technology
ACRL	Association of College and Research Libraries
AFI	Application Family Identifier
AI	Artificial Intelligence
AICTE	All India Council for Technical Education
AIU	Association of Indian Universities
ALA	American Library Association
ALIA	Australian Library and Information Association
A-LIEP	Asia-Pacific Conference on Library and Information Education and Practice
ASIS	American Society for Information Science
BCI	Bar Council of India
BD	Blu Ray Disc or Blue Ray Disc

BIS	Bureau of Indian Standards
BPMS	Business Process Management System
BPR	Business Process Re-engineering
CABE	Central Advisory Board of Education
CALIBER	Convention on Automation of Libraries in Education and Research Institutions
CCH	Central Council of Homeopathy
CCIM	Central Council of Indian Medicine
CD	Compact Disc
CD-ROM	Compact Disc – Read Only Memory
CD-RW	Compact Disc – Re-Writable
CeRA	Consortium for e-Resources in Agriculture, India
CLIS	Centre for Library and Information Science, KAU
COA	The Council of Architecture
CONSER	Cooperative ONline SERials (Earlier the name was CONversion of SERials)
CPD	Continuous Professional Development
CPFR	Collaborative Planning, Forecasting and Replenishment
CRISP	Customer Resolution and Information Services Project
CRM	Customer Relationship Management
CSCW	Computer Supported Cooperative Work
CSF	Critical Success Factors
CSIC	Consejo Superior de Investigaciones Científicas, Spain
CSIR	Council of Scientific and Industrial Research
CUSAT	Cochin University of Science and Technology

DAE	Department of Atomic Energy
DAM	Digital Asset Management
DBMS	Database Management System
DCI	Dental Council of India
DDS	Document Delivery Services
DEC	Distance Education Council
DELNET	Developing Library Network
DFSS	Design For Six Sigma
DL	Digital Library
DLP	Digital Light Projector
DOI	Digital Opportunity Index
DPMO	Defects Per Million Opportunities
DRDO	Defence Research and Development Organisation
DRTC	Documentation Research and Training Centre
DSIR	Department of Scientific and Industrial Research
DSL	Digital Subscribe Lines
DVB	Digital Video Broadcasting Group
DVD	Digital Video Disc or Digital Versatile Disc
EAN-UCC	European Article Numbering – Uniform Code Council
ECL	Educational Community License
ELiMS	Electronic Library Management System
EPA	Environmental Protection Agency
ERP	Enterprise Resource Planning
ETD	Electronic Theses and Dissertations
FAIFE	Freedom of Information Laws and Social Responsibilities

FAO	Food and Agricultural Organization
FEDORA	Flexible Extensible Digital Object Repository Architecture
FID	International Federation for Information and Documentation
FRAD	Functional Requirements for Authority Data
FRBR	Functional Requirements for Bibliographic Records
FRPAA	Federal Research Public Access Act
FTP	File Transfer Protocol
GE	General Electric
GEC	General Education Courses
HP	Hewlett Packard
HRM	Human Resource Management
HTML	HyperText Markup Language
HTTP	HyperText Transfer Protocol
IAMAI	Internet And Mobile Association of India
IARIS	Integrated Agricultural and Rural Information System
IASLIC	Indian Association of Special Libraries and Information Centres
ICADL	International Conference of Asian Digital Libraries
ICAR	Indian Council of Agriculture Research
ICMR	Indian Council of Medical Research
ICSD	International Conference on Semantic Web and Digital Libraries
ICSSR	Indian Council of Social Science Research
ICT	Information and Communication Technologies

ICT-OI	Information and Communication Technologies-Opportunity Index
IFLA	International Federation of Library Associations and Institutions
IIIT	Indian Institute of Information Technology
IIM	Indian Institute of Management
IISc	Indian Institute of Science
IISD	International Institute for Sustainable Development
IIT	Indian Institute of Technology
ILP	Information Literacy Programmes
ILS	Information Literacy Skills
IM	Instant Messaging
IMC	Indian Medical Council
INB	Indian National Bibliography
INC	Indian Nursing Council
INDEST	Indian National Digital Library in Science and Technology
INFLIBNET	Information and Library Network Centre
INLIS	Integrated National Library and Information System
INSDOC	Indian National Scientific Documentation Centre (Now NISCAIR)
IP	Internet Protocol
IPv6	Internet Protocol Version 6
IR	Institutional Repository
IS	Information Society
ISBN	International Standard Book Number
ISD	Information Services Division
ISI	Indian Statistical Institute

ISO	International Standards Organization
ISRO	Indian Space Research Organisation
ISSD	Information Society and Sustainable Development
IT	Information Technology
ITU	International Telecommunication Union
JISC	Joint Information Systems Committee
JIT	Just In Time
KALA	Kerala Agricultural Library Association, Thrissur, India
KAM	Knowledge Access Management
KAU	Kerala Agricultural University, Thrissur
KAULIS	Kerala Agricultural University Library and Information System
KLA	Kerala Library Association
KM	Knowledge Management
KSCSTE	Kerala State Council for Science, Technology and Environment
KU	Kannur University, Kannur
LAN	Local Area Network
LCD	Liquid Crystal Display
LCI	Library Council of India
LIS	Library and Information Science
MCI	Medical Council of India
METS	Metadata Encoding and Transmission Standard
MGU	Mahatma Gandhi University, Kottayam
MIT	Massachusetts Institute of Technology
MOD	Media on Demand
MPEG	Moving Pictures Expert Group

NAAC	National Assessment and Accreditation Council
NAIP	National Agricultural Innovation Programme
NAL	National Agricultural Library, USA
NASA	National Aerospace and Space Administration
NASSDOC	National Social Science Documentation Centre
NATP	National Agricultural Technology Programme
NCERT	National Council of Education Research and Training
NCSI	National Centre for Science Information
NCTE	National Council for Teacher Education
NGO	Non Governmental Organizations
NIH	National Institute of Health, USA
NISCAIR	National Institute of Science Communication and Information Resources (Formerly INSDOC)
NIST	National Institute of Standards and Technology, USA
NKC	National Knowledge Commission, India
NLB	National Library Board of Singapore
NPTEL	National Programme on Technology Enhanced Learning
NSF	National Science Foundation, USA
OA	Open Access
OAI	Open Archive Initiative
OAI-PMH	Open Archives Initiative Protocol for Metadata Harvesting

OCLC	Online Computer Library Centre
OCR	Optical Character Recognition
OD	Organization Development
OFC	Optical Fibre Cable
OI	Opportunity Index
OPAC	On-line Public Access Catalogue
OPAL	Online Programmes for All Libraries
OSM	Open Source Movement
OSS	Open Source Software
PCI	Pharmacy Council of India
PDP	Professional Development Programme
PRIMO	Peer Reviewed Instructional Materials Online
RCI	Rehabilitation Council of India
RDA	Resource Description and Access
RFID	Radio Frequency Identification
RLG	Research Libraries Group
RLIN	Research Libraries Information Network
ROI	Return of Investment
RSS	Really Simple Syndication or Rich Sites Summary or RDF Site Summary or Real-time Simple Syndication
RTSP	Real-Time Streaming Protocol
SAFARI	Skills in Accessing, Finding, and Reviewing Information
SALIS	Society for the Advancement of Library and Information Science, Chennai, India
SCM	Supply Chain Management
SIS	Society for Information Science, India
SLA	Special Libraries Association

SM	Streaming Media
SM	Synchronous Messaging
SSUS	Sree Sankaracharya University of Sanskrit, Kalady, Ernakulam
TA	Transactional Analysis
TQM	Total Quality Management
TRAI	Telecom Regulatory Authority of India
UAP	Universal Availability of Publications Programme of IFLA
UB	University of Botswana
UBC	Universal Bibliographical Control
UBL	University of Botswana Library
UGC	University Grants Commission
UH	University of Houston
UIUC	University of Illinois at Urbana-Champaign
UNCTAD	United Nations Conference on Trade and Development
UNDP	United Nations Development Programme
UNESCO	United Nations Educational, Scientific and Cultural Organisation
UN-GAID	United Nations Global Alliance for Information and Communication Technologies
UNLV	Libraries of the University of Nevada, Las Vegas
UOC	University of Calicut, Malappuram
UOK	University of Kerala, Thiruvananthapuram
USNP	United States Newspaper Program
UW	University of Washington
VCI	Veterinary Council of India
VDSL	Very High Bit Rate Digital Subscriber Line

VPN	Virtual Private Network
VPT	Village Public Telephones
V-SAT	Very Small Aperture Terminal
WAN	Wide Area Network
WDLP	World Digital Library Project
WebCT	Web Course Tools
WEI	World Education Indicators
WiFi	Wireless Fidelity
WiMax	Worldwide Interoperability for Microwave Access (Telecommunications technology that provides wireless data over long distances in a variety of ways)
WLL	Wireless in Local Loop
WSIS	World Summit on the Information Society
WWW	World Wide Web
XHTML	Extensible Hypertext Markup Language
XML	Extensible Markup Language
YZU	Yuan Ze University

1
Introduction

Information and communication technologies are the tools that underpin the emerging "Information Society" or "Knowledge Society". It can be described as a society in which the creation, distribution, and manipulation of information and knowledge have become the most significant economic and cultural activity. Information exchange between people and through networks of people has always taken place. But the Information and Communication Technologies (ICT) - enablement of information exchange has radically changed the magnitude of this exchange, and thus factors such as timeliness of information and information dissemination patterns have become more important than ever.

ICT, like other tools, are not essentially or inherently good, or bad. They can, however, have positive as well as negative effects on development. This dual nature of ICTs, and the increased reliance on knowledge and information in general, have put the intersection of information society and sustainable development at the forefront of national policy-making. (Willard and Andjelkovic, 2005).

Library and Information Centres have a key role in the acquisition, processing, preservation and dissemination of information and knowledge. In conventional meaning, library is a collection of books used for reading or study, or the building or room in which such a collection is kept. Libraries collect, stock, process, organize, disseminate and distribute information/ knowledge. Since knowledge and information are so vital for all round human development, libraries and institutions that handle and manage information and knowledge are indeed invaluable. From their historical beginnings as places to keep the business, legal, historical, and religious records of a civilization, libraries have emerged since the middle of the 20th century as a far-reaching body of information resources and services that do not even require a building.

A library is a public institution or establishment charged with the care of a collection of books, the duty of making them accessible to those who require the use of them and the task of converting every person in its neighbourhood into a habitual library goer and reader of books (Ranganathan, 1940). In his book, Five Laws of Library Science, Ranganathan (1957a) observed on the functioning of libraries as follows: "Even those working in the same sector did not show much evidence of team work. There was no evidence of an overall view. All these factors tended to hide the common point of emergence of the trends in the different sectors. Consequently, what could be seen was only an aggregate diverse practice without an integral relation. It looked as if future developments were totally unpredictable. It all appeared to be a matter of rule of thumb, and severely empirical". This observation is relevant also to most of the libraries in India. In the era of modern ICT also, the management style of our libraries need thorough modification to fulfill the vision of Dr. S.R. Ranganathan. That is, our libraries should be able to convert the potential users into actual users by appropriate management.

In the traditional sense of the word, a library is a collection of books and periodicals. It can refer to an individual's *private collection*, but more often it is a large collection that is funded and maintained by a *city* or *institution*. This collection is often used by people who choose not to – or cannot afford to – purchase an extensive collection by them. In the modern context, the term 'book' refers to information sources and documents of different types such as printed, handwritten, engraved materials and digital such as books, microfilms, photographs, gramophone records, tape records, CDs, DVDs, BDs, Websites, online documents etc.

However, with the invention of media other than books for storing information, many libraries are now also repositories and access points for *maps*, *prints* or other *artwork*, *microfilm*, *microfiche*, *audio tapes*, *CDs*, *video tapes* and *DVDs*, and provide public facilities to access *CD-ROM* and subscription databases and the *Internet*. Thus, modern libraries are increasingly being re-defined as places to get unrestricted access to *information* in many formats and from many sources. The term 'library' has itself acquired a secondary meaning: "a collection of useful material for common use", and in this sense it is used in fields such as *computer science*, *mathematics* and *statistics*, *electronics* and *biology*.

More recently, libraries are understood as extending beyond the physical walls of a building, providing assistance in navigating and analyzing tremendous amounts of knowledge with a variety of digital tools. A modern library is regarded as a service institution. Its aim is to enable the users to make available and accessible the required information and facilitate the most effective use of such resources.

For the growth and development of a modern society, communication of knowledge has become increasingly important. The knowledge is becoming increasingly complex and the same is true about the means of communication of knowledge. (Krishan Kumar, 2000).

Rapid developments in computers, telecommunications, and other technologies have made it possible to store and retrieve information in many different forms and from any place with a computer and a telephone connection. The terms digital library and virtual library have begun to be used to refer to the vast collections of information to which people gain access over the Internet, cable television, or some other type of remote electronic connection. (Encyclopaedia Britanica, 2007).

Creative learning provides a sound and clear grasp of fundamentals, which is an asset and starting point for a creative individual. Attempting an innovation requires knowledge of inter-disciplinary ideas, and an up-to-date knowledge of that which has already been invented (Khare, 1976). The real goal of the libraries and librarians is to make all the published works of humankind accessible to everyone, no matter where they are in the world. It may be difficult for a student or a researcher to access to a library, but access to information is a key ingredient to education and an open society. Because the creation and dissemination of knowledge is important for building societies that grow and prosper. Many in the library community agree that universal access to all knowledge could stand as one of the greatest achievements of humankind (Kahle, 2005).

1.1 HIGHER EDUCATION IN INDIA

The higher education has always occupied a place of prominence in Indian history. In ancient times, Nalanda, Taxila and Vikramsila universities were renowned seats of higher learning, attracting students not only from all over the country but from far off countries like Korea,

China, Burma (now Myanmar), Ceylon (now Sri Lanka), Tibet and Nepal. Today, India manages one of the largest higher education systems in the world.

The present system of higher education dates back to Mountstuart Elphinstone's minutes of 1823, which stressed on the need for establishing schools for teaching English and the European sciences. Later, Lord Macaulay, in his minutes of 1835, advocated "efforts to make natives of the country thoroughly good English scholars". Sir Charles Wood's Dispatch of 1854, famously known as the 'Magna Carta of English Education in India', recommended creating a properly articulated scheme of education from the primary school to the university. It sought to encourage indigenous education and planned the formulation of a coherent policy of education. Subsequently, the universities of Calcutta, Bombay and Madras were set up in 1857, followed by the University of Allahabad in 1887.

The Inter-University Board (later known as the Association of Indian Universities) was established in 1925 to promote university activities, by sharing information and cooperation in the field of education, culture, sports and allied areas.

The first attempt to formulate a national system of education in India came in 1944, with the Report of the Central Advisory Board of Education on Post War Educational Development in India, also known as the Sargeant Report. It recommended the formation of a University Grants Committee, which was formed in 1945 to oversee the work of the three Central Universities. In 1947, the Committee was entrusted with the responsibility of dealing with all the then existing Universities.

Soon after Independence, the University Education Commission was set up in 1948 under the Chairmanship of Dr. S Radhakrishnan "to report on Indian university education and suggest improvements and extensions that might be desirable to suit the present and future needs and aspirations of the country". It recommended that the University Grants Committee be reconstituted on the general model of the University Grants Commission of the United Kingdom with a full-time Chairman and other members to be appointed from amongst educationists of repute.

Central Government is responsible for major policy relating to higher education in the country. It provides grants to the UGC and establishes central universities in the country. The Central Government is also responsible for declaration of Educational Institutions as 'Deemed to be University' on the recommendation of the UGC. State Governments are responsible for establishment of State Universities and colleges, and provide plan grants for their development and non-plan grants for their maintenance.

The coordination and cooperation between the Union and the States is brought about in the field of education through the Central Advisory Board of Education (CABE). Special Constitutional responsibility gives exclusive Legislative Power to the Central Government for co-ordination and determination of standards in Institutions of higher education or research and scientific and technical institutions.

1.2 HIGHER EDUCATION AND UNIVERSITY LIBRARIES

Education aims at the exchange of knowledge, the inculcation of values and the imparting of vocational skills. Education may be formal or informal. Higher education is education provided by universities and other collegial institutions that award *academic degrees*, such as *career colleges*. Post-secondary or tertiary education, also referred to as third-stage, third level education, or higher education, is the non-compulsory educational level following the completion of a school providing a *secondary education*, such as a *high school*, *secondary school*, etc. Tertiary education is normally taken to include *undergraduate* and *postgraduate education*, as well as *vocational education and training*. *Colleges* and *universities* are the main institutions that provide tertiary education. Higher education includes teaching, research and social services activities of universities, and within the realm of teaching, it includes both the *undergraduate* level and postgraduate level. In most developed countries a high proportion of the population (up to 50%) now enters higher education at some time in their lives. Higher education is therefore very important to national *economies*, both as a significant industry in its own right, and as a source of trained and educated personnel for the rest of the economy.

Modern universities make significant contributions in the areas of social sciences, humanities and science and technology. They are supposed to perform the functions such as teaching, research, extension, etc. At the earlier stages of education like the school, reading books and the process of imbibing knowledge should be done to supplement the class room teaching. At later stages, particularly in colleges and universities, the focal point of learning should gradually shift from the class room to the library. University Library or Library system established, administered, and funded by a university to meet the information, research, and curriculum needs of its students, faculty, and staff. Some large universities maintain separate undergraduate and graduate libraries. Large university libraries with comprehensive collections are considered research libraries.

A university library is a part of a university set-up. Therefore, it exists to serve the objectives of its parent organisation. In other words, a university library should aim at the advancement of the functions of its university.

It should reflect the character of the university. According to Wilson and Tauber (1956), "the well-administered university library directs its activities towards the fulfillment of these functions. By accumulating and organising books, manuscripts, journals, and other materials, the university library serves as an active force in the teaching, research and extension programmes of the university. Through direct assistance to the members of the faculty and research staff and through the service of members of the library staff as instructional officers, the university library participates in the interpretive function of the university. Through its many bibliographical and other reference services, the library aids individuals of the instructional and research staff who are engaged in the preparation of materials for publication".

The library, which is still a combination of the past (print collections) and the present (new information technologies), must be viewed with a new perspective and understanding if it is to fulfill its potential in adding value to the advancement of the institution's academic mission and in moving with that institution into the future. Rather than threatening the traditional concept of the library, the integration of new information technology has actually become the catalyst that transforms the library into a more vital and critical intellectual center of life at colleges and universities today. ... The library is the only centralized location where new and emerging information technologies can be combined with traditional knowledge resources in a user-focused, service-rich environment that supports today's social and educational patterns of learning, teaching, and research. ... The academic library as place holds a unique position on campus. No other building can so symbolically and physically represent the academic heart of an institution. If the library is to remain a dynamic life force, however, it must support the academic community in several new ways. Its space must flexibly accommodate evolving information technologies and their usage as well as become a "laboratory" for new ways of teaching and learning in a wired or wire-less environment. At the same time, the library, by its architectural expression and sitting, must continue to reflect the unique legacy and traditions of the institution of which it is part. It must include flexible spaces that "learn" as well as traditional reading rooms that inspire scholarship. By embracing these distinct functions, the library as a place can enhance the excitement and adventure of the academic experience, foster a sense of community, and advance the institution into the future. The library of the future remains irreplaceable (Freeman, 2005). Successful library planning will involve collaboration among faculty, academic officers, librarians, and architects. It will be rooted in how students learn, how faculty members teach, and how teaching and learning patterns will change over time. Planning will be based on what students are actually doing in the library, on what they really need in a learning environment, and on changes in scholarly communication (Demas, 2005).

1.3 EDUCATION COMMISSIONS AND LIBRARIES

After the independence of India, several efforts were made to improve the standard of higher education, particularly university education. The Government of India appointed the University Education Commission in 1948 with Dr. S. Radhakrishnan as Chairman. The Commission enquired into the existing conditions of university education and made important recommendations to bring it to the level of universities abroad. The Commission stressed the importance of university libraries and their services to the university community in the following statement (India. University Education Commission, 1948-49):

"The Library is the heart of all the University's work; so as regards its research work, and indirectly as regards its educational work, which derives its life from research work. Scientific research needs a library as well as its laboratories, while humanistic research the library is both library and laboratory in one."

The University Grants Commission (UGC) has constituted a Library Committee, headed by Dr. S.R. Ranganathan, in 1957 to advice on the matters relating to the proper functioning and management of college and university libraries in the country. The Committee made suitable recommendations on: Grants to libraries; book purchase; reading habits; documentation work; departmental libraries; library personnel; library buildings and furniture. (UGC, 1959). The UGC accepted most of the recommendations of this committee and provided liberal grants to universities for strengthening their libraries. However, many universities did not implement some of the recommendations and standards forwarded by the Committee. The Education Commission, 1964-66, chaired by Dr. D.S. Kothari remarked: "with ever increase in the enrolment in the universities and colleges, the demand for library service has been mounting. Unlike in the past, the library staff has now to cater to the diverse needs of undergraduates, post graduates and research scholars". (India. Education Commission, 1964-66).

The Indian Council of Agricultural Research (ICAR) has appointed a Committee in 1956, consisting of Dr. Ralph R. Shaw and Dr. D.B. Krishna Rao, to conduct a study on library and bibliographic services for agricultural teaching and research in India. Though the Committee has made several recommendations (Shaw and Krishna Rao, 1957), any of these were not implemented because of lack of proper administrative support. In 1960, the Government of India appointed a Committee headed by Dr. Ralph W. Cummings of the Rockfeller Foundation to advise the State Governments on the legislation for the establishment of agricultural universities. On the basis of the recommendations made by this Committee, ICAR prepared a Model Act, which could be adopted by the newly developing agricultural universities (India. Cummings Committee, 1962). This was a significant event in the development of these universities.

In 1967, the ICAR appointed the Indo-American Agricultural Library Survey and Study Team, chaired by Dorothy Parker to make recommendations for the improvement of the libraries of ICAR Institutes and agricultural universities. The Team submitted 69 recommendations for the development of the libraries (ICAR. Indo-American Agricultural Library Survey and Study Team, 1969). The ICAR got these recommendations reviewed by a Committee known as the Ramaiah Committee. But, unfortunately, many recommendations of vital importance were either not accepted or were modified by this Reviewing Committee. The final recommendations of the Committee caused a setback to the pace of development of agricultural libraries in India (Prasher, 1991). Several other studies and recommendations were also made on the university libraries in India. Though the studies and recommendations could revamp the library and information services in the universities and colleges in the country, much more improvement and thorough reorganization is needed to suit the system to the present situation.

1.4 UNIVERSITY GRANTS COMISSION AND PROFESSIONAL COUNCILS

As recommended by the University Education Commission, the University Grants Commission was constituted in 1953 and it was made as a statutory body of the Government of India in 1956 through an Act of Parliament. The UGC has the unique distinction of being the only grant-giving agency in the country which has been vested with two responsibilities: that of providing funds and that of coordination, determination and maintenance of standards in institutions of higher education. It is the body that provides recognition for universities in India. (India. Department of Higher Education, 2006). Professional Councils are responsible for recognition of courses, promotion of professional institutions and providing grants to undergraduate programmes and various awards. The statutory professional councils functioning in the country are:

i. All India Council for Technical Education (AICTE)
ii. Distance Education Council (DEC)
iii. Indian Council for Agriculture Research (ICAR)
iv. Bar Council of India (BCI)
v. National Council for Teacher Education (NCTE)
vi. Rehabilitation Council of India (RCI)
vii. Medical Council of India (MCI)
viii. Pharmacy Council of India (PCI)
ix. Indian Nursing Council (INC)
x. Dental Council of India (DCI)
xi. Central Council of Homeopathy (CCH)
xii. Central Council of Indian Medicine (CCIM)
xiii. Veterinary Council of India (VCI)
xiv. The Council of Architecture (COA)

1.5 ROLE OF UNIVERSITIES ON LIBRARIES

Well-known educationists agree that teaching in a university is a cooperative endevour. Books and other information documents are tools which help teachers to teach and students to learn. For research, control and access of related information is essential. The role of library in a university aimed at realising the educational and research goals of the university. It is not merely to provide stimulus to reading by procuring materials for study and research, by introducing open access systems, by providing long hours of open, by organising the library resources in a systematic way, but, it should feed the intellect of the student, encourage the research programmes (Lazarus, 1979). The importance of University Libraries has been recognised by the Radhakrishnan Commission. It asserted libraries as the heart of all University work and recommended to earmark 6.25 percent of the total university expenditure for the purchase of books, journals, etc. As a library is the heart of a university, naturally the aim of university education should be the aim of a University Library. The aims as defined by Radhakrishnan Commission are the "dissemination of learning, search for new knowledge, unceasing effort to plumb the meaning of life, provision for professional education to satisfy the occupational needs of our society and to find its guiding principle in the aims of the social order for which it proposes, in the nature of the civilization it hopes to build" (India. University Education Commission, 1948-49).

1.6 INFORMATION AND COMMUNICATION TECHNOLOGIES

Several decades back, Dr. S.R. Ranganathan (1956) highlighted the necessity of mechanization of library routine as follows. "Perhaps, the most over-worked sector in the mechanization of library routine is that the literature search. The Laws of Library Science demand that every reader should be supplied with all his documents, exactly, exhaustively, and expeditiously. This is the demand of first Four Laws. But, the Fifth Law puts a hurdle in the way. When the number of documents – particularly micro – documents – increases beyond a certain measure, the fulfillment of the other Laws becomes difficult". Ranganathan's Five Laws of Library Science serve as guiding principles for assessing the usefulness of IT in library and information services (Kaur, 2000). Information and Communication Technologies deal with the use of electronic computers, computer software and communication systems to convert, store, protect process, transmit, and retrieve information. ICT in education can be understood as the application of digital technology to all aspects of teaching and learning. The growth of use of ICT and its tools in the field of education has seen tremendous growth in the recent past. Technology has entered the classroom in a big way, to become part of a teaching learning process.

ICT is a broad subject concerned with technology and other aspects of managing and processing information, especially in large organisations. ICT can be defined as the application of computers and other technologies to the acquisition, organization, storage, retrieval and dissemination of information. It is used as a generic term for a group of electronic and digital technologies such as computer technologies, communication technologies, etc.

According to the United Nations Development Programme (UNDP): 'ICTs are basically information-handling tools- a varied set of goods, applications and services that are used to produce, store, process, distribute and exchange information". They include the 'old' ICTs of radio, television and telephone, and the 'new' ICTs of computers, satellite and wireless technology and the

Internet. These different tools are now able to work together, and combine to form our 'networked world' – a massive infrastructure of interconnected telephone services, standardized computing hardware, the internet, radio and television, which reaches into every corner of the globe'. The older and more familiar ICTs are referred to under the collective heading of "analogue media" while the newer computer and Internet based technologies are called the "digital media". Revolutions in information and communication technologies have reduced national boundaries to meaningless lines drawn on maps. And in the new scenarios, education has been identified as one of the major services, which need to be opened up for free flow of trade between countries (Reddi, 2006).

As stressed by the World Summit on the Information Society (WSIS) held during 2005, information and communication technology must be effectively integrated into development activities if the internationally agreed development goals, including the Millennium Development Goals, are to be achieved within the agreed time frame (UN-GIAD, 2006).

The WSIS envisaged an Information Society for all and put forwarded some Key Principles to achieve that goal. Amongst these, ICT has a prominent role. The summit resolved to ensure that everyone should benefit from the opportunities offered by ICTs. According to WSIS, in order to meet these challenges, all stakeholders should work together to: improve access to information and communication infrastructure and technologies as well as to information and knowledge; build capacity; increase confidence and security in the use of ICTs; create an enabling environment at all levels; develop and widen ICT applications; foster and respect cultural diversity; recognize the role of the media; address the ethical dimensions of the Information Society; and encourage international and regional cooperation. It identified the above key principles for building an inclusive Information Society. The summit declared the information and communication infrastructure as an essential foundation for an inclusive Information Society. The WSIS document further described as follows:

"Connectivity is a central enabling agent in building the Information Society. Universal, ubiquitous, equitable and affordable access to ICT infrastructure and services constitutes one of the challenges of the Information Society and should be an objective of all stakeholders involved in building it. Connectivity also involves access to energy and postal services, which should be assured in conformity with the domestic legislation of each country. A well-developed information and communication network infrastructure and applications, adapted to regional, national and local conditions, easily-accessible and affordable, and making greater use of broadband and other innovative technologies where possible, can accelerate the social and economic progress of countries, and the well-being of all individuals, communities and peoples.

Policies that create a favourable climate for stability, predictability and fair competition at all levels should be developed and implemented in a manner that not only attracts more private investment for ICT infrastructure development but also enables universal service obligations to be met in areas where traditional market conditions fail to work. In disadvantaged areas, the establishment of ICT public access points in places such as post offices, schools, libraries and archives, can provide effective means for ensuring universal access to the infrastructure and services of the Information Society.

Access to information and knowledge: The ability for all to access and contribute information, ideas and knowledge is essential in an inclusive Information Society.

The sharing and strengthening of global knowledge for development can be enhanced by removing barriers to equitable access to information for economic, social, political, health, cultural, educational, and scientific activities and by facilitating access to public domain information, including by universal design and the use of assistive technologies.

A rich public domain is an essential element for the growth of the Information Society, creating multiple benefits such as an educated public, new jobs, innovation, business opportunities, and the advancement of sciences. Information in the public domain should be easily accessible to support the Information Society, and protected from misappropriation. Public institutions such as libraries and archives, museums, cultural collections and other community-based access points should be strengthened so as to promote the preservation of documentary records and free and equitable access to information.

Access to information and knowledge can be promoted by increasing awareness among all stakeholders of the possibilities offered by different software models, including proprietary, open-source and free software, in order to increase competition, access by users, diversity of choice, and to enable all users to develop solutions which best meet their requirements. Affordable access to software should be considered as an important component of a truly inclusive Information Society. We strive to promote universal access with equal opportunities for all scientific knowledge and the creation and dissemination of scientific and technical information, including open access initiatives for scientific publishing" (WSIS, 2005).

A summary of the 2007 ICT-OI (Opportunity Index) results showed that significant progress has been made across almost all economies and all areas of the telecommunication/ICT sector since the beginning of this century. At the same time, major differences remain. The study highlighted that the digital divide, which is understood as the relative difference in ICT Opportunity levels among economies and groups, needs to be seen in perspective and will show different results, depending on which economies or groups are being compared. The ICT-OI highlights that between 2001-2005 the divide increased between those economies that already have very high ICT levels and the rest of the world. It decreased between the *medium* group and the *low* group, indicating that countries with low levels of somewhat been able to catch up and reduce the divide compared to countries in the *medium* level. An indicator-centric analysis suggests that the majority of countries are lagging behind in terms of broadband uptake and the difference in broadband penetration between economies with *high* ICT-OI levels and the rest of the world is significant and greater than for any other indicator. For policy makers, this finding suggests that more efforts need to be undertaken to integrate and strengthen broadband policies and strategies (ITU and UNCTAD, 2007). The tables 2.3.2 and 2.3.3 show the level of use of ICT and Internet in different types of economies.

Key Trends in the development of ICTs

During the marching of world economies towards information societies, we could see the following trend in the development of ICTs:

1. Cutting the cord : The DOI shows that fixed lines in homes are declining, mainly in response to the rise of mobile communications. This trend makes it likely that countries will never achieve 100 per cent fixed household penetration. In India also the phenomenon of abandoning the fixed lines for Wireless in Local Loop (WLL) or Cellular phones has happened.

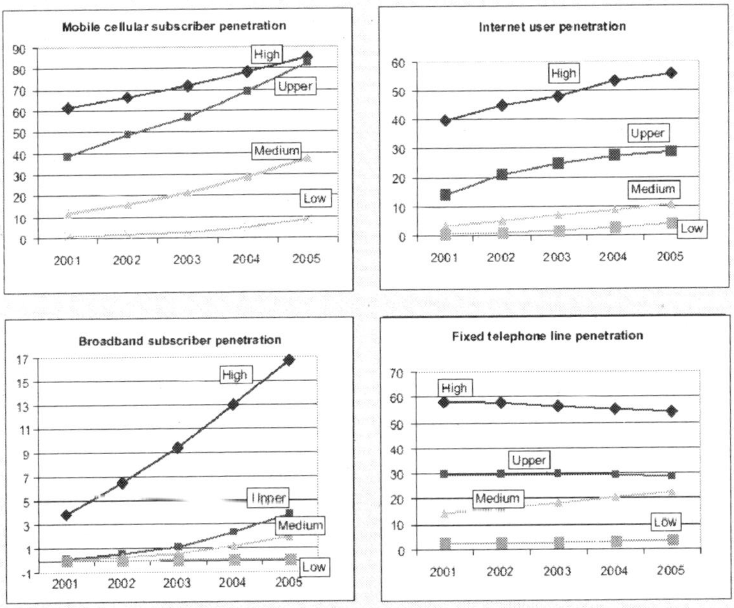

Source: ITU

Fig. 1.6.1. 2001-2005 Penetration rates for mobile cellular subscribers, fixed telephone lines, internet users and broadband subscribers, by ICT-OI category

2. Getting connected to the Internet : It is common practice that having bought a computer, most households would then want to connect it to the Internet. In developed economies, access to the Internet is more likely to be from home than from the workplace, with high household Internet and PC penetrations in all high-DOI economies. It is reported that many households, professionals and technocrats accessing the Internet through mobile phones.

3. The death of dial-up : The DOI tracks access to new and advanced technologies, including fixed and wireless broadband. The telecommunication industry reached a key milestone in 2005, when broadband subscribers exceeded dial-up for the first time as the primary way of accessing the Internet. By the end of 2005, there were nearly 218 million broadband subscribers around the world, accounting for 53 per cent of all Internet subscriptions. At current rates of growth, the vast majority of Internet subscriptions should be at broadband speeds (equal to or greater than 256 kbit/s) by the end of this decade. Meanwhile, the speed and choice of services available are growing. Meanwhile, for many developing countries, wireless broadband offers an attractive way of reaching greater number subscribers at reduced costs.

4. Growth in Third Generation Mobile : The third generation (3G) mobile services are at an increasing faster rate of growth, particularly in Asia and Europe. As operators introduce these advanced mobile services, they are now deriving a greater proportion of their revenues from data services.

1.7 THE DIGITAL REVOLUTION

An information network is a set of interrelated information systems associated with communication facilities, which are cooperating through more or less formal agreements and institutional agreements, in order to jointly implement information handling operation, with a view to pooling their resources and to offer better services to the user (Mittal, 2005). The recent advancement in digital technologies has contributed lot to the establishment of functional information networks. The Digital Revolution represents the ongoing improvement of digital devices used in ICTs by replacing or emulating analog devices and which results in rapid drop in cost and, enabling former unthinkable innovations like the Internet, World Wide Web, online information retrieval, etc. It includes changes in technology and society, business processes, public administration, etc.

In multimedia applications, the digital revolution marked the transition from the storage of information on fixed material objects dedicated to specific purposes (books for words, phonograph records or audio cassettes for sound, film for images), to the storage of all information in a binary digital format, which is readily stored on a variety of media. Of equal importance to the revolution was the ability to easily move the digital information between media, and to access or distribute it remotely. The digital revolution goes far beyond multimedia applications. By having digital copies of records stored in databases, and having those databases accessible over digital networks, the digital revolution essentially put an end to privacy as previous generations understood it. As the revolution moves forward, virtually every aspect of life is captured and stored in some digital form.

Underlying the digital revolution was the development of the digital electronic computer, the personal computer, and particularly the microprocessor with its steadily increasing performance, which enabled computer technology to be embedded into a huge range of objects and applications. Equally important was the development of transmission technologies including computer networking, the Internet and digital broadcasting.

Socio-economic Impact : The economic impact of the digital revolution has been large. Without the World Wide Web, for example, globalization and outsourcing would not be nearly as viable as they are today. The digital revolution radically changed the way individuals and companies interact. Concepts such as On-demand services and manufacturing and rapidly dropping technology costs made possible new innovations in all aspects of industry and everyday life.

The *Internet*, opened new avenues for communication

and information sharing. The ability to easily and rapidly share information on a global scale brought with it a whole new level of freedom of speech. Any type of information available world over can be accessed by the users within seconds. Individuals and organizations were suddenly given the ability to publish on any topic, to a global audience, at a negligible cost, particularly in comparison to any previous communication technology. Many people considered ready access to such diverse and vast amounts of information only as a benefit. Large cooperative projects such as Open-source software projects, Digital Repositories of information documents, Consortia Models for journal subscription, Cooperative and shared development of information documents, etc. could be endeavored.

Issues of copyright and trademark also found new life in the digital revolution. The capability to exactly reproduce original information and files, coupled with information sharing, complicated matters of intellectual property rights. The digital revolution, especially regarding privacy, copyright, censorship and information sharing remain a controversial topic.

Security issues in the use of ICTs : The Internet has transformed almost all aspects of modern life. Use of the Internet continues to grow and it might have exceeded the number of Internet users by one billion worldwide at the end of 2006 and an estimated 113 million websites. It runs a monthly survey of websites. In April 2007, it registered some 113,658,468 sites, an increase of 3.2 million sites from the previous month's survey. Of these sites, around 50 million were "active". (Netcraft, 2007). The total sites rose to 176,748,506 and active sites rose to 65 million by August 2008 (Netcraft, 2008). According to a projection published by the Computer Industry Almanac, the 2 billion Internet users milestone is expected to reach by the year 2011. People around the globe and from all walks of life have been hearing about the promised improvements the Internet will bring to their lives. While some of these promises have materialized, the full potential of the Internet has not yet been realized. One of the main reasons is that many users lack trust in the Internet for conducting transactions or storing sensitive information. An online survey conducted by ITU in 2006 found that almost two-thirds of respondents had refrained from certain activities online due to security concerns, while users' greatest fears were theft of personal information (e.g., identity theft, credit card fraud etc.), computer viruses and spyware (ITU, 2006). Building trust and confidence is one of the key enablers of future growth and use of the Internet (ITU and UNCTAD, 2007).

The expansion of the Internet is opening up many new opportunities for criminals to exploit online vulnerabilities to commit cyber crime acts or even deliberately attack the critical infrastructures. Viruses, spyware, identity theft, zero-day exploits, Denial of Service (DoS) attacks, and other vulnerabilities are endangering cyberspace and jeopardizing the very future of the Internet. With spam and other exploitation now accounting for up to 90 per cent of e-mail traffic over the Internet, This poses critical issues in the reduction of digital divide and further development of the Information Society. Unless there is progress in building confidence and security in the use of ICTs, users' trust in the Internet may diminish and this could limit its growth and potential.

Concerns of Information Management : While there have been huge benefits to the digital revolution, especially in terms of the accessibility of information, there are a number of concerns. Expanded powers of communication and information sharing, increased capabilities for existing technologies, and the advent of new technology brought with it many potential opportunities for exploitation. The digital revolution helped to usher in a new age of mass surveillance, generating a range of new civil and human rights issues. Reliability of data became an issue as information could easily be replicated, but not easily verified. The digital revolution made it possible to store and track facts, articles, statistics, etc. Quantity and quality of information became relevant issues of the day. Digital records are easy to create but also easy to delete and modify. Changes in storage formats can make recovery of data difficult or near impossible, as can the storage of information on obsolete media for which reproduction equipment is unavailable. Information passed off as authentic research or study must be scrutinized and verified. With such massive proliferation of information it became possible to write an article citing wholly false sources, also based on false sources. These problems are further compounded by the use of digital rights management and other copy prevention technologies which, being designed to only allow the data to be read on specific machines, may well make future data recovery impossible. Digital information today is far too easy to reproduce, and far too hard to destroy. Once a piece of digital data is put onto the Internet, it is copied by search engines, various archives and other places. A piece of information posted in Internet would be readily available to anyone searching the Internet for years, regardless of the authenticity or truthfulness of the information.

1.8 INTERNET, LIBRARIES AND LIBRARIANS

Internet through its open standard has set the foundation for global communication. It provides access to resources that millions of computer users enjoy today. It is commonly said that any system can prove to be only as good as the manner of its use and its upkeep (Ramesh

Babu and Gopalakrishnan, 1998). The introduction of the Internet into libraries has changed the way information resources are provided to users. The Internet takes the revolution caused by printing one stage further and provides information to the user wherever he is – all that is needed is the appropriate technology. At the same time the Internet continues the revolution in communications caused by printing thanks to the speed and low cost of distributing information. The crucial difference, however, is the way the Internet, in its multimedia format, blurs the lines between information provision and consumption. This has changed information provision in libraries by allowing the library user far more control over how he or she accesses information. Sreekumar (2005) established thc potential of Internet in enhancing the information sharing process of libraries.

Prior to the Internet, the Universal Availability of Publications (UAP) Programme initiated by the International Federation of Library Associations and Institutions (IFLA) and United Nations Educational, Scientific and Cultural Organization's (UNESCO), demonstrated the commitment of libraries in providing the widest possible access to information. Networks of libraries, at local, national and international levels co-operated to offer printed publications to users. Internet technology changed this situation and enabled libraries to offer wider access to information than previously, far quicker and, in theory, more cheaply for users. Introducing public access Internet into libraries lets users select information, bypassing the librarian as mediator and leaving the user dependent on his own skills at finding information that may or may not be valid. Availability of information on the Internet, therefore, differs from 'traditional' library stock in that librarians select the stock to go in their libraries. If selection in a traditional sense were applied to the entire Internet, libraries would make available only specific sites actively located, evaluated and added to their systems. On the Internet, no such selection procedures exist. Information is posted to the Web, and then users do the selecting.

The process of information retrieval, for both librarians and library users, is therefore now both simpler and more complex than ever before. It is simpler thanks to the speed and simplicity of search mechanisms that return keyword matches in seconds. On the other hand, it is more complex due to the staggering size of the Internet and the lack of organisation to found amongst the information online (IFLA/UNESCO, 2006). Despite the undeniable benefits and opportunities these new developments offer, many problems for librarians and their users have become apparent. New skills must be learned in information retrieval, and provision made for users to better utilise online technologies. Additionally, because it is impossible for librarians to know everything on the Internet (unlike before, when a library catalogue theoretically contained all available holdings) there are new problems regarding the types of information users are accessing. The Internet, which has sometimes been referred to using analogies of the Wild West, can be seen as a minefield of (mis) information, pornography, hoaxes, scams and ephemera of all kinds. Such a situation has led to the increased use of filtering software – at the level of national telecommunications infrastructure and in libraries themselves. The use of filtering software is slowly becoming more favoured by library associations and more common in the library itself (IFLA/FAIFE, 2005).

The IFLA/UNESCO Internet Manifesto Guidelines clearly defines the changed role of librarians in the Internet environment. It has listed the areas of re-engineering to be introduced in modern libraries. The areas identified by the document are; Public Access of Information; Public libraries and other public access points; Information Users; Enablers of Local Content, Language and Open access; E-services, E-governance and E-democracy; Technological choices, Development and network management; Barriers as – Filtering, Privacy/ Security, Copyright, Net Neutrality, Charges for access; User Training and support; and Internet Use Policies (including user responsibilities and disruptive use).

Sherman (2006) assigns the distinctive role of libraries and librarians in the Internet era. He concluded that, "society is not ready to abandon the library, and it probably won't ever be. Libraries can adapt to social and technological changes, but they can't be replaced. While libraries are distinct from the internet, librarians are the most suited professionals to guide scholars and citizens toward a better understanding of how to find valuable information online. Indeed, a lot of information is online. But a lot is still on paper. Instead of regarding libraries as obsolete, state and federal governments should increase funding for improved staffing and technology. Rather than lope blindly through the digital age, guided only by the corporate interests of web economics, society should foster a culture of guides and guideposts. Today, more than ever, libraries and librarians are extremely important for the preservation and improvement of our culture".

1.9 AVAILABILITY OF INFORMATION RESOURCES, INDIAN SCENARIO

Knowledge and information are factors of indisputable importance in society. Their availability and use determines new economic patterns, creates new types of undertakings, generates new patterns of growth, and changes our way of life. Society makes intense use of knowledge and of information, resting on these pillars to guarantee its growth and maintenance. A society's economic and social growth and development can be understood by its level of access to knowledge, which are both the cause and the consequence of development. It is an accepted fact that one of the major problem every user faces in Internet environment is the junk overload of unwanted information.

Knowledge and Development

Economic growth has already been related to knowledge on some occasions, as in the example of Paul Romer's ***new theory of growth*** which relates access to knowledge to productivity in work (Romer, 1990). Romer also gives clues in other works on the role of knowledge in the development of poor countries, as in "Economic Growth," where he speaks of the reuse of ideals already existing in other countries to raise the technological level of productive activities in poor countries (Romer, 1993). Still in the field of the theory of economic development, the recent work of Chen and Kee (2005) develops a new model of development, where the principal force for economic growth is knowledge. The model shows the direct linkage between the growth of human capital and stable economic growth. Chen and Dahlman (2004) describe four preconditions which must be in place for knowledge to be an effective force for growth. According to them, the four preconditions, or four pillars, of the economy of knowledge are:

i. Education and Training;
ii. Information Infrastructure;
iii. Economic Incentive and Institutional System; and
iv. Innovation Systems (A network of businesses, research centres, universities, consultants and other organizations for using the growing global stock of knowledge, assimilating it and adapting it for local

needs, and creating new knowledge).

Chen and Dahlman postulate that the quantity of knowledge, and how it is used, are essential determinants of the total productivity factor. They emphasize that the strengthening of these four pillars induces the increase of the quantity and quality of knowledge available for economic production, consequently increasing economic growth. India is a developing economy with powerful symptoms of a fast growing country. But, at the same time it shows several weaknesses such as disparity in distribution of income and wealth, wide gap in education and health levels, etc. In the case of availability and use of information also there prevails the predominance of "haves" and "have nots". It is a fact that with regard to ICT applications, many places of the country are advanced and comparable to that of advanced societies of the world. The popularizations of telephone, computer and Internet, especially the cellular phone and broadband Internet, have done much impetus to this advancement. But, the country as a whole, wide disparity still prevails and information rich and information poor individuals, institutions and societies are abundant, especially in rural areas. The narrowing down of digital gap in rural India is a major challenge. The new economic policies and liberalization coupled with the application of modern ICTs have contributed much towards this endevour.

1.10 DISPARITY IN INFORMATION AVAILABILITY

Wide disparity prevails in the availability and accessibility of information not only within a country but between countries. The advanced nations have supremacy in this respect also. IFLA/FAIFE (2007) World Report has compared its findings for the years 2001, 2003, 2005 and 2007 on Internet access to different types of libraries, that is, public, school and university libraries. The digital format and digitized instant communication is the great technological revolution of our times. It has streamlined business and shopping and delivered more information more quickly to more people than ever before. It has accelerated both basic and applied research in all subjects. Scientists have created virtual communities that share data and ideas in important fields like medicine and the environment. Both the problems and the researchers who work on them are widely scattered around the world, but they now come together in a common focus on the World Wide Web. Even with these technologies, possibilities and efforts, many scientists and societies are facing acute shortage of relevant and authentic information. UNESCO, the Library of Congress, USA and several other libraries and institutions world over are striving for universal availability of information by reducing digital divide. UNESCO and the Library of Congress were arranged a meeting on 01-12-2006 at UNESCO Paris Headquarters to pave the way for the launch of a World Digital Library, an internet-based repository of knowledge from all cultures and in all languages. In this respect, James H. Billington, the Librarian, Library of Congress has remarked that, "Most important for the possibility of building a World Digital Library, we are working with all the stakeholder communities on finding answers to two crucial and still unsolved questions: (1) how to strike the proper balance between protecting copyright and maximizing accessibility on the Internet; and (2) how to create metadata (the online equivalent of cataloging) and the interoperability that can create a unified and usable online library that is multimedial and transcultural. If we can solve these problems reasonably well at the national level, we should have a better chance of dealing with them internationally" (Billington, 2006). Digital Library (DL) is a capital – intensive and technology intensive project. It is a challenge for research and academic libraries in developing countries like India to develop DL due to high initial and recurring expenditure and shrinking budget, in addition to socio-economic problems of illiteracy, population growth, health, nutrition and weak infrastructure (Parvathamma, 2001).

According to Prasad (2006), Director, National Assessment and Accreditation Council (NAAC), India, the students and research scholars should be able to access library and information resources round-the-clock, overcoming time and space limitations students and research scholars should be able to access library and information resources round-the-clock, overcoming time and space limitations. Libraries in academic institutions should share knowledge, expertise and facilities with others. Prasad said that on a visit to the Hong Kong Open University, he had found the library at the institution accessible round-the-clock to students, because it was technology-based. Most of the users accessed resources from 10 p.m. to 6 a.m. He said that students and research scholars in India should be able to obtain library and information resources in a similar manner, overcoming time and space limitations. Library resources, knowledge, experience and facilities should not be limited to elite institutions alone, but should be shared with others through networks, without creating a "digital divide".

The information explosion has posed several challenges to the modern libraries. On one side, it is a boon to the academic and research community. At the same adequate measures are needed to manage these information resources with a view to provide effective services to all types of users. Though the modern ICTs offer solutions to many of the problems faced, Indian libraries need policies and their proper implementation to adapt to the situation. Absorption of new technologies poses several management issues that have to be addressed with utmost care and precision in order to reap maximum efficiency and good results. Whatever be the situation, the library system should be able to manage the information resources available world over and provide services to the user community.

1.11 RE-ENGINEERING AND RE-DEFINING: A TECHNIQUE FOR MANAGING ICT

The whole human activity of today is highly affected by the influence of modern ICTs and hence revolutionary changes had happened in all institutions and business houses to re-define their programmes and processes. The process of re-engineering and re-defining has received much of impetus from necessity, as old methodologies have proved ineffective in the context of many present day situations and must, therefore, give away to new approaches. The proponents argue that the re-engineering has the advantages like cost savings, increased customer or user satisfaction, improved sales and service effectiveness, and greater ability to respond to competitive threats, etc. All libraries are striving to provide information services to their clientele based on the resources available within the library as well as that are available elsewhere. The Universal Bibliographical Control (UBC) and the Universal Availability of Publications (UAP) are the target lines of all information professionals and striving with all technologies towards this goal. Achieving these goals in its real sense is a difficult task. But, the application of modern ICTs has made significant contribution in the acquisition, processing and delivery of information and towards the fulfillment of UBC and UAP. The digital revolution and three main advancements of ICT, that is, the processing speed of the computers, digital storage technology and bandwidth have made remarkable contribution in this line. The advent of

Internet, especially the World Wide Web (WWW), has given unprecedented impetus to the information professionals and information users.

Geoffrey T. Freeman, principal of a famous design firm categorically remarked the need for reinventing the Library with technology as catalyst. While information technology has not replaced print media, and is not expected to do so in the foreseeable future, it has nonetheless had an astonishing and quite unanticipated impact on the role of the library. Contrary to the predictions of diminishing use and eventual obsolescence of libraries, usage has expanded dramatically—some-times doubling or even tripling. These increases are particularly common at libraries and institutions that have worked with their architects and planners to anticipate the full impact of the integration of new information technologies throughout their facilities. At institutions where such collaborative planning has occurred—for our firm, at the University of Southern California, Emory University, and Dartmouth College, and more recently, at Fordham University, Illinois Wesleyan University, and Lake Forest College—new library usage speaks for itself: The demand for services and technological access to information, regardless of format, is beyond expectations (Freeman, 2005).

Jagdish Arora, the Director, INFLIBNET Centre and former Coordinator, INDEST Consortium & Librarian, IIT, Bombay highlighted the importance of re-engineering in libraries as follows: "The present digital networked environment has changed the whole structure of 'knowledge organizations', i.e., libraries. The pace of such changes is very fast. To cope up with the above changes, it requires a radical change in our thinking, our organization, our people, and the usage of technologies. And this radical change is possible by way of re-engineering only."

The library, which is still a combination of the past (print collections) and the present (new information technologies), must be viewed with a new perspective and understanding if it is to fulfill its potential in adding value to the advancement of the institution's academic mission and in moving with that institution into the future. Rather than threatening the traditional concept of the library, the integration of new information technology has actually become the catalyst that transforms the library into a more vital and critical intellectual center of life at colleges and universities today.

Recommending a major overhaul of the information service and library sector in the country including the inclusion of libraries in the Concurrent list of the Constitution, a National Library Fund of Rs 1,000 crore to upgrade all existing libraries, a permanent national commission on libraries and a national level survey to assess the requirements and reading habits, the National Knowledge Commission (NKC) has submitted its report to the Government of India on how to re-define the information services in India. The NKC has been set up with the mandate to transform the country into a knowledge society. Underlining the need of including libraries in the concurrent list, the NKC report says that it would facilitate coordinated development of libraries across different sectors. It also suggests that a specified percentage of Central and State education budgets must be earmarked for libraries.

On the service front, the NKC insists that all libraries must have the following facilities — "motivated, courteous and adequate staff, easy access and user friendly retrieval system, effective signages and computers with internet access and photocopiers". It asks the government to issue a library charter to all libraries to take appropriate steps to ensure that libraries meet the objectives set by the commission which includes dissemination of knowledge as widely as possible, serving as a major vehicle to facilitate creation of knowledge, facilitating optimal use of knowledge by all sectors, and easy access to knowledge relevant to their needs. It also recommends a national committee for the identification, documentation and preservation of private collections available in the country. It also suggests that every state should establish a registry and archives of knowledge based digital resources which should be made accessible to all.

The committee has also suggested research and development activities in identifying user needs for different groups, organisation of community information and development of appropriate standards, standardisation of Indian names and vocabulary control over Indian subjects developed in terms of multi-lingual thesauri, development of open sources software and development of digital libraries both in English and Indian languages.

Regarding the public library collections, the NKC suggests that the size and nature of the collection should reflect the population and local requirements and that at least 10 per cent of the book collection should be less than five years old. It also says that libraries should be open on all days, except on national holidays. The NKC adds that library services should initiate imaginative services apart from offering routine library services including lectures and discussion centering on books, cultural programmes, support to students' homework and project and IT training at different levels (India. National Knowledge Commission, 2006).

1.11.1. Re-engineering and Re-defining

Aiming at improving organisational performance through the effective use of production capability and technology, operations strategy such as total quality management (TQM), business process re-engineering (BPR), just in time (JIT), benchmarking, performance measurement and many others are commonly used (Ahmed and Montagno, 1996). Standing out in the literature is TQM and BPR approaches. TQM is based on the principle of continuous improvement of products and processes aimed at continually satisfying customer expectations regarding quality, cost, delivery and service.

Several experts have defined re-engineering in different ways. It was one of the hottest management philosophy and experiment in the nineties. Many have explained this concept as BPR because it deals with the radical *redesign* of an *organization*'s *processes*, especially its *business processes*. Rather than organizing a firm into functional specialties (like production, accounting, marketing, etc.) and looking at the tasks that each function performs, we should, according to the re-engineering theory, be looking at complete processes from acquisition, to production or services, to marketing and distribution. Hence, the institution or firm should be re-engineered into a series of processes.

The original philosophy of BPR was first introduced to the business world by *Frederick Winslow Taylor* when he published his article, "The Principles of *Scientific Management*" in the *1900s*. Following on from the earlier ideas of *Time and Motion Studies* pioneered by *Frank* and *Lillian Gilbreth*, Scientific Management was the first step to the introduction of BPR which turned out to be unsuccessful due to the many issues which were not resolved. During Taylor's time, not many knowledgeable workers were employed in the manufacturing workforce, which at the time was the main wealth generator. Scientific Management involved breaking the manufacturing process down to a thoughtless cycle of simple sequences which were to be carried out in the least amount of time possible with the minimum amount of effort. This often raised the factory workers' salaries but also cause the workers to work just as hard in back-breaking manual labour. This practice of improving efficiency in manufacturing often raised the concern of "dehumanization of the workplace" (Kock, 2003).

The Scientific Management method gave birth to TQM in *Japan* after *World War II*, which eliminated many of the discrepancies that the previous method of improving the business structure. *William Deming* and *Joseph Juran* helped Japan become a super economic power by taking over market share from *North American* businesses with quality goods and services. TQM's main goal is to improve the manufacturing operations.

The term BPR was first introduced by Michael Hammer in 1990 at a Harvard Business Review article, "Re-engineering Work: Don't Automate Obliterate". Davenport also has done some pioneering contributions in this philosophy. Michael Hammer and James Champy also have considered as main proponents of the re-engineering. In a series of books including Re-engineering the Corporation, Re-engineering Management, and The Agenda, they argue that far too much time is wasted passing-on tasks from one department to another. They claim that it is far more efficient to appoint a team who are responsible for all the tasks in the process. In The Agenda they extend the argument to include suppliers, distributors, and other business partners. Michael Hammer once said, "Serving the customer is not a mechanical act but one that provides an opportunity for fulfillment and meaning".

Michael Hammer and James Champy have defined re-engineering in the book, "Re-engineering the Corporation" as follows: "Re-engineering is the fundamental rethinking and redesign of business processes to achieve dramatic improvements in critical, contemporary measures of performance, such as cost, quality, service and speed" (Hammer and Champy, 1993). Hammer and Champy suggested seven principles of re-engineering that would streamline work processes, achieve savings, and improve product quality and time management:

Seven principles of re-engineering

1. Organize around outcomes, not tasks.
2. Identify all processes in an organization and prioritize them in order of redesign urgency.
3. Integrate information processing work into the real work that produces information.
4. Treat geographically dispersed resources as though they are centralized.
5. Link parallel activities in the workflow instead of just integrating their results.
6. Put the decision point where the work is performed, and build control into the process.
7. Capture information once and at the source.

Increase in consumer requirements for both product and service efficiency and effectiveness have resulted in BPR.

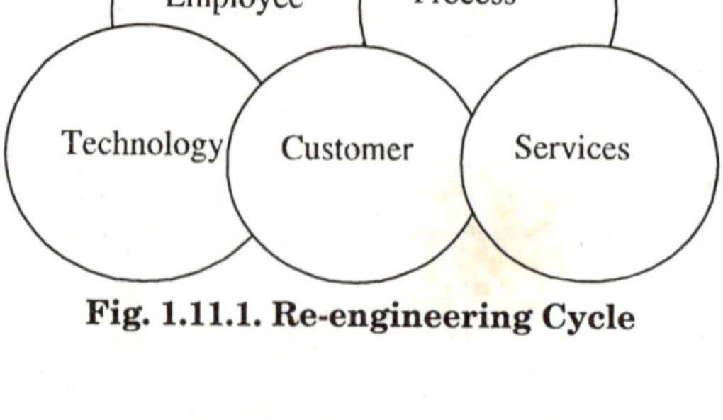

Fig. 1.11.1. Re-engineering Cycle

The National Academy of Public Administration (NAPA) recast this definition for government as, "Government business process reengineering is a radical improvement approach that critically examines, rethinks, and redesigns mission product and service processes within a political environment. It achieves dramatic mission performance gains from multiple customer and stakeholder perspectives. It is a key part of a process management approach for optimal performance that continually evaluates, adjusts or removes processes." (Caudle, 1995).

Al-Mashari and Zairi (2000) suggest that re-engineering of business processes involves changes in people (behaviour and culture), processes and technology. Re-engineering is a rapid and radical re-designing of processes, services, policies and the organizational structure of an organization. It can be defined as an art of changing an organization's way of thinking and consequently, of doing things in a radical way. It involves changing processes, organizational structure, management style and behaviour, compensation and reward systems, as well as relationships with external and internal business partners. Sometimes the term re-engineering is considered as synonymous to TQM. But, it has a much wider connotation because it takes into its fold not only TQM but other related aspects of management services also such as automation, re-designing, re-organization and downsizing. It is more effective than TQM in the sense that the TQM is measure to improve the existing system, whereas re-engineering management is applied from the beginning. It often uses technology in creative and innovative ways. It is time bound process and necessitates to work within a prescribed time frame. The ultimate aim of re-engineering management is to provide customer satisfaction by efficient and effective services, and to lay down a set of effective and efficient processes for the organization.

In a re-engineering process, firstly, resources need to be generated. Secondly, operations have to be stabilized and thirdly, when the operations become familiar, the focus shifts to the customers. The systems can be improved and refined on the basis of feed back from the users. Re-engineering requires hard work, sincerity and timely action, and most importantly, an in depth knowledge of operations activities and services (Gaur, 2003).

Re-engineering is the basis for many recent developments in management. The cross-functional team, for example, has become popular because of the desire to re-engineer separate functional tasks into complete cross-functional processes. Also, many recent management information systems developments aim to integrate a wide number of business functions. *Enterprise Resource Planning* (ERP), *Supply Chain Management* (SCM), *Knowledge Management* (KM) Systems, *groupware and collaborative systems*, *Human Resource Management (HRM) Systems* and *Customer Relationship Management* (CRM) Systems all owe a debt to re-engineering theory. Although BPR has gained tremendous popularity in business management as a new innovative theory; many of its premises are similar to previous management theories that have failed. Specifically, the theory and notoriety of BPR suggests that it is "the process" and not "the people" that will make businesses successful. On the contrary, proven success of a business is getting people to perform efficiently together. The true benefit to BPR if implemented successfully will be in the human element, or the people, and not solely processes.

Learning Organisations : The goal of BPR is change. BPR purists advocate dramatic change to organisations and process. But many organisations which have implemented BPR find that change is constant, and that the people in the organisations must learn to adapt quickly to all change. The key for these organisations is to learn from all aspects of implementing change, even mistakes along the way, and quickly implement action to resolve these problems. Firms that recognise this and implement these techniques of continuous learning are called Learning Organisations (Young, Pieters and Cherin, 1994).

Learning Organisation extends to all levels of an organisation, striving to keep up with customer needs. Keeping up with new customer needs means that a fundamental change must take place through all people within an organisation, even people who have no impact on customers and/or products. A Learning Organisation is more than a training programme, it is the establishment of a learning process which is a collective state-of-mind for all people. It is a dedication of people, time, talent and money for continuous learning and new knowledge transformed into new behaviour and action. When creating a Learning Organisation programme, there are primarily two categories that must be considered. The first is awareness-based training and the second is skills based training (Campbell and Kleiner, 2001). Both awareness-based training and skills based training are separate training initiatives, but they complement each other and tend to reinforce the goals of the firm, resulting in a synergistic Learning Organisation training programme.

1.11.2 Steps involved in Re-engineering

The activities which constitute business process management can be grouped into three categories, that is, process design, process execution and process monitoring.

1. Process design : This encompasses either the

design or capture of existing processes. In addition the processes may be simulated in order to test them. The software support for these activities consists of graphical editors to document the processes and repositories to store the process models. An emphasis on getting the design of the process right will logically lead to better results as the flow on effect of problems at the design stage logically affects a large number of parts in an integrated system. Evolution of business processes requires a change to the process design to flow on into the live system. Integrating business process is also a current research area. Integration of software for process design to be used both for creating graphical representations of workflows and implementing and maintaining these workflows makes evolution of business processes less stressful, given that requirements are not as static as *information systems*.

2. Process execution : The traditional way to achieve the automatic execution of processes is that an application is developed or purchased which executes the steps required. However, in practice, these applications only execute a portion of the overall process. Execution of a complete business process can also be achieved by using a patchwork of interfacing software with human intervention needed where applications are not able to automatically interface. In addition, certain process steps can only be accomplished with human intervention (for example, deciding on a major credit application). Due to the complexity that this approach engenders, changing a process is costly and an overview of the processes and their state is difficult to obtain. As a response to these problems, the Business Process Management System (BPMS) category of software has evolved. BPMS allows the full business process (as developed in the process design activity) to be defined in a *computer language* which can be directly executed by the computer. The BPMS will either use services in connected applications to perform business operations or will send messages to human workers requesting they perform certain tasks which necessitate a human attribute such as intuition as opposed to automated processes. As the process definition is directly executable, changes in the process can be relatively quickly moved into operation. In order to work effectively a BPMS often requires that the underlying software is constructed according to the principles of a *service-oriented architecture*. Thus, it is often difficult to make a suite of existing legacy systems fit with a BPMS.

3. Process monitoring : This monitoring encompasses the tracking of individual process so that information on their state can be easily seen and the provision of statistics on the performance of one or more processes. An example of the tracking is being able to determine the state of a customer or user requirement (e.g. ordered for Inter library loan, documents arrived, awaiting delivery of documents, invoice paid on that, etc.) so that problems in its operation can be identified and corrected. In addition, this information can be used to work with customers and suppliers to improve their connected processes. Examples of the statistics are the generation of measures on how quickly a customer or user order is processed, how many orders were processed in the last month etc.. These measures tend to fit into three categories: cycle time, defect rate and productivity. Although such functions may be within the scope of current applications, the use of a BPMS is expected to ease the development of such reporting. Manufacturers of BPMSs will often offer process monitoring software as well as MIS and execution.

Business process modeling is an activity performed by business analysts within a company or institution. Analysts use modeling tools to depict both the current state of an enterprise and the desired future state. The activity of modeling a business process usually predicates a need to change processes or identify issues to be corrected. This transformation may or may not require the involvement of ICT, although that is common driver for the need to model a business process. *Change management* programmes are desired to put the processes into practice. BPM has always been a key aspect of *business process re-engineering*, and continuous improvement approaches seen in *Six Sigma*.

Key targets

Business Process Re-design and Re-engineering is the analysis and design of workflow and processes within and between organizations. It has three key target areas:

1. Customer Friendly : One of the main goals of introducing BPR is to get a competitive edge and that can only be gained by providing the customers more than what the others in the market are asking for. If a customer is looking for products tailored to their needs, for example: a car customized to the customer's taste, then that car-maker would most probably gain more customers over the competition due to the customization option.

2. Effectiveness : How effective is the product or service that the business or manufacturing company providing the customer? If whatever product or service the business might be providing to the customer is successful, then the customers would automatically want to buy that product or service again. For example: Japanese made cars like Honda and Toyota, even though they are more expensive compared to the domestic cars, they are very reliable cars causing the customers to continue going back to those brands for generations.

3. Efficiency : How efficient is the company that is manufacturing the product before introducing it to the market to minimise costs? This is one of the key categories that are believed to be more important than any others. If a manufacturing company can master the skill of being efficient then they can automatically be more customers friendly and effective. Efficiency is not just about being efficient at the production floor level but the management level also has to be efficient. An example of only the production floor being efficient and not the management level would be the Japanese manufacturing companies. Now they are going through turmoil to repair their problems.

Successes of BPR : BPR, if implemented properly, can give huge returns. BPR helped giants like *Procter and Gamble* Corporation and *General Motors* Corporation succeed after financial drawbacks due to competition. It helped *American Airlines* somewhat get back on track from the bad debt that was haunting their business practice. BPR is about the proper method of implementation.

General Motors Corporation implemented a 3-year plan to consolidate their multiple desktop systems into one. It was known internally as "Consistent Office Environment". This re-engineering process involved replacing the numerous brands of desktop systems, network operating systems and application development tools into a more manageable number of vendors and technology platforms. The BPR could lay a foundation for the successful implementation of a common business communication strategy across General Motors. *Lotus Development Corporation* and *Hewlett-Packard* Development Company also gained similar achievements due to BPR by reducing costs and increasing quality and efficiency. *Southwest Airlines*, American Airlines, etc. have achieved successful results by re-engineering their companies and using Information Technology (Furey and Diorio, 1994). In order to sustain in the results, they have to continuously re-engineer their strategy.

Motivation : In order for BPR to succeed, staff and management must be motivated to achieve the vision and goals of BPR. When motivating the staff on a BPR project, one must not forget some of the classic management theories such as reinforcement theory, learning theory, and expectancy theory. These management theories will provide practical and proven techniques for motivating employees and are equally applicable and effective for BPR. A quick review of these management theories will be helpful prior to discussing their effect on BPR (Rause and Watson, 1994).

In a publication for the National Academy of Public Administration, Sharon L. Caudle identified six critical success factors that ensure government reengineering initiatives achieve the desired results (Caudle, 1995):

1. Understand reengineering.
   - Understand business process fundamentals.
   - Know what reengineering is.
   - Differentiate and integrate process improvement approaches.
2. Build a business and political case.
   - Have necessary and sufficient business (mission delivery) reasons for reengineering.
   - Have the organizational commitment and capacity to initiate and sustain reengineering.
   - Secure and sustain political support for reengineering projects.
3. Adopt a process management approach.
   - Understand the organizational mandate and set mission-strategic directions and goals cascading to process-specific goals and decision-making across and down the organization.

- Define, model, and prioritize business processes important for mission performance.
- Practice hands-on senior management ownership of process improvement through personal involvement, responsibility, and decision-making.
- Adjust organizational structure to better support process management initiatives.
- Create an assessment program to evaluate process management.

4. Measure and track performance continuously.
    - Create organizational understanding of the value of measurement and how it will be used.
    - Tie performance management to customer and stakeholder current and future expectations.
5. Practice change management and provide central support.
    - Develop human resource management strategies to support reengineering.
    - Build information resources management strategies and a technology framework to support process change.
    - Create a central support group to assist and integrate reengineering efforts and other improvement efforts across the organization.
    - Create an overarching and project-specific internal and external communication and education program.
6. Manage reengineering projects for results.
    - Have clear criteria to select what should be reengineered.
    - Place the project at the right level with a defined reengineering team purpose and goals.

- Use a well-trained, diversified, expert team to ensure optimum project performance.
- Follow a structured, disciplined approach for reengineering.

Criticisms of Re-engineering : Re-engineering has earned a bad reputation because such projects have often resulted in massive staff downsizing and layoffs. This reputation is not altogether warranted. Many companies have often downsized under the banner of re-engineering. Further, re-engineering has not always lived up to its expectations. The main reasons seem to be that: Re-engineering assumes that the factor that limits organization's performance is the ineffectiveness of its processes (which may or may not be true) and offers no means of validating that assumption. Re-engineering assumes the need to start the process of performance improvement with a "clean slate", i.e. totally disregard the *status quo*.

Abrahamson (1996) showed that fashionable management terms tend to follow a lifecycle, which for re-engineering peaked between 1993 and 1996 (Ponzi and Koenig 2002). While arguing that re-engineering was in fact nothing new (as e.g. when Henry Ford implemented the assembly line in 1908, he was in fact re-engineering, radically changing the way of thinking in an organization), Dubois (2002) highlights the value of signaling terms as re-engineering, giving it a name, and stimulating it.

The biggest problem that businesses usually face with BPR is overzealous expectations. BPR is a business tool with a high price and gradual returns. BPR is quoted as having a 30% success rate due to the time and cost involved. BPR has been used by corporations as an excuse for job cuts which has tarnished the name with employees. Specifically, in *1995*, *Pacific Bell* called for 10,000 job cuts, followed by *Apple Computer* Incorporated. Both used the word re-engineering to explain the job cuts.

The future : *Six Sigma* and TQM are terms often confused with BPR, and are not its replacements. All are change initiatives, with the main difference being BPR is focused on radical, "big bang" change, and Six Sigma and TQM both focused on continuous, incremental improvement. Business Process Management (BPM) is presently taking a similar road toward many failures by focusing too heavily on automation and failing to consider people in processes. BPM refers to activities performed by businesses to optimize and adapt their *processes*. *BPR*, which was popular in the 1990s, dealt with one-off changes to the organization and it deals with the continuity and embedding of process orientation in the organization. BPM has evolved as technology has caught up with management processes to the point that technology should no longer be the limiting factor in BPM. BPM encompasses other process elements, such as TQM, *Six Sigma*, *Performance Management*, etc.

1.11.3 Re-engineering v/s Total Quality Management

Total Quality Management is a *management* strategy aimed at embedding *awareness* of *quality* in all organizational processes. TQM has been widely used in *manufacturing*, *education*, *government*, and *service industries*. It is considered as one of the most popular management innovation and change programmes that have emerged over the last few decades. TQM is connected with quality improvement on a company wide basis. It is a comprehensive approach to improving competitiveness, effectiveness and flexibility through planning, organizing, and understanding all the activities and tasks undertaken by people within an organization. The core of TQM is about improving customer and supplier relationships. According to the *ISO*, "TQM is a management approach of an organization, centered on quality, based on the participation of all its members and aiming at long-term success through customer satisfaction, and benefits to all members of the organization and to society."

In Japanese, TQM comprises four process steps, namely (Wilson, 1998):

1. *Kaizen* : Focuses on Continuous Process Improvement, to make processes visible, repeatable and measurable.
2. *Atarimae Hinshitsu* : Focuses on intangible effects on processes and ways to optimize and reduce their effects.
3. *Kansei* : Examining the way the user applies the product leads to improvement in the product itself.
4. *Miryokuteki Hinshitsu* : Broadens management concern beyond the immediate product.

The application of TQM in a library and information science environment requires deep and full dedication of employees. This can be achieved by appropriate human resources management, by participative management, by ensuring autonomy to work culture management, etc. TQM requires that the organisation should maintain *quality standard* in all aspects of its business process. This requires ensuring that things are done right the first time and that defects and waste are eliminated from operations.

BPR places considerable emphasis on exploiting IT opportunities, while in the TQM programmes the focus is on automated systems for collecting data and controlling processing variation (Davenport, 1993).

Virtually all efforts to redesign business process today have their roots in two movements: Total Quality Management (TQM) and Re-engineering. Both have provided managers with a powerful means of reshaping individual processes so that they serve existing categories of customers more efficiently. Re-engineering in particular, has helped managers harness formidable power information technology to improve process performance. But several managers have attributed many limitations to the TQM and Re-engineering.

Lee and Asllani (1997) consider that TQM and BPR are two management approaches designed to improve organizational performance and quality. Because of the pace, time required, and initiatives for change, TQM and BPR are regarded as two completely different improvement programmes. They also share common features, which create the basis for a possible integration of TQM and BPR under the endless quality improvement concept. Organizations that can effectively combine TQM and BPR would be very successful in gaining a sustainable competitive advantage. According to them, TQM is based on a broad organizational commitment to make continuous quality enhancements in products and services for customers over a long term. BPR allows for radical changes in organizational processes intended to make quantum leaps in performance by taking advantage of the advances in the information and telecommunication technology. While they seem to be two completely opposite approaches, TQM and BPR can well be combined into the "endless quality improvement" concept. Under a system context, they conclude that moving from TQM to BPR is a transition from an adaptive to a proactive approach, from an evolutionary to a revolutionary process improvement. Finding ways to improve quality is a major concern for today's organizations. To ensure sustainable competitive advantage, an integration of TQM and BPR appears to be the best management approach for many organizations. Although TQM and BPR represent two different approaches, a careful combination of these methods can help to achieve long term breakthrough results. The best integration of programmes intended for radical improvements and gradual improvements can be achieved under the concept of the re-engineering life cycle.

The factors such as BPR, TQM, etc. have important roles to play in enterprise resource planning (ERP) implementation which have significant impact on business performance and successfulness (Schniederjans and Kim, 2003). The application of the principles and techniques of TQM in a library and information service environment requires deep commitment of all levels of employee for achieving excellence (Biswas, Jalal and Ghosh, 2003).

1.11.4 Re-engineering and Re-defining in Libraries

Towards this approach, it is worth considering the remark of the National Agricultural Library (2008), USA. "*NAL must be omnipresent and always on providing constant access to quality information in the digital environment in line with consumer needs and expectations. To succeed, NAL must build upon its current services by developing entirely new ways to deliver information for a broad and demanding customer base, but the new must not come at the expense of the old*". Although most of the university libraries in India have played significant role in the evaluation of the use of new information technologies, it is a recognized fact that there is a significant difference between the evaluation and implementation of these technologies. Organizational changes are necessary in order to utilize effectively the new information resources. Aggressive outreach services are needed to provide the basis for timely and effective information delivery.

While considering the issue of re-engineering and re-defining libraries, it is better to note the remark of McGahan (2004) in a "*Harvard Business Review*" article entitled 'How industries change'. She argues strongly that to develop strategy and make appropriate investments in innovation within the organisation requires a real understanding of the nature of change within the industry. This is of course easy to say but difficult to assess, particularly to take a long-term look in a rapidly changing short-term context. The business world is littered with misinterpretations of signs. She suggests, however, four distinctive trajectories of change – radical, progressive, creative, and intermediating. It can be seen that libraries and information services are operating in an environment between intermediating and radical change. An industry on a radical change trajectory is entirely transformed, probably over a timescale of decades, with an end result of complete reconfiguration.

In the context of modern ICT, all the conventional activities of libraries such as acquisition, classification, cataloguing, maintenance, preservation, binding, weeding out, documentation and information services, circulation, inter library services; serials control, etc. have to be re-defined. Many of these activities have lost relevance in its traditional definition and its application. Most of the libraries have overweighed with the digital form of information resources in comparison with the other forms such as paper, micro film, micro fiche, tapes, etc. The nature and preference of the users also have changed. Instead of physical presence of the users, many users approach the libraries or would like to approach the libraries for services through remote access, via World Wide Web or some other ICT means such as telephone, mobile phone, fax, e-mail, etc. In this context, in order to achieve management efficiency, service effectiveness and user satisfaction, re-defining the activities and processes of the libraries and their re-engineering is advocated.

Since operations of an institution, including library,

are in general managed from a functional perspective, mapping the business processes is a fundamental step to understand the flow of information and resources through the business processes of the internal value chain. It may also help to understand relationships of processes and dimensions and consequently focus attention on the processes and activities that most impact performance on critical competitive dimensions. Mapping can also bring the benefit of helping in assessing performance of operational and supporting processes.

Moreover, assessment of performance is essential to diagnose the root causes of problems or weakness so as to determine what areas or activities are the weak points and need to be addressed. Information on process performance can be gathered with qualitative assessment of current situation (Carpinetti, Buosi and GeroÂlamo, 2003).

Wilson (1998) clearly explains the need for Business process re-engineering (or redesign) in academic libraries in the digital age. The transformation from the handling of artefacts to the handling of electronic sources may be effected with maximum benefit to the information user. He advocates a special role of Information Officer with high degree of competencies and built-in intelligence in the reliable and robust integrated systems. He argued that in the changed scenario, the academic library and its role, and the roles of academic librarians will need to be redesigned. At present, academic libraries function mainly as systems that acquire and organise physical artefacts in the form of books, journals and other information-bearing products. Of course, the system has changed and is changing – access to online information services has become a standard part of library practice (although financial pressures have meant that the services are not as widely available as might be wished), and libraries have acquired CD-ROMs and have mounted them on campus networks for university-wide access. However, the structure of library systems has still geared to acquiring objects, organising them and making them generally available and accessible. Scholarly publication and, indeed, many other forms of publication, however, are increasingly moving towards electronic delivery to the end user. Under these circumstances, how can the university library redefine its role? Leaving aside the continuing need to acquire books, journal issues and other artefacts, this will require the same systems as at present, although possibly on a reduced scale, some radical rethinking will be necessary. One possibility will be to focus even more closely upon the client and the experience of business process redesign in the insurance industry offers the model of the 'case officer' – interestingly this is also the terminology adopted in other client-serving organisations.

As the new management approach of re-engineering and re-defining has been tried in many American and European organizations, libraries also have made use of this approach. Gaur (2002) has made a detailed study on the applicability of re-engineering in management libraries in India. He further stressed this need in his book; "Re-engineering Library and Information Services", described several such examples (Gaur, 2003).

The revolutionary management principles of F.W. Taylor had re-defined the management processes with much emphasis on the principles of the division of labour and his theory of scientific management. But, the new movement of Re-engineering rejects many of the principles and assumptions that have shaped the business landscape for the last two centuries. This movement is receiving much of its impetus from necessity as old methodologies are proven ineffective in the context of present circumstances and therefore give way to new approaches.

1.11.5 ICTs and Changes in Knowledge Management Scenario

The modern ICTs have made radical changes in the conventional system of information processing and its delivery. The higher education sector is experiencing an unprecedented growth rate. This trend is largely a result of new enabling technologies that have facilitated the virtual delivery of academic programs (Moyo and Cahoy, 2003). This has in turn led to:

i. Globalization of academic programs;

ii. Emergence of virtual academic communities; and

iii. Libraries becoming key success factors in the virtual academic environment.

Knowledge Management (KM) may refer to the ways organizations gather, manage, and use the knowledge that they acquire. The term "knowledge management" has also served as an umbrella term by practitioners advocating a variety of organizational processes and practices for identifying and capturing knowledge, know-how, expertise and other intellectual capital, and for making such knowledge assets available for transfer and reuse across the organization. Knowledge is treated more and more as a principal success factor – or the major driving force behind business success. Knowledge-intensive processes tend to be characterized by dynamic changes of goals, information environment, constraints, and highly individual and ad-hoc communication and collaboration patterns (Papavassiliou and Mentzas, 2003).

The approach of Probst, Raub and Romhardt (2000) specifies eight building blocks to manage knowledge: *knowledge goals*, *knowledge identification*, *acquisition*, *development*, *sharing*, *utilization*, *retention* and *assessment*. Knowledge is considered to be a resource used in the business process. The idea of building blocks for knowledge management has been proposed by Wiig (1995) with examples of building blocks for knowledge creation and dissemination. The model-based knowledge management approach proposed by Allweyer (1998) adds a new perspective to the modelling of existing business processes, especially of knowledge-intensive processes. Knowledge management activities are considered as an integral part of existing business processes. The four level architecture of business process management is adopted for knowledge management and the method is renamed knowledge process redesign. The approach aims to the description of required and used knowledge as well as generated and documented knowledge.

A survey study based on 400 academic journal publishers conducted by the Association of Learned and Professional Society Publishers (ALPS, 2006) reveals the following trend in the publications of journals:

1. Ninety percent of the journals are now available online.
2. A fifth of the publishers are experimenting with open access Journals.
3. 40 percent of publishers use previous print subscriptions as the base for pricing for bundles.
4. Most publishers make agreements for either one year or three years.
5. Ninety one percent of publishers make back volumes available online; 20 percent charge for access to back volumes.
6. Forty two percent have established formal arrangements for the long-term preservation of their journals.
7. Eighty three percent require authors to transfer copyright in their articles to the publisher.

The management doyen, Peter F. Drucker observed that, "knowledge workers, even though only a large minority of the work force, already give the emerging knowledge society its character, its leadership, its central challenges and its social profile. They may not be the "ruling" class of the knowledge society, but they already are its "leading" class. In their characteristics, their social positions, their values and their expectations, they differ fundamentally from any group in history that has ever occupied the leading, let along the dominant position" (Drucker, 1994). He continued that education will become the center of the knowledge society and schooling its key institution. What knowledge mix is required for everyone? What is quality in learning and teaching? All these will, of necessity, become central concerns of the knowledge society and central political issues.

He predicted the high probability of the need of re-define the meaning of an educated person. He added that increasingly, an educated person, will be someone who has learned how to learn, and throughout his or her lifetime continues to learn, especially in and out of formal education. This society, in which knowledge workers dominate, is in danger of a new class conflict: the conflict between the large minority of knowledge workers and the majority of people who will make their living through traditional ways, either by manual work, whether skilled or unskilled, or by services work, whether skilled or unskilled. The productivity of knowledge work still abysmally low will predictably become the economic challenge of the knowledge society. On it will depend on the competitive position of every country, industry and institution within society.

The points asserted by Drucker are absolutely true in the context of Indian knowledge economy, especially, the library and information service sector. The libraries and librarians not capable to absorb new technologies upgrade skills and increase productivity as a continuous and lifetime process will be ousted from the society or their position will be assumed by some other agencies or persons. Bavakutty, Abdul Majeed and Nasirudheen (2008) also have narrated much needed similar changes in the knowledge management scenario of libraries and the role of modern librarians.

1.11.6 Transformation of Organisations and Services

The radical evolution from print to electronic resources and services pose significant challenges for the modern academic libraries. Higa et al (2005) explains the case of transformation of information resources and services in the Library of the University of Texas South Western Medical Center at Dallas. In 1995, the library had one e-journal in 1995; by 2004, it had more than 5000. The library's most popular journal, "*Nature*", illustrated the users' clear preference for electronic option. In 2003, the *Nature's* electronic version generated more than 51,000 uses, whereas the print version received fewer than 1,300 uses.

At the same time, the whole organisation was not adapting to the drastically changing situation. Resistance to change is a term used either diagnostically or pejoratively, to describe a person who for some reason or another is perceived as needing to adapt their views or conduct in certain areas, often at the suggestion or requirement of an authority figure, senior manager or advisor, but is seemingly unable or unwilling to do so. In organizational development, as business change practitioners assist their clients with managing change, they almost always find themselves dealing with some form of resistance to change from those whose roles, status, responsibilities, or conditions will be affected.

Managing national information resources in all sectors has taken on new meaning in the last few years. Not only is the nature of information resources changing as a result of new information technologies, but all the sectors itself are undergoing a radical transition as it moves into the information age. Fierce competition in the marketplace, sophisticated technology and changing consumer demands make timely access to accurate and comprehensive information crucial. Both the changing nature of information and the changes in the concerned sectors have profound effect on the management of their programmes and services. The National Agricultural Library (NAL) of the United States has played a leading role in the evaluation of the use of new information technologies in libraries; they recognized that there was a significant difference between the evaluation and implementation of these technologies and anticipated that organizational changes are necessary in their vision of the future. Along with the regular services as the National Library, the NAL has undertaken several extension services to the public, employees of the Department of Agriculture, agriculturalists, businessmen, etc. The library participates in local, national and international networks and co-operative activities which promote the sharing of information, access to recorded knowledge, and the support and advancement of scholarly communication. In its dual role as a national and a departmental library, NAL and land-grant university libraries work together on programmes to improve access to, and maintenance of, the nation's agricultural knowledge. In recent years, this has been done more and more frequently through the application of new electronic technology. Work has been done with digitizing agricultural collections and mounting them on CD-ROM and other electronic media; developing and using hypertext, hypermedia and expert advisory systems; and transmitting digitized documents over the Internet. As a result of these activities, NAL and the land-grants have developed an international reputation in the exploration of the uses of new technologies in library and information science settings (André and Pisa, 1994).

As a result of rapid environmental changes, organizations of all types are rethinking their organizational structures in an attempt to provide greater effectiveness and efficiency. A few years ago the BPR was considered the most promising way to restructure an organization, but has become less popular as shortcomings associated with the process have become evident. Citing the examples of academic libraries in North America, Moran (2001) reported that today, greater emphasis is being placed upon modifying the actual organizational structure of modern libraries. Most re-structured organizations have moved away from rigid hierarchies to flatter, more flexible structures. Many of the forces like increased automation, changing information needs and expectations of users, reduced budgets, the need for staff to have more autonomy over their own work, etc. have precipitated the reshaping of other organisations have also affected the organizational re-structuring of academic libraries. Grimshaw (1995) opines that the BPR is a continuous and ongoing process which includes emerging new processes and tools, process redesign, etc. and it is becoming a competitive imperative for all industry sectors.

2

Re-Engineering and Redefining Applications in Libraries

Information and Communication Technologies warranted thorough re-structuring of operations of any organization. Though normally the academic, research and special libraries form the part of any parent institution, in management aspect, libraries takes the nature of an independent institution with all complexities. Hence, while planning the application of ICTs, libraries should be considered as an independent organization.

2.1 PLANNING FOR RE-ENGINEERING AND RE-DEFINING

Modern ICTs have made tremendous changes in the functioning of the university libraries. University libraries in Inida also have tried to adopt many of these technologies. Muhammed Salih has made a detailed study on the computerization of university libraries in Kerala (Salih, 2004). The study identified the level of automation of university libraries in Kerala and revealed that the libraries could not exploit the possibility of computer technologies to the maximum and finally this reflected in the quality of information services and utilization of available information resources. He has underlined several reasons such as lack of fund, manpower, skills, cooperation and collaboration between libraries, etc. to this situation. This study gave a preliminary insight to formulate the objectives of the current study. Since the advancement of ICTs during the last few years has made a quantum leap as compared to the situation prevailing at that time, as ICT has a central role in re-engineering and redefining, several findings of that study would helped to do in-depth analysis of the problem.

Based on an Italian experience on one-stop shops, Ongaro (2004) advocates the Process management style and approach characterised by the focus on business processes that can provide an important contribution to the management of public sector organizations. This experiment about the reduction of "red tape" for businesses shows that one-stop shops for businesses have been created with the purpose of easing businesses of most of their administrative burden by identifying a single interface for issuing business licences between the public administration and the entrepreneur and by increasing co-ordination among public entities involved in regulatory management. The implementation of this reform has required many public organisations to engage in radical process re-engineering interventions. At the same time, the reform has created conditions favourable to the spread of process management approaches in the Italian public sector, which, in a number of cases, developed much beyond the activation of the one-stop shop according to the requirements of this reform. The results of the new processes was that the "throughput" time for issuing business licenses has been significantly reduced (from an average of about 150 days to less than 90 days). Also the quality of the interface with users has in general improved. Other important results identified were enhanced customer-orientation, increased output quality, output-oriented organization, greater organisational flexibility, increased capacity of monitoring users' needs and quickly adapting the outputs accordingly, etc.

The role of information in community activities has been studied by several experts. Communities in the more remote parts of areas which themselves are considered to be peripheral may feel doubly isolated. Access to information can help reduce negative effects of living and working in such communities, but, in turn, this peripherality creates barriers to information access. The relationship between access to information and the effects of peripherality; has been studied by Sue Beer in Shetland and the Western Isles of Scotland as case studies (Beer, 2004). The study was concerned with all types of information need from within the target communities and which point to a strong interdependency between geographical peripherality and exclusion from information, in remote communities where accessing information is described as being both more difficult and more necessary. Travel from Isles to the mainland and beyond is time consuming and expensive, and can be exhausting for the traveller; this affects the ability of island residents to access information. For those in remote parts of these island groups, their need for information may be greater, but their opportunity to access it is further diminished by distance from information providers and training, inferior telecommunications, erratic electricity supply and poor public transport; this can be exacerbated by intolerance on the part of those that are centrally located who do not all make allowances for the needs of their more remote clients through flexible provision of information services.

Strong networks and intimate knowledge of who does what within the community allow individuals and groups to reach the "right" person to answer their information enquiry, and the long service record and continuity of staff helps facilitate the sharing of appropriate knowledge, as does the commitment of many individuals to a number of committees, coupled with good partnership working. Access to better telecommunications, ideally broadband, was identified by the study as being crucial to effective information access; the peripherality indicators most often referred to as providing the barriers to information flow were, however, the traditional spatial indicators such as travel cost and accessibility. An IT solution with enough and effective provision for training was envisaged for a remote islander who has difficulties in travelling to access information in person.

Schäffler (2004) reported the results of a re-engineering process at the Bayerische Staatsbibliothek (Bavarian State Library) in Munich, Germany, the central regional library of the State of Bavaria and one of the largest academic research libraries in Europe with local, regional and supra-regional responsibilities. The introduction of digital resources has not only had considerable impact on the role of libraries in the information society, but it has also had a remarkable effect on back office procedures, i.e. on the way the library is organised. The study indicated that due to the multiple roles of the library, it was particularly important not only to bridge the gap between traditional and new material, but also to create a flexible organisational platform for the various tasks at the different levels. In order to cope up with the new situation, the library utilized the principles of re-engineering and change management.

Based on a questionnaire study on organizational learning, particularly in the context of evaluation and organizational change in 67 academic libraries in Taiwan, Chen (2006) reported that the perceptions of library employees concerning the use of routines to solve problems, the consideration of innovative ideas, the nature of discussions held, the development of new routines, the existence and nature of organizaticnal change, the support for any such change, and the use of information technologies are the key components of library communication and behaviour which provide a pathway to effective library organizational change. The study stressed the need for professional development activities for positive and effective change. Management itself must provide an appropriate learning climate if the library as an organization is to make progress. As more library workers gain a Library and Information Science degree, this aspect may improve. A refined organizational learning model framed by Chen is shown in the Fig. 2.1.1.

It identifies the barriers to double-loop learning and also suggests that interventions and increased management leadership could be of benefit. Innovative ideas can be present, interpreted and even integrated but they fail to progress to institutionalization. Thus, it is argued that there is always some degree of organizational learning even in a relatively primitive form. Of course the point is that the innovative learning must progress or otherwise the organization as a whole cannot be considered a true learning organization.

In the keynote speech to the Bielefeld Conference, Lynne Brindley gives a panoramic picture of the need for re-defining libraries. Based on the case study experience of the British Library and reviewing a wide range of materials published between 2003–2006, Brindley (2006) establishes that the challenge for libraries in the 21st century is to find new ways to add value and remain

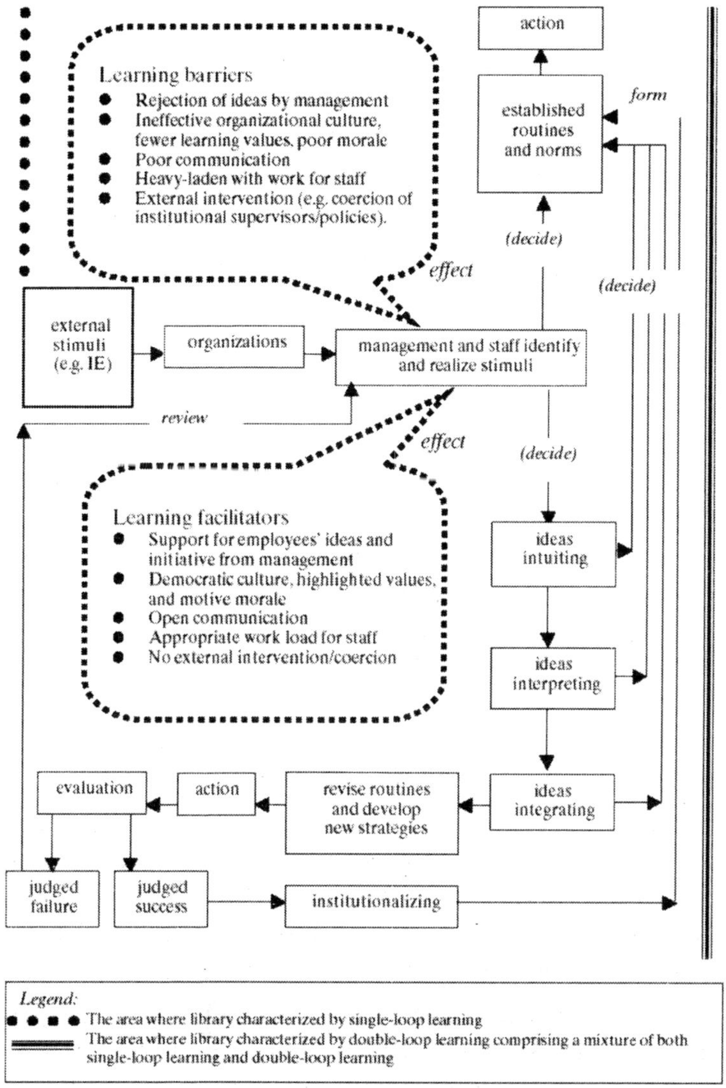

Fig. 2.1.1. Model of organizational Learning.

Source: Chen (2006).

relevant in this rapidly changing, confusing and competitive environment and stressed the need for continuing re-definition and re-positioning of libraries to remain relevant in the 21st century. Through this study, Brindley identified the following seven themes as central to re-defining the library in the 21st century:

1. Know the library users and keep close to them : Using expertise from commercial marketing, the British Library identified clear audiences, all of whom had specific ideas of what they needed from the Library . Since the needs of the users are varied and distinct, defining the library functions with balance on the needs was a challenge. But their new, focused understanding of the individual users was an important catalyst for creativity in approaching the rest of the core themes and activities of the library.

2. Re-think the physical spaces and create a desirable draw : Libraries should aim to be uplifting, innovative and inspiring cultural, social and intellectual spaces, encouraging debate and collaboration, and desirable as places to be in, even in the age of ubiquitous Internet access. While rethinking the physical space, it need not always mean rebuilding it.

3. Integrate marketing into the organization : Exhibitions and series of seminars and lectures were arranged by the British Library which attracted new audiences to hear a range of speakers and experts. This in turn could generate revenues to the library.

4. Open up legacy print collections to digital channels and reveal them through digitization : There are several great opportunities for libraries to find new channels, deliver public value and ensure business models that enable sustainability by digitizing primary collections of archives, manuscripts and rare materials and therefore made infinitely more visible and accessible to the world is enormous.

5. Reduce legacy costs and continue to improve productivity in traditional activities : Underpinning the functioning of the libraries are many traditional processes and activities – selection, acquisition, cataloguing, fetching and retrieving, preserving, and so on. Vigilant on these activities to ensure that these well-worn routines continue to be challenged both in the way the library do them and the priority give for them.

6. Invest more in innovation and digital activities : Value added activities and services to the user communities have been provided by the library through new roles such as institutional repository management, digital asset management and audit, digital scholarship, e-learning activities, and so on. Some of these roles required new kinds of consortial and other partnerships across the public and the private sector. The Legal Deposit Libraries Act 2003 has given new responsibility for archiving the UK's digital output and they have prepared infrastructure and methodology for this.

7. Develop our people and ensure the right mix of skills : The information professionals of the future need to be outward-going people, with really sharp business skills and a huge understanding of technology and the implications of the Internet. They need to be able to understand and engage with users to bring their collections to life, in a way that a search engine on someone's desk simply cannot. They need to concentrate on what they are good at - information management, metadata, reference services, to name but a few - and be ruthless about bringing in specialisms they need from outside to add value to their core tasks.

A study by Childerhouse et al. (2003) and similar other studies have put forward several issues related to the BPR in supply chain management. Though the study dealt with supply chain management, many of the points identified by this study are applicable to the planning and implementation of LIS systems. As per the study, four generic areas have been identified which are barriers to improving performance of an organisation. These are cultural, organizational, technological and financial. It was reported that integrated information flow strategy could offer substantial improvement and this could help for optimal decision support system (DSS). Information flowing upstream has been identified as vital to the elimination of many costs associated with poor scheduling and inventory control.

Several experts have previously acknowledged customer satisfaction and marketplace understanding as crucial elements for consideration when attempting to establish a new supply chain strategy. They have used the uncertainty circle as a means of focusing on opportunities for improving real-world supply chain performance (Childerhouse, Towill and Disney, 2001). But, as shown in Figure 2.1.2, this can easily become a vicious circle in real-world supply chains. According to them, there are three feedback loops therein, each capable of causing instability and hence chaos within the supply chain. Thus distortion, both deliberate and accidental, masking, delays, and missing data all feed through our information flow, leading to further infidelities in vendor orders, and via uncertain deliveries to more infidelities in customer orders. Hence the vicious circle continues to fuel yet further distortion and so on. It would appear elementary to state the need for transparent and timely information throughout the supply chain. However, there are many barriers to be overcome.

The Cardiff business process change model

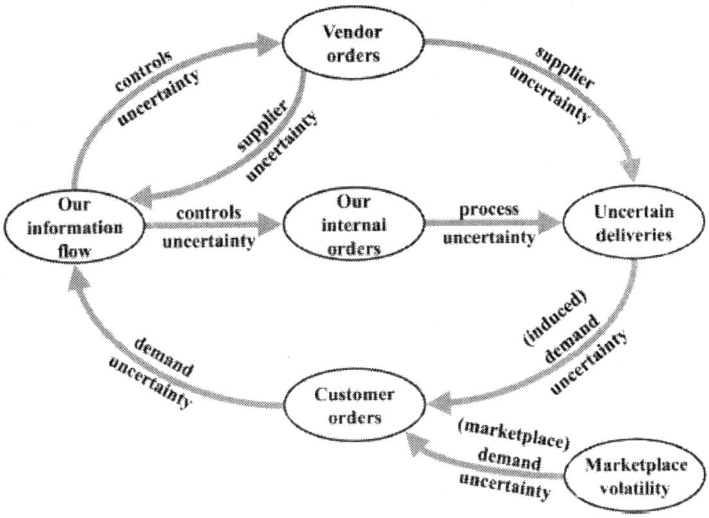

Fig. 2.1.2. The "Vicious Circle" caused by uncertainty Source: Childerhouse, Towill and Disney (2001).

In determining an approach to the barriers of change it is helpful to use an established framework like the Cardiff BPR change model. This is shown in diagrammatic form in Figure 2.1.3. It is very useful for identifying blockages to change and subsequently taking action to free them up (Towill, 1991). The model is based on the experience of business process engineering in European manufacturing industry, initially at the shop floor level (Kaloo and Towill, 1978), and identifies the major barriers to successful design and implementation. As the diagram shows, the barriers are not independent, since there is often considerable overlap between the various enablers. However, in diagnosing problems and offering possible solutions, it is helpful to classify them as primarily technological, cultural, financial, and organisational in origin.

Cardiff process change model adapted to illustrate interactive barriers to supply chain information flow.

The people perspective is particularly important in changing business processes. It is an issue that needs to be carefully considered and handled. Loughman, Fleck and Snipes (2000) listed the following "*people factors*" to be addressed:

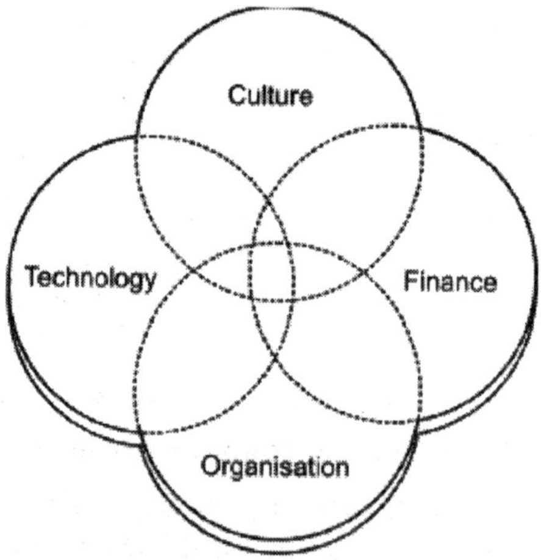

Source: Mason-Jones *et al.* (2001), based on Towill (1991)

Fig. 2.1.3. Cardiff Process Change Model

Technological Barriers

Despite the fact that the technology already clearly exists to achieve the necessary supply chain information sharing, there are many IT hurdles to be overcome. There are two major issues: the cost aspect to which we shall return again later, and the constraints on implementation. In some instances implementation of an IT system that would enable transparent information sharing could well be prohibitively expensive, especially where a chain containing many members is concerned. A major barrier to implementation is then agreeing the format of the information between the members of the supply chain. This is further complicated by the degree to which ordering systems are embedded within the operating IT system within each echelon of the chain. Furthermore, many companies suffer from an already strained IT department and therefore shrink from embarking on a project of the magnitude required to implement transparent information sharing. In a paper on information sharing, Palmatier (1988) emphasized the need for establishing closer links with customers so as to improve demand planning. Cost benefits obtained via closer collaboration and information transparency are also well documented.

More or less similar technological barriers are persisting in the change process of the libraries in the ICT context. The cost of ICTs, various related costs to implement such technologies put strong hurdles in the transformation of library and information services in a proper way.

Cultural barriers

Given the increasing sophistication of insights into, and compelling evidence of the importance of information flow to, supply chain performance, and the increasing power of information technology to facilitate communication, it is necessary to ask why cultural barriers to achieving desired and identifiable improvements still persist. Andraski (1994) has claimed that in real-world retail supply chains "80 per cent of problems that arise are due to people, not technology". This is no doubt true and the evidence presented by Childerhouse *et al.* (2003) provides a good manifestation of "interference" by the human element in what ought to have been an industrial "seamless" supply chain. However, from an institutional perspective we would argue, in turn, for the importance of recognising that people are embedded in real-world structures and situations. This must have a significant impact on culture and hence on behaviour.

Clark and Hammond (1997) have noted how in grocery supply chains the emergence of trust (and hence information sharing) has been inhibited by the persistence of traditional "adversarial win-lose negotiations". They go on to observe that retailers "are only willing to share information if they perceive that the benefits of this information sharing offset the perceived risks involved". This type of cultural or people oriented barriers are visible in our libraries. The users as well as professionals to some extend are reluctant to accept the changes open heartedly and in a desired speed.

Financial Barriers

Here the "visible" costs of enabling information flow is being considered. There are four obvious major sources of expenditure as follows:

1. Feasibility studies/system design costs;
2. Hardware costs;
3. Software costs; and
4. Management costs.

The financing of feasibility studies, systems design, and management effort to oversee, de-bug, and start up new supply chain communication channels combine to make a substantial barrier to implementation. In the context of digital information, several new forms of expenditure have emerged. These became new barriers to be tackled by the modern libraries.

Organisational Barriers

There are significant financial and technological barriers towards establishing an integrated information architecture that enables information sharing. But there are also more general and equally pressing barriers in integrating the services. In particular, the disintegrated structures of supply chains and information services, comprising, as they do independent companies or agencies, give rise not only to transactions and their associated costs and tensions but also to issues of co-ordination and governance. Many discussions and meetings were conducted in the library and information sector to formulate a coordinated effort for the pooling and sharing of available information resources in the country. But, all such movements could not achieve desired result mainly due to organizational barriers.

2.2 INTEGRATED SYSTEM FOR INFORMATION

In many organizations such as universities, colleges, research institutions, etc., separate and almost isolated units such as library, computer section, publication division, etc. are functioning. As Lunin and D'Elia (1991) indicated, each delivery system specialized in different formats and types of information; each developed its own mechanisms and culture for acquiring, maintaining, and distributing information; and each rendered its services independently of the others. That means, information was processed and provided to campus information users and knowledge workers through separate subsystems instead of through an integrated system. These disintegrated system resulted in fragmentation and duplication of resources and services, which caused confusion, especially when the users' needs were for integrated and/or cross media information services. Hence, it is clear that an integrated information service unit is called for, first, to streamline the administration and implementation of technologies into more efficient and effective ways and, second, to satisfy campus information users' increasing needs. Concurrent with this conceptualization, this call for integrated information services within academic environments has already been set in action in a number of instances, such as University of Wisconsin at Parkside (Meachen, 1997), University of Montana (Samson, Pengelly and Brown, 1997), University of Wisconsin at Whitewater (Liang and Yin, 1996), University of Minnesota (Bowers, Debeau-Melting, DeVries and Schellinger, 1996; and (Branin, D'Elia and Lund, 1993), University of California (Sharrow, 1995), University of Maryland at Baltimore (Lunin and Ball, 1994), and University of Iowa (Creth, 1993). In observing the above cases, we realize that although the idea of integration is universal, the action is full of local considerations. Each case has its unique background and campus culture, which, in turn, engenders its own political considerations and change processes.

2.3 ADVANCEMENT OF ICTs

Libraries and Information Services (LIS) are being heavily transformed by technology, especially, the ICTs. Consequently, LIS have to adapt to meet their users' changing needs and growing expectations. Terminological and ideological transformation has also happened for the conventional concept of library management. The concept of library management had been transformed to library and information management and now take the shape of knowledge management.

According to a study conducted by IBM and The Economist magazine, although the digital divide remains considerable for some countries, the gaps are shrinking. The study assessed both availability and use of technology in 68 countries and assigned each an "e-readiness" score on a scale of 1 to 10. The study noted that nearly every country's score improved from last year but that countries nearer the bottom of the list saw greater gains than those in the upper tiers, indicating a shrinking digital divide overall. The digital divide is narrowing as citizens in emerging markets get online via computers and mobile phones, with some regions now on a par with developed nations. Beyond the issue of connectivity lies the question of what efforts each country makes to use technology. (Economist Intelligence Unit, 2006). The e-readiness continues to advance across the globe. Indeed, the average e-readiness score of the 70 countries in this year's rankings rose to 6.39, up from 6.24 in 2007. This overall progress, however, masks some backtracking among a handful of countries, notably within the top ten. After four consecutive years as the world's most e-ready country, Denmark has fallen four places, as has Switzerland. Similarly, Finland has dropped three places and has been supplanted in the top 10 by Austria. The United States is now the global e-readiness leader, with a score of 8.95, followed closely by Hong Kong, which has advanced two places. In order for citizens to be online, countries need them to be Internet literate. Or rather technoloy needs to accommodate their literacy levels in order to get them online. India is one country leading the world to include such programmes (Economist Intelligence Unit, 2008).

Table 2.3.1. E-Readiness Rankings of the world countries, 2008

2008 e-readiness rank (of 70)	*2007 rank*	*Country*	*2008 e-readiness score (of 10)*	*2007 score*
1	2	United States	8.95	8.85
2	4	Hong Kong	8.91	8.72
3	2	Sweden	8.35	8.85
4	9	Australia	8.83	8.46
5	1	Denmark	8.83	8.88
6	6	Singapore	8.74	8.60

7	8	Netherlands	8.74	8.50
8	7	United Kingdom	8.68	8.59
9	5	Switzerland	8.67	8.61
10	11	Austria	8.63	8.39
11	12	Norway	8.60	8.35
12	13	Canada	8.49	8.30
13	10	Finland	8.42	8.43
14	19	Germany	8.39	8.00
15	16	South Korea	8.34	8.08
16	14	New Zealand	8.28	8.19
17	15	Bermuda	8.22	8.15
18	18	Japan	8.08	8.01
19	17	Taiwan	8.05	8.05
20	20	Belgium	8.04	7.90
21	21	Ireland	8.03	7.86
22	22	France	7.92	7.77
23	24	Malta	7.78	7.B6
24	23	Israel	7.61	7.B8
25	25	Italy	7.55	7.45
26	26	Spain	7.46	7.29
27	27	Portugal	7.38	7.14
28	28	Estonia	7.10	6.84
29	29	Slovenia	6.93	6.66
30	32	Greece	6.72	6.31
31	31	Czech Republic	6.68	6.32
32	30	Chile	6.57	6.47
33	34	Hungary	6.30	6.16
34	36	Malaysia	6.16	5.97
35	33	United Arab Emirates	6.09	6.22
36	39	Slovakia	6.06	5.84
37	37	Latvia	6.03	5.88
38	41	Lithuania	6.03	5.78
39	3B	South Africa	5.95	6.10
40	38	Mexico	B.88	5.86

41	40	Poland	B.83	5.80
42	43	Brazil	5.65	5.45
43	42	Turkey	5.64	5.61
44	44	Argentina	5.56	5.40
45	45	Romania	5.46	5.32
46	46	Saudi Arabia	5.23	5.05
47	49	Thailand	5.22	4.91
48	48	Bulgaria	B.19	B.01
49	46	Jamaica	5.17	5.05
50	-	Trinidad & Tobago*	5.07	-
51	51	Peru	5.07	4.83
52	50	Venezuela	5.06	4.89
53	52	Jordan	8.03	4.77
54	54	India	4.96	4.66
55	54	Philippines	4.90	4.66
56	56	China	4.85	4.43
57	53	Egypt	4.81	4.26
58	53	Colombia	4.71	4.69
59	57	Russia	4.42	4.27
60	61	Sri Lanka	4.35	3.93
61	60	Ukraine	4.31	4.02
62	62	Nigeria	4.25	3.92
63	59	Ecuador	4.17	4.12
64	63	Pakistan	4.10	3.79
65	65	Vietnam	4.03	3.73
66	64	Kazakhstan	3.89	3.78
67	66	Algeria	3.61	3.63
68	67	Indonesia	3.59	3.39
69	63	Azerbaijan	3.29	3.26
70	69	Iran	3.18	3.08

The statistics on Performance Indicators of Telecom Services in India, released by the Telecom Regulatory Authority of India (TRAI, 2007) reveals the following:

i. Wireless Market grew at 15.5% in the quarter ending December 2006 by adding 20.08 million subscribers.

ii. Internet Subscribers base reached 85.47 Lakhs in the quarter ending December 2006 by registering a growth of 5.9%.

iii. Broadband subscriber base reached 20.19 Lakhs in the quarter ending December 2006 by registering a growth of 11.12%.

iv. The gross subscriber base of the wire-line and wireless services together reached 189.92 million in the quarter ending December, 2006 from 170.02 million as on 30th Sept 2006, showing an increase of 11.70% during the quarter. The overall growth for the year (December 2005 to December 2006) was 52.20%.

v. The tele-density in the quarter ending Dec' 2006 has reached 17.16 compared to 15.41 at quarter ending Sept' 2006.

vi. The subscriber base for wireless services has increased from 129.54 million to 149.62 million and that of Fixed Line service has decreased from 40.5 million to 40.3 million.

vii. The number of Public Call Offices (PCO) in the country has increased to 5.30 million from 5.12 million by registering a growth of 3.51% in quarter ending Dec' 2006.

viii. Rural Wireline subscriber base has reduced from 12.56 million in quarter ending Sept 2006 to 12.48 million in quarter ending Dec'2006 by registering a negative growth of 0.64%.

ix. The number of Village Public Telephones (VPT) in the country has increased to 5.59 lakhs from 5.52 lakhs registering a growth of 1.26%.

Statistics released during 2008 show the following indications towards the availabililty of connectivity and Internet facilities in India (TRAI, 2008):

i. Subscribers base to cross 300 million in April 2008.

ii. Wireless subscribers base reaches 250 million mark. India to become second largest wireless network in the world by April 2008.

iii. Wireless Subscribers addition is 8.53 million in February 2008.

iv. Broadband continues to grow in the country.

v. Tele-density cross 25% mark. Total 8.49 million telephone connections have been added during February 2008 as compared to 8.74 million connections added in January 2008. The total number of telephone connections reaches 290.11 million at the end of February 2008 as compared to 281.62 million in January 2008. The overall tele-density is 25.31% at the end of February 2008 as against 24.63% in January 2008.

Another study by the Internet in India (I-Cube) jointly organized by the Internet And Mobile Association of India (IAMAI) and IMRB International shows the following pattern on the use of Internet in India:

Mumbai with 3.24 million ever users and 2.6 million active users, leads the pack of top 8 internet using metros. Delhi was second with 2.66 and 1.80 million of ever and active users respectively. The findings of the study are given in the following tables (I-Cube, IAMAI and IMRB International (2006):

While top metros continue their dominance, there was a clear cut trend of small metros, non-metros and small towns catching up fast. Among the ever user category, the share of top 8 metros has declined from 58 per cent in 2001 to 41 per cent in 2006. The corresponding decline in

Table 2.3.2. The Internet Users Base across top eight Metro Cities in India, 2006

Top 8 Metros (figures in millions)	*Ever Internet Users (13.12mn of 17.36 mn)*	*Active Internet Users (10.21mn of 13.23 mn)*	*% of Active Internet users*
Mumbai	3.24 mn	2.60 mn	82%
Delhi	2.66 mn	1.80 mn	67%
Kolkata	1.34 mn	1.05 mn	78%
Chennai	1.48 mn	1.26 mn	85%
Bangalore	1.31 mn	0.97 mn	74%
Hyderabad	1.29 mn	0.95 mn	74%
Ahmedabad	0.78 mn	0.59 mn	75%
Pune	1.02 mn	0.92 mn	90%

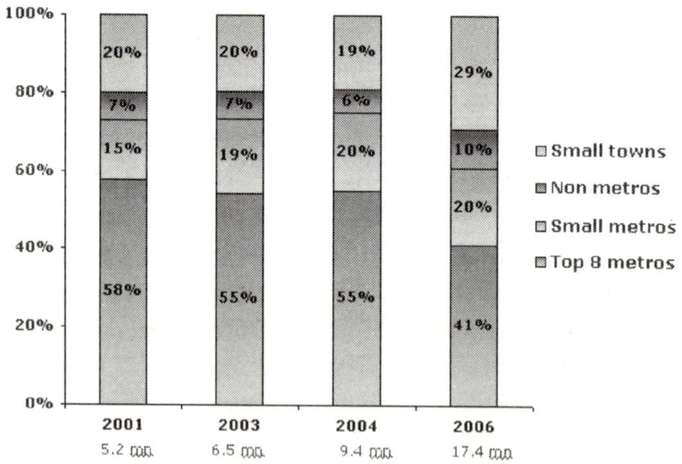

Fig. 2.3.1. The Trend of Internet Users small metros, non-metros and small towns in India, 2006

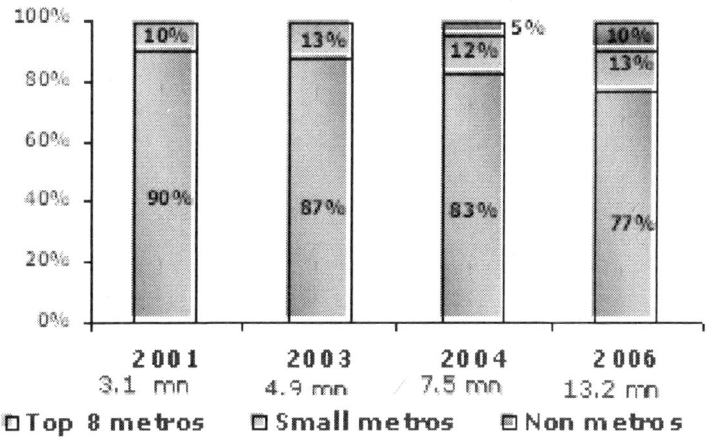

Fig. 2.3.2. The Declining Trend of percentage of Internet Users in small metros, non-metros and small towns in India, 2006

the active users was from 90 per cent in 2001 to 77 per cent in 2006. The figures 2.3.1 and 2.3.2 give a clear picture of this trend.

In terms of access points, proportion of users accessing from home was the highest in Hyderabad and lowest in Pune. The proportion of users accessing from offices was highest in Mumbai and lowest in Hyderabad. Cyber cafes continue to be the most important access point in Pune and Bangalore. While except in Bangalore, access from schools continues to be dismal. The schools/colleges as access point were ranging from 2-17 percent only. This implies that there was enough scope for libraries for re-engineering and re-defining their web based information services. This also implies that the Internet facilities, that is, the number of computers, speed of the Internet, working hours of the libraries, etc., in the schools/colleges need to be upgraded to improve the situation. Another point to be stressed was the necessity of information literacy programmes. The figures 2.3.3 and 2.3.4 show the access points of Internet users.

Among the various town classes, cyber cafes continue to serve as access points to 50 per cent of users in non-metros with home use showing a healthy 30 plus per cent in all four town classes.

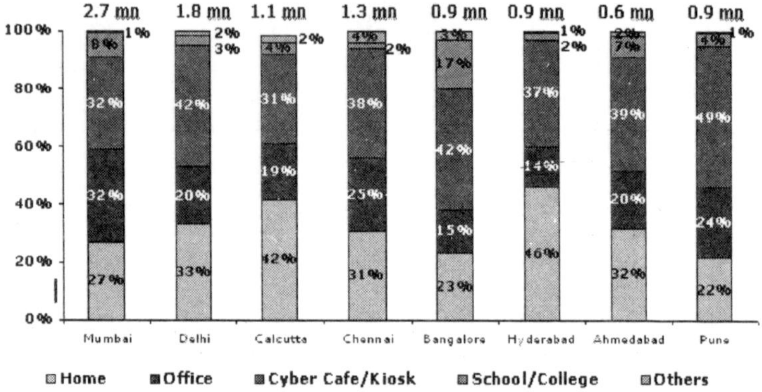

Fig. 2.3.3. The Access Point of Internet Users in India, 2006

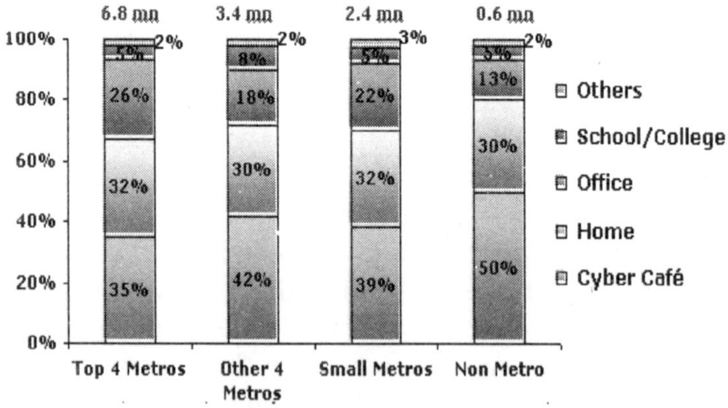

Fig. 2.3.4. Percentage of Access Point of Internet Users in India, 2006

The study also indicates the trend in Internet application usage in India. The figures 2.3.5 and 2.3.6 reveal this trend.

The proportion of internet users accessing internet for information search was significant in non metros. As observed earlier, almost 40% of the internet users were school/college going students. Lack of availability and accessibility of reliable sources for information was driving users from non metros towards Internet, mainly for education.

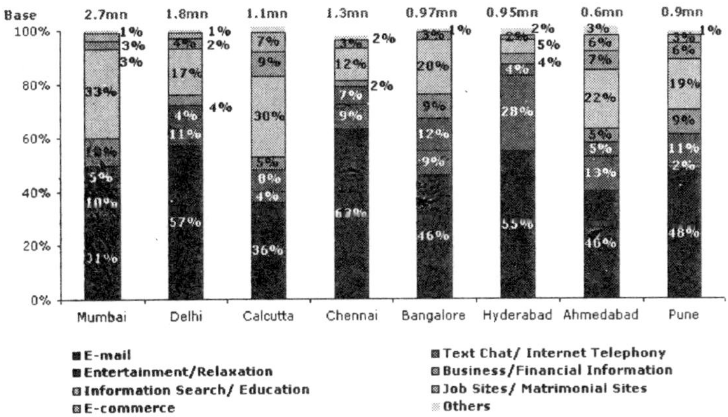

Fig. 2.3.5. Application Usage of Internet in India, 2006

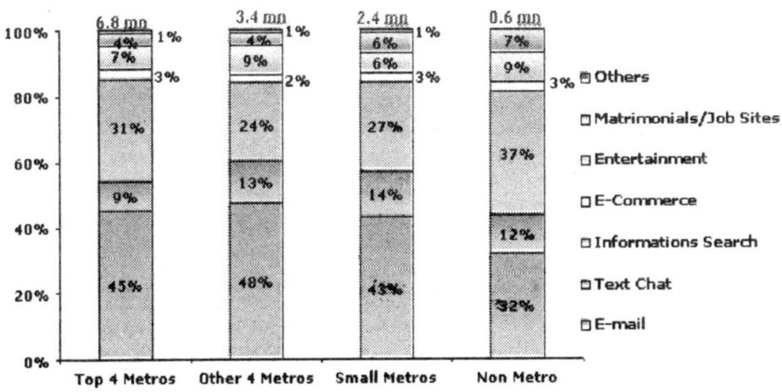

Fig. 2.3.6. Percentage of Application Usage of Internet in India, 2006

The reports released during 2007 by I-Cube, IAMAI and IMRB International (2007) show that among all categories of users, e-mail is the most used service of Internet and Information seeking is the second. Figures 2.3.7 and 2.3.8 gives a clear picture of this nature.

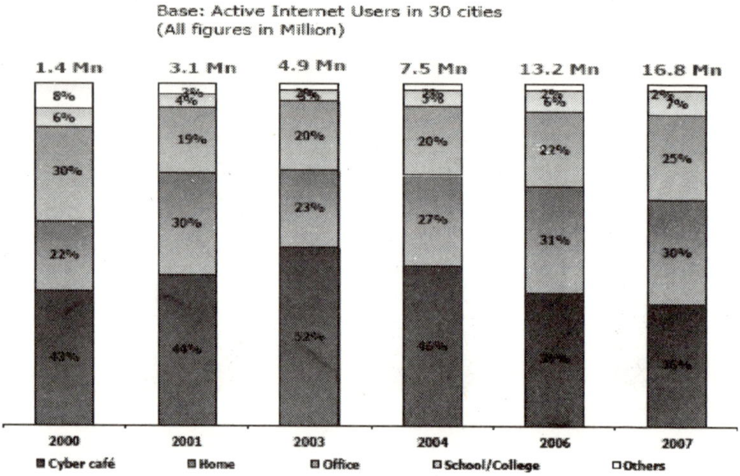

Fig. 2.3.7. Active Internet users in 30 cities India, 2007
Source: I-Cube, IAMAI and IMRB International (2007)

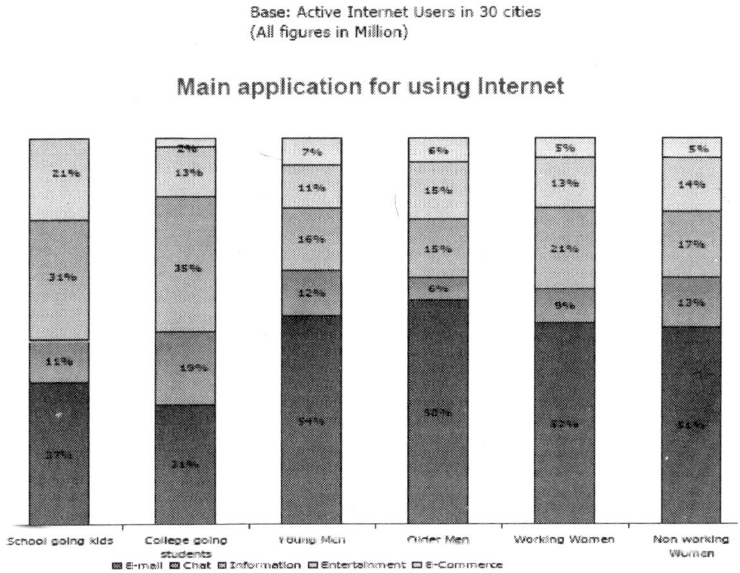

Fig. 2.3.8. Main application for using Internet by active users in 30 cities in India, 2007

Source: I-Cube, IAMAI and IMRB International (2007)

The world's top economies were highly utilizing Internet technologies for their all activities. The reports of the International Telecommunication Union (ITU) show a clear picture of the use of such technologies. (ITU, 2005)

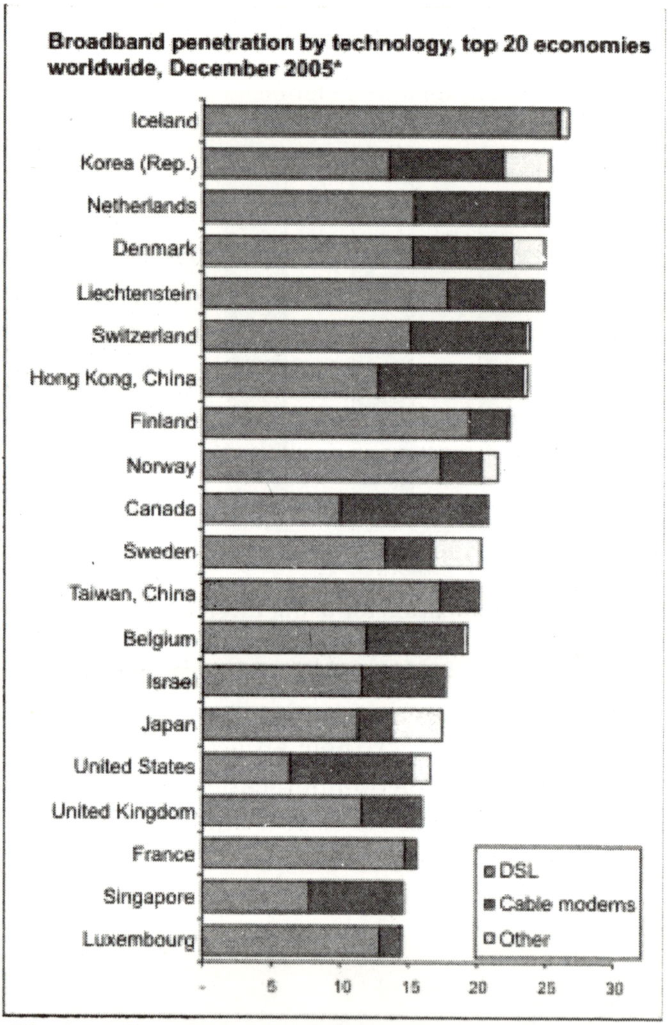

Fig. 2.3.9. Broadband penetration by technology, top 20 economies of the World

***Source:* International Telecommunication Union (ITU) adapted from national reports.**

i. In 2004, the developing world had 4 times fewer fixed telephones than the developed world. They had 4 times fewer mobile subscribers per 100 people than the developed world. In 2004, the developed world still had 8 times the Internet user penetration rate of the developing world.

ii. In 2004, less than 3 out of every 100 Africans use the Internet, compared with an average of 1 out of every 2 inhabitants of the G8 countries (Canada, France, Germany, Italy, Japan, Russia, the UK and the US). There were roughly around the same total number of Internet users in the G8 countries as in the rest of the world combined. That is, 429 million Internet users in G8 countries and 444 million Internet users in non-G8 countries. To explain more, the G8 countries - home to just 15% of the world's population - had almost 50% of the world's total Internet users.

iii. There were more than 8 times as many Internet users in the US, three times as many Internet users in Japan, and more than twice as many Internet users in Germany than on the entire African continent. The entire African continent - home to over 50 countries - has fewer Internet users than France alone.

iv. There were major discrepancies in international Internet bandwidth - the critical infrastructure that dictates the speed at which websites in other countries can be accessed. Denmark – a country roughly the size of Costa Rica - had more than twice the international Internet bandwidth than the whole of Latin American and the Caribbean combined.

v. The high cost of international bandwidth was often a major constraint, with developing countries often having to pay the full cost of a link to a hub in a developed country. Many countries today have less than 10 Mbps of international Internet bandwidth, whereas in Belgium, a 9 Mbps ADSL high-speed

Internet package was available for just EURO 60 a month.

vi. Around 30 countries were with an Internet penetration of less than 1%.

Asia-Pacific Region in 2004

i. Internet penetration ranges from below 1% in countries like Bangladesh, Cambodia and Lao, to above 65% in countries like Australia and the Republic of Korea.

ii. Mobile penetration ranges from below 1% in countries like Bhutan, Myanmar, Nepal and Papua New Guinea to 90% or more in countries like Hong Kong (China) and Singapore.

iii. China remains the region's powerhouse. During 2004, the country added an average 5.4 million new mobile subscribers every month. China already represents almost 50% of the entire Asian mobile market in terms of subscriber numbers, yet domestic penetration still hovers at around just 25%. That translates into another one billion more potential mobile customers.

iv. India has overtaken China to become one of the region's fastest-growing mobile markets, with growth rates of over 90% per annum every year since 1999. With just total mobile penetration rates of just over 4%, potential for growth is enormous.

v. The Republic of Korea leads the world in broadband penetration, with high-speed lines serving more than a quarter of the population.

The table 2.3.3 given below shows the picture of Internet Usage in India:

Table 2.3.2. Internet Usage Status and Population Statistics, 2006

Year	*Users*	*Population*	*% Pen.*	*Usage Source*

1998	1,400,000	1,094,870,677	0.1 %	ITU
1999	2,800,000	1,094,870,677	0.3 %	ITU
2000	5,500,000	1,094,870,677	0.5 %	ITU
2001	7,000,000	1,094,870,677	0.7 %	ITU
2002	16,500,000	1,094,870,677	1.6 %	ITU
2003	22,500,000	1,094,870,677	2.1 %	ITU
2004	39,200,000	1,094,870,677	3.6 %	C.I. Almanac
2005	50,600,000	1,112,225,812	4.5 %	C.I. Almanac
2006	40,000,000	1,112,225,812	3.6 %	IAMAI

International Telecommunication Union (ITU), Internet & Mobile Association of India (IAMAI), Computer Industry Almanac (C.I. Almanac)

Another statistics on Internet usage by leading countries of the world is shown in the table 2.3.4.

Table 2.3.4. Internet usage by leading countries of the world

	Country	*Internet Users*	*Internet Penetration*	*% users of world*
1	USA	2,05,326,680	68.6 %	20.1 %
2	China	1,11,000,000	8.5 %	10.9 %
3	Japan	86,300,000	67.2 %	8.4 %
4	India	50,600,000	4.5 %	5.0 %
5	Germany	48,721,997	59.0 %	4.8 %
6	UK	37,800,000	62.9 %	3.7 %
7	South Korea	33,900,000	67.0 %	3.3 %
8	Italy	28,870,000	48.8 %	2.8 %
9	France	26,214,173	43.0 %	2.6 %
10	Brazil	25,900,000	14.1 %	2.5 %

Source: Business Today, June 4, 2006, p. 16

This table indicates that while more than 50 percent of the people of the advanced countries using Internet, that ratio in India was only 4.5 percent which is a clear indication that wide gap prevails in the use of modern knowledge management platform and the related tools. At the same time, it was revealed that India continues to be one of the fastest growing major ICT power in the world. Sweeping reforms introduced by successive Indian governments over the last decade have dramatically changed the nature of telecommunications and Internet in the country. In order to tap this potential of these technologies, the library and information sector and the LIS professionals should take dynamic role.

2.4 CONVERGENCE OF LIS AND IT

Convergence and the subsequent emergence of hybrid form of libraries are the creation of modern ICT and such libraries are common now. Hybrid libraries are described as 'the continuum between the conventional and digital library, where electronic and paper-based information sources are used alongside each other' (Pinfield et al., 1998). When seeking to define convergence, Field (2001) explains that multiple meanings can be attached to the phrase, including organizational or formal convergence involving management structures, and operational or informal convergence whereby functions or operations of the service are changed or merged. Operational convergence between the two library and computing disciplines offers the following possibilities: collaboration between the two sets of staff on information services and development projects; joint training of users in information technology skills; joint enquiry desk services and potential multi-skilling for staff; increased liaison with academic departments.

Kerry M. Wilson and Eddie Halpin reported the result of a case study done in academic LIS departments of four British Universities as follows. The study was done in City Campus Learning Centre at Leeds Metropolitan

University; Aldham Robarts Learning Resource Centre at John Moores University, Liverpool; City Learning Centre at the University of Northumbria at Newcastle and Adsetts Learning Centre at Sheffield Hallam University. The phenomenal growth and rate of change in information communication technology and electronic information services have had a profound and far reaching effect upon learning and information services (LIS) in British academia. During the past decade, the effects of these changes have been reported widely in terms of the advent of converged services, and the subsequent financial implications and impacts upon management, resources and staff training and development. Such changes in the deployment of staff resources, and the changing role and duties of academic library staff, have encouraged a new professional philosophy within the sector. To complement the hybrid library environment, academic LIS professionals have evolved to become new hybrid information professionals, encouraged by a process of work assimilation between disciplines and across professional boundaries, posing questions about the true professional identity of contemporary academic librarianship.

The hybrid librarian draws on a wealth of generic, transferable skills, which are dominated by a commitment to customer care and standards of service. The contemporary LIS professional has embraced new, transferable skills, and does not consider them to be a threat to professional standards within the sector, but an inevitable consequence of convergence and changing service dynamics. The role of the traditional subject librarian has become subsumed by the role of the hybrid librarian, and the assimilated, generic duties associated with this post. As a result, the LIS professional has acquired new job titles that reflect this new professional identity. This has raised some issues for staff in terms of professional identity, as it is generally felt that job titles do not communicate the extent of their skills and experience. Job descriptions have been revised as a result of convergence, and are more regularly updated to reflect the constant changes. Essential and desirable skills have become more diverse and demanding. (Wilson and Halpin, 2006).

Dr. APJ Abdul Kalam, an eminent scientist and former President of India mooted the idea of 'World Knowledge Platform' at the IBM Investors meet at Bangalore on June 07, 2006. Dr Kalam proposed this to achieve and integrate the core competencies of the partner countries to develop knowledge products. He continued by saying that this platform will enable joint design, development, cost effective production and marketing of the knowledge products in various domains. He asked IBM to look at possible collaborations or consortium with Indian industries for the development of integrated hardware, software integrated system of tablet PC, which will be useful to the 300 Million Indian students alone apart from the other common users, professionals and executives of multiple countries. He added that the joint design, development and manufacture of a handheld tablet Personal Computer (PC) with multilingual capability in a cost effective manner with open source operating system and software configured for the school students and the common world citizens. The students should be able to use this as a digital book, notebook and as an e-learning device. This tablet PC will have the wireless connectivity so that it can take care of the communication needs and possibly the telephone and will have sufficient video capability to act as an entertainment platform and for tele-education and telemedicine and even a hand writing recognizer that will also permit authentication for secure e-business transactions.

Giving a glimpse of technology revolution to come, Dr. Kalam, asked whether a computer can challenge the human brain? Most of the computers of the future and accessories will be micro sized, wearable and will have wireless communication with each other. Moderately priced PCs capable of performing about a billion calculations per second today will be able to perform about a trillion calculations per second within next 10 years. It is predicted that by 2019, the computational ability of an ordinary PC would exceed the capability of human brain. He added that by 2029, the capability of a normal PC would be around 1000 times that of the human brain. However, he said that the creativity of the human mind will always be superior to the most powerful computers in the horizon. By the end of this century, there would be a strong trend towards convergence of human thinking with the world of machine intelligence that the human species initially created. When there would no longer be any clear distinction between human and computers, how would the molecular biologists help us to retain the supremacy of man over machine? Computers are going to give us a challenge. It is not only for the ICT and biotechnologists; the entire scientific community would have greater responsibility of keeping the mankind above the man-made computers, human creativity being the prime mover (Kalam, 2006). The views of Kalam clearly indicate the future issues to be addressed by the Library and Information Professionals as Knowledge Workers. The convergence of different technologies poses several tasks to be managed by the future libraries. Change management, rapid re-engineering and re-defining to the tune of technologies and situations will have to be addressed by the libraries properly.

The convergence of ICT and LIS has necessitated

re-defining many of the roles of the conventional librarian as digital librarian, especially in the context of Digital Information Systems (DIS). The need for such transformation has been strongly advocated by Gopinath (1996) and Sreenivasulu (2000). Prof. M.A. Gopinath, Documentation Research and Training Centre, Bangalore identified several competencies required for a library and information specialist in the modern era.

Sreenivasulu stresses that the multimedia nature of the next generation of digital libraries requires the digital librarians (DL) to be essentially a type of specialist librarian who has to manage and organize the digital library, handle the specialized tasks of massive digitization, storage, access, digital knowledge mining, digital reference services, electronic information services, search co-ordination, and manage the archive and its access. The digital librarian acts as guardian of the information superhighway / the universal digital library or the global digital library and acts as a symbiotic human-machine 'guru'. He also highlights the roles and functions of a DL in information retrieval, content delivery, navigation, and browsing and envisages the professional education and training for digital librarians in the management of digital information systems. According to him, as huge digital libraries are emerging as knowledge warehouses, Digital librarians are required to: manage the digital libraries; organize digital knowledge and information; disseminate digital information from the computer-held digital information; provide digital reference services and electronic information services; provide knowledge mining from the emerging knowledge warehouses; handle the tasks of massive digitization, digital storage process, and digital preservation; provide universal access and retrieval of digital knowledge, ultimately access to all; catalogue and classify digital documents and digital knowledge.

He describes the Competencies and skills of a digital librarian and their importance in the management of DIS / digital libraries. Such competencies can be represented by different sets of skills, attitudes and values that enable a digital librarian to work as digital information professional or digital knowledge worker and digital knowledge communicator. The skills and competencies that the digital librarian should develop are web navigation, browsing, filtering, retrieving, accessing, digital document analysis, digital reference services, electronic information services, searching network databases in a number of digital sources and Websites, creating home pages, content conversion, downloading techniques, Web publishing, electronic publishing, archiving digital documents, locating digital sources, digital preservation and storage, electronic messaging, connectivity skills, Web authoring, Multimedia technology, digital media processing, multimedia indexing, image processing, object-oriented processing, interactive digital communications and visualization, cataloguing and classification of digital documents, digital content, searching and retrieval of text, images and other multimedia objects, speech recognition, image visualization, advanced processing capabilities, exploiting digital medium, videoconferencing techniques, Digital information system, online, optical information, interfacing online and off-ramps, twists and turns of digital knowledge, development of digital information sources, digitization of print collections, competency to manage CD-ROM network stations, development of machine readable catalogue records, design and development of databases, design and development of software agents for digital libraries, conversion of print media into digital media, knowledge in digital knowledge structures, etc.

Allan Foster reported that many universities in UK and USA were in the line of integrating libraries and computer services. He quoted the pioneering initiatives done by Columbia University and Carnegie Mellon University using the concept of the 'Chief Information Officer' role that can be traced back to the early 1980s. This kind of integration, in one flavour or another, has become a popular strategy, with more than 70 per cent of universities in the UK adopting some kind of serious convergence and common management. The cross functions that have been tried for convergence are: Library, Academic computing service; Audio-visual/media/educational development unit, Administrative computing, Website management, Telephone services, Reprographic services (photocopying, printing, etc.), Teaching/learning initiatives and/or staff development, etc. (Foster, 2006). However, it became much more widely adopted in the UK in the late 1980s and first half of the 1990s. This was encouraged in part by the influential Follett Committee Report (1993) published in 1993, which pushed UK university libraries to re-evaluate their changing roles and how they work with IT.

2.5 INFORMATION LITERACY

IFLA/UNESCO (2006) Internet Manifesto Guidelines defined Information Literacy as follows:

"The concept of information literacy generally implies the ability to make effective use of information sources, including analysing and evaluating information, and organising and using it in an individual or group context. If users cannot understand or process information correctly then freedom of access to information may come to nothing. The development of critical tools for dissection of information is crucial therefore, and information literacy programs can be integral to the creation of an appropriate framework for access to information in libraries".

Information Literacy is defined by the Association of College and Research Libraries in the United States as "*the set of skills needed to find, retrieve, analyze, and use information.*" These skills are critical to the creation of an equitable global 'Information Society' in which both developed and developing nations can share in social and economic development. (Sayers, 2006).

Conception of information literacy, used primarily in the library and information studies field, and rooted in the concepts of library instruction and bibliographic instruction, is the ability "*to recognize when information is needed and have the ability to locate, evaluate and use effectively the needed information*". In this view, information literacy is the basis for life-long learning, and an information literate person is one who: recognizes that accurate and complete information is the basis for intelligent decision making recognizes the need for information knows how to locate needed information formulates questions based on information needs identifies potential sources of information develops successful search strategies accesses sources of information including computer-based and other technologies evaluates information no matter what the source organizes information for practical application integrates new information into an existing body of knowledge uses information in critical thinking and problem solving uses information ethically and legally (Doyle, 1994).

Since information may be presented in a number of formats, the term information applies to more than just the printed word. Other literacies such as visual, media, computer, network, and basic literacies are implicit in information literacy. A seminal event in the development of the concept of information literacy was the establishment of the American Library Association's Presidential Committee on Information Literacy whose final report outlined the importance of the concept. The concept of information literacy built upon and expanded the decades-long efforts of librarians to help their users learn about and how to utilize research tools (e.g., periodical indexes) and materials in their own libraries. Librarians wanted users to be able to transfer and apply this knowledge to new environments and to research tools that were new to them. Information literacy expands this effort beyond libraries and librarians, and focuses on the learner, rather than the teacher (Grassian, 2004; Grassian and Kaplowitz, 2001, pp.14-20). The user's knowledge about the options in OPAC also is an important factor in utilizing the possibilities. Many of the users are still unaware of these options. This necessitates thorough user education about the use of OPAC in the computerized environment (Hussain and Raza, 2002). Based on a study on electronic journals at IIT, Delhi, Ali and Hassan (2003) reported that only 45.45 percent of users were aware about the list of online journals subscribed by the library and 34.34 percent of users were utilizing these services.

Because information literacy skills are vital to future success, it is the normal notion that the Information literacy skills must be taught in the context of the overall process; and the instruction in information literacy skills must be integrated into the curriculum and reinforced both within and outside of the educational setting. In United States proper standards and guidelines have been evolved in this direction. With the passage of the Goals 2000: Educate America Act (1994), subject matter organizations were able to obtain funding to develop standards in their respective subject areas. Information literacy skills are implicit in the National Education Goals and national content standards documents. Individual states are creating initiatives to ensure that students attain information literacy skills by the time they graduate from high school (Comings, Garner and Smith, 2007).

Educational reform and restructuring make information literacy skills a necessity as students seek to construct their own knowledge and create their own understandings. Educators are selecting various forms of resource-based learning (authentic learning, problem-based learning and work-based learning) to help students focus on the process and to help students learn from the content. Information literacy skills are necessary components of each. Web based information literacy tutorials are being created and integrated with curriculum areas, or being used for staff development purposes. Library media programs are fostering information literacy by integrating the presentation of information literacy skills with curriculum at all grade levels.

Information literacy efforts are not being limited to the library field, but are also being employed by regional educational consortia. Parents are encouraging their children to develop information literacy skills at home by contacting KidsConnect, the Internet help and referral service for K-12 students.

Efforts in higher education are also effective. The inclusion of information competencies as a graduation requirement is the key that will fully integrate information literacy into the curricula of academic institutions. Information literacy instruction in higher education can take a variety of forms: stand-alone courses or classes, online tutorials, workbooks, course-related instruction, or course-integrated instruction.

State-wide university systems and individual colleges and universities are undertaking strategic planning to determine information competencies, to incorporate instruction in information competence throughout the curriculum and to add information competence as a graduation requirement for students. Librarians often are required to teach the concepts of information literacy during "one shot" classroom lectures. There are also credit courses offered by academic librarians to prepare college students to become information literate. Academic library programs are preparing faculty to facilitate their students' mastery of information literacy skills so that the faculty can in turn provide information literacy learning experiences for the students enrolled in their classes.

Now that information literacy has become a part of the core curriculum at many post-secondary institutions, it is incumbent upon the library community to be able to provide information literacy instruction in a variety of formats, including online learning and distance education. The Association of College and Research Libraries (ACRL) addresses this need in its Guidelines for Distance Education Services (ACRL, 2000):

"Library resources and services in institutions of higher education must meet the needs of all their faculty, students, and academic support staff, wherever these individuals are located, whether on a main campus, off campus, in distance education or extended campus programs — or in the absence of a campus at all, in courses taken for credit or non-credit; in continuing education programs; in courses attended in person or by means of electronic transmission; or any other means of distance education."

The American Library Association (ALA) states that

"Information literacy is a survival skill in the Information Age" (ALA, 1989), and calls for re-defining and a restructuring of the learning process itself, rather than the curriculum. Revamping the process would ensure that students should:

- know when they need information
- identify what information will address a particular problem
- find the needed information
- evaluate the information
- organize the information
- use the information effectively in addressing the problem

ALA, ACRL, American Association for Higher Education) and the Council of Independent Colleges set the following five Information Literacy Competency Standards for higher education (ALA, 2000). It also provided performance indicators for each standard:

Standard 1: The information literate student determines the nature and extent of the information needed.

Performance Indicators

Indicator 1. The information literate student defines and articulates the need for information.

Indicator 2. The information literate student identifies a variety of types and formats of potential sources for information.

Indicator 3. The information literate student considers the costs and benefits of acquiring the needed information.

Indicator 4. The information literate student reevaluates the nature and extent of the information need.

Standard 2 : The information literate student accesses needed information effectively and efficiently.

Performance Indicators

Indicator 1. The information literate student selects the most appropriate investigative methods or information retrieval systems for accessing the needed information.

Indicator 2. The information literate student constructs and implements effectively designed search strategies.

Indicator 3. The information literate student retrieves information online or in person using a variety of methods.

Indicator 4. The information literate student refines the search strategy if necessary.

Indicator 5. The information literate student extracts, records, and manages the information and its sources.

Standard 3: The information literate student evaluates information and its sources critically and incorporates selected information into his or her knowledge base and value system.

Performance Indicators

Indicator 1. The information literate student summarizes the main ideas to be extracted from the information gathered.

Indicator 2. The information literate student articulates and applies initial criteria for evaluating both the information and its sources.

Indicator 3. The information literate student synthesizes main ideas to construct new concepts.

Indicator 4. The information literate student

compares new knowledge with prior knowledge to determine the value added, contradictions, or other unique characteristics of the information.

Indicator 5. The information literate student determines whether the new knowledge has an impact on the individual's value system and takes steps to reconcile differences.

Indicator 6. The information literate student validates understanding and interpretation of the information through discourse with other individuals, subject-area experts, and/or practitioners.

Indicator 7. The information literate student determines whether the initial query should be revised.

Standard 4: The information literate student, individually or as a member of a group, uses information effectively to accomplish a specific purpose.

Performance Indicators

Indicator 1. The information literate student applies new and prior information to the planning and creation of a particular product or performance.

Indicator 2. The information literate student revises the development process for the product or performance.

Indicator 3. The information literate student communicates the product or performance effectively to others.

Standard 5: The information literate student understands many of the economic, legal, and social issues surrounding the use of information and accesses and uses information ethically and legally.

Performance Indicators

Indicator 1. The information literate student understands many of the ethical, legal and socio-economic issues surrounding information and information technology.

Indicator 2. The information literate student follows laws, regulations, institutional policies, and etiquette related to the access and use of information resources.

Indicator 3. The information literate student acknowledges the use of information sources in communicating the product or performance.

Addressing Information Literacy Needs and in response to the challenges of incorporating technology into teaching and learning and the creation of community at a large public university, the University of Washington (UW) had developed a holistic, campus-wide approach called UWired. The primary goal of UWired was to create an electronic community in which communication, collaboration, and information technologies were integral to teaching and learning; ultimately, the aim was for information literacy to be a hallmark of a UW degree. In this process of restructuring both pedagogy and paradigm, librarians were active partners in the development and implementation of UWired initiatives, which address faculty development, active student learning, and facilities redesign. Librarians, faculty, computing staff, administrators, and students from a number of units across campus were collaborating in this project, including Undergraduate Education, Computing & Communications, University Libraries, and University Educational Outreach. UWired seeks to go beyond technology as an end in itself, and instead offered sustained discipline-specific instruction, useful educational applications of technology, faculty and librarian development, and the requisite facilities and infrastructure (Williams and Zald, 1997).

In a study at the East Carolina University, Colaric

(2003) observed that the Users searching the Web have difficulty in using search engines and developing queries. Searches tend to be simple, and Boolean operators were used infrequently and incorrectly. Users also were unaware that search engines operate differently from other information retrieval systems. The number of users accessing the Web was increasing, as was the amount of information on the Web. Although efforts were being made to increase the usability of the search engine itself, progress was slow. It was further observed that effective instruction would be the key to increase the return of relevant results and decreasing user frustration while searching the Web. This observation stresses the importance of re-defining the information literacy programmes in the line of the ever increasing digital information resources and web based services.

OCLC has conducted a survey on "Students' Perceptions of Libraries and Information Resources" (OCLC, 2006). On "Awareness of Library Electronic Resources", most college students responded that they that were aware of library electronic resources. But, this awareness among total respondents was low. Respondents were asked to indicate if their library provides various types of electronic resources. College students surveyed show high levels of awareness of library electronic resources across all eight categories. Nearly three quarters or more were aware their library has a library Web site (87 percent), an online library catalog (86 percent) and online reference materials (71 percent). Nearly half or more of college students were aware their library has electronic books (47 percent), an online librarian question service (45 percent), electronic magazines/journals (62 percent) and online databases (62 percent). The awareness of whether their library has audio books (downloadable/ digital) was mixed; with 43 percent who are aware the library has this resource and 44 percent who were not sure if their library has audio books.

Results also indicated that awareness among total respondents was low for most of the library's electronic resources. For example, 58 percent of all respondents were not sure if their library offers access to online databases. Of the eight library electronic resources evaluated, total respondents show the highest level of awareness for the library Web site and online library catalog, with at least 60 percent who are aware the library has these resources.

Regarding the familiarity with the library web site, it was revealed that most of the college students have used a library Web site. Respondents were asked about their familiarity with library Web sites, the main point of access to libraries' catalogs and resources. College student respondents were more familiar with library web sites than the total respondents. Most college students know the library Website exists, and 35 percent were either extremely familiar or very familiar with the library website. Among college students who have never used an online library Website, the main reason was that other websites have better information (44 percent). Nineteen percent of college students said that they did not know it was existed or it does not exist and 15 percent reported they could not find the library Website. For the total respondents who reported they have never visited an online library Website, they did not know the Website existed/does not exist was the primary reason cited for lack of use. Fifty-five percent of total respondents report they did not know the library Website exists or said it does not exist.

Barbara Valentine reported that studies on research behavior have demonstrated that students are drawn to information sources based on ease of use and favoring convenience of access over quality of information. It also revealed that students tend to avoid resources they are unfamiliar with or believe are difficult to use, returning to tools they have used successfully in the past (Valentine, 1993). In a separate study conducted by Debbie Malone and Carol Videon, students most frequently cited ease of use as their reason for selecting electronic resources over print materials (Malone and Videon, 1997). Several other researchers found that students favour electronic resources primarily for their convenience and efficiency and indicated a strong preference for full-text access to information.

Similar results were also reported by Lombardo and Miree (2003) based on a study on business students. It indicated that the development of more comprehensive, relevant, and easily searchable subject directories and search engines (e.g., Yahoo, Google) and the ubiquity of the Web have resulted in a generation of students who now perceive the Internet as the most familiar, convenient, and expedient source of information. They asserted that after proper library instruction, students held more favorable attitudes toward print resources and used them in their research more.

This was a clear indication that the library instruction and information literacy programmes have to be re-structured in order to get the users a proper understanding on different types of information resources in different formats. In a study by Biradar and Sampath Kumar (2005) in universities in Karnataka state, it was found that the most common obstacles to the use of Internet and Web based sources to research scholars and faculty members were lack of Internet facility and lack of training regarding the Internet use.

Oladokun (2006) describes an example of the University of Botswana (UB). It was running a research project on e-learning pilots since 2003. Already there was a clear institutional strategy for online teaching of students, combined with interactive video conferencing, e-learning and other educational technologies, to create virtual classroom. The teaching of information literacy skills by the librarians (discussed below) was part of the agenda. The library has its own University of Botswana electronic learning (UBel) team, which has been working to put some of the course contents in WebCT (Web Course Tools) for online delivery. In the meantime the library database was accessible via Internet. Accessibility to several thousands of articles from electronic journals was ensured through the University of Botswana Library (UBL) web page. The library systems also have self-help and self-service functions, whereby individual borrowers could carry out book renewal from any computer with an Internet connection, anywhere within or outside the university campus.

Teaching of Information Literacy Skills

The new pedagogic paradigm in vogue tends towards accentuating the empowerment of students and encouraging them to take control of their own learning. This move towards a knowledge-based society in a rapidly changing educational pattern was driving universities to prepare their students for lives and careers in the Information Age. For its part, the University of Botswana Library, as custodian of information, indubitably believed that it has a strong role to play in this exercise. The teaching of information literacy skills (ILS) was perceived as a sine qua non to equip the students to be able to cope effectively with the demands of the new age of information and lifelong learning. At the UBL, the information literacy skills programme was regarded as a fundamental service to be rendered in order to guarantee resource-based and independent learning by University of Botswana students. Lumande, Ojedokun and Fidzani (2006) note that ILS programmes at UBL were aiming at empowering students with life-long skills that are necessary for accessing, analysing and using information regardless of where the information may be found. The students were offered general information literacy skills that emphasize theory as well as skills in the use of printed and electronically based information sources, including Motswedi on-line public access catalogue (OPAC), and CD-ROM databases and now . . . teaching of Internet. For a long time the UBL had been clamouring for official recognition of the teaching of information literacy skills at the university. The library's efforts appear to have yielded some dividend of late, with the librarians now not just playing the role of 'the sage on the stage' but also functioning as 'the guide on the side'. The librarians, in conjunction or collaboration with the lecturers in the Computer Science Department, jointly developed the curriculum of, and teach, General Education Courses (GEC) 121 and 122. It should, however, be emphasized that prior to the integration of ILS into the curricula of the University, the different departments and faculties had been teaching ILS skills in a sporadic and uncoordinated manner. The respective faculties and the University Library were responsible for handling the ILS course (Ojedokun and Lumande, 2005).

The integration of Information Skills into the University curriculum also required the introduction of a computing skills component. The skills-based courses were taught for two semesters, with GEC 121 in the first semester serving as a requirement for GEC 122 in the second semester. The two credit courses were mandatory for all first year students of the University, irrespective of the course of study for which they were registered – be it certificate, diploma or degree programme. The job of the librarians at the University of Botswana involves active teaching on how to find, use and evaluate information as part of a lifelong learning continuum. The information skills component taught in the first semester includes such topics as the Concept of Information, Organization of Information, Information Access Tools and Reference Sources. In the second semester topics taught include Introduction to Periodical Literature, Introduction to Electronic Databases (Indexes, Abstracts and Full electronic databases), Legal Issues of Information Use and Citation Styles and Evaluation of Information Resources. With the new 'learning to learn' slogan at the university, the students endeavour to master new competencies in information skills as they were being guided on how to function appropriately in the constantly changing society. Based on the experiences at the University College Dublin, McGuinness (2007) suggested institution level re-structuring of the ILP and it may be offered as curriculum based programme. The Librarians should be aware of major curriculum reforms that may offer them a chance to reposition and integrate IL on a more permanent basis within the pedagogical structure of the institution.

In order that the distance learners of the University of Botswana might not be left behind, the content of the information literacy skills courses has been developed into modules and given to distance learners in the same manner as they receive other courses. During the occasional residential or study weekend sessions, librarians were given slots and deployed to the four study centres presently available across the country to provide tutorial lessons to distance learners in the same way as was done for other courses. This provided opportunities for face-to-face practical sessions, enabling distance learners to have hands-on experience and also to ask questions. It thus attempts to bridge the gap and bring a human face to the seemingly faceless system of distance education. Based on a study on the use of Internet in engineering colleges in Karnataka State, Kumbar and Raju (2007) reported that 92.22% of the respondents use Internet only for e-mail and stressed the need for training facilities for the faculty and students to make use of the information resources available on the Internet.

In India, though the Information Literacy Programme (ILP) is not conducted as a compulsory course by all libraries, several university and college libraries are effectively organizing such programmes. The NAAC (2006) has reported the best practices on ILP conducting by some colleges and universities in India. Such practices of the College of Horticulture (Constituent College of the Kerala Agriculture University), Thrissur and the Loyola College Social Sciences (Affiliated College of the Kerala Universty), Thiruvananthapuram, were reported by NAAC from the Kerala State. Considering the importance of knowledge management skills, the Mahatma Gandhi University has recently introduced a curriculum based ILP module for its MSc botany course and discussions were going on to include such programmes for other courses also.

Whilst evaluation of the teaching of information literacy skills may not yet have been carried out, no one is in any doubt that the students who undergo the study are much better with the training than without it, as they are equipped with lifelong learning skills. For instance, among many other things, it is observed that the students and other users seem to be more familiar with the use and application of electronic information resources.

2.6 WEBSITES AND HOME PAGES

The pre-dominance of digital information has posed several related problems in the access and use of such information. Most academic librarians regard the library as the primary gateway to information for the university community. They believe that they have a significant responsibility for information literacy instruction, specifically for the selection, use, and evaluation of information resources, including Internet resources. But experience is that many libraries are failing to maximize their ability to present the Internet to users in an organized manner. In the presentation of collections and services on library home pages, libraries often provide inadequate paths to resources, guides for selection, evaluation and use of search engines, and other navigational tools necessary for users to make intelligent and informed choices about resources beyond those owned and licensed in the institution's collections.

A library's Web page is the most common vehicle for the delivery of instruction and information. McGillis and Toms (2001) reiterated that, "*in the digital environment, a library web site is the virtual public face—the quasi-equivalent of the front door, signage, pathfinders, collections, services, and, to an extent, people*". Many studies have reported the difficulties users experience in navigating academic library Websites. In a study on user perceptions of the library's Webpages at Texas A&M University, researchers found that "there was an obvious need for clearer, simpler terminology to facilitate navigation and decision making (Crowley et al, 2002). Mark Spivey also has emphasized the need for clarity of the home page and usage of clear terminology for successful navigation of a large library website (Spivey, 2000).

Wright (2004) observed that academic libraries have the opportunity through their Web pages to present to the university community recommended sites and appropriate techniques for searching the Internet. But in the design and organization of home pages, academic libraries often provide inadequate navigational paths to sites that provide search engine selection and evaluation criteria. He noted that libraries are increasingly using the Web to direct users to resources beyond their own licensed collections, but there is a striking and disturbing inconsistency among libraries in the presentation of these Internet-searching resources. This research found that 67 percent of the sites studied have dedicated Internet-searching pages that include search engines, guides, and tutorials. Moreover, libraries that do not offer high-quality Internet search engine links, user guides, and instruction lose a great opportunity to attract students and to position themselves as the primary gateway for information.

An OCLC (2002) study on web based information services conducted during 2001-02 among college students revealed the following:

Seven-in-ten students use the campus library website for at least some of their assignments, and one-in-five use it for most assignments. College students find out about the library's website from multiple sources, including from their professors and teaching assistants (49%), by looking it up themselves (45%), from classes about using the library (34%), and from librarians (27%). Among the students who do not use the campus library's website, some (20%) did not know the library had a site, and some (29%) say it doesn't have what they need, but nearly half (43%) feel other sites have better information. During their most recent electronic visit, most used full texts of journal articles (67%), the library's catalog (57%), databases and journal indexes (51%), and electronic books (21%). Few college students use any "Ask-a-librarian" services.

Perceived barriers

From their points of view as library users, students

identify several major barriers to their successful use of library resources. Regardless of whether or not these barriers are genuine, students perceive that access is denied, because of the following: Inability to access databases remotely due to password requirements and/or license restrictions; Difficulty in searching and navigating within the library and its website; Costs of copying and printing at the library; Shortage of knowledgeable librarians; Lack of the customer orientation they have come to expect as consumers.

A sampling of their verbatim comments is below:

i. *"Allow remote access to catalog / periodicals / reserve information for students with Internet access at home."*

ii. *"The whole point to a library is to have information that can be accessed EASILY and used for one's [own] uses. When that information is there, however, it is too difficult to get it ...what good does it do...?"*

iii. *"Librarians are always too busy to help you when you need help. You have to be an expert to be able to navigate through their system."*

The awareness that librarians have more information than they make available to remote. The University of Houston (UH) Libraries had undertaken a project to reshape and restructure its Website. At the time, all content was passed through the Web services department before becoming part of the site. As a result, making updates was a time-consuming task and significant portions of the site were out-of-date. In addition, the site's structure was rigid and inflexible and provided no space for staff or users to participate. Assessment revealed that staff members wanted to control their own content and to have a way to make the site more engaging and interesting to their users. Based on this assessment, it was decided to make the Website that was more "Web 2.0" in nature. Web 2.0 is often defined by the technologies that are part of it: social software, Weblogs, linklogs, folksonomies, wikis, podcasts, RSS feeds, and Web services. "Web 2.0" is transforming the Web into a space that allows anyone to create and share information online—a space for collaboration, conversation, and interaction; a space that is highly dynamic, flexible, and adaptable. Based on the experimental study at Houston, they designed six pillars of Web 2.0 that can be used as the foundation for rebuilding the library Websites. These pillars are (Jadav, 2007):

i. Radical decentralization
ii. Small pieces loosely joined
iii. Perpetual beta
iv. Re-mixable content
v. User as contributor
vi. Rich user experience

For exploiting the possibilities of Library Websites and homepages, Indian libraries were not crossed the real take off. Even though, it was noteworthy to consider the best practices on library websites and homepages of Madurai Kamaraj University, Bangalore University and University of Hyderabad, reported by the NAAC (2006).

2.7 EVALUATION OF RE-ENGINEERING AND RE-DEFINING

An experience of the re-engineering of Hewlett-Packard's CD-RW supply chain management system has been evaluated by Hammel, Kuettner and Phelps (2002). Their goal was to identify the most cost-effective supply chain network for the CD-RW product line, relative to a required level of customer service. To do this, they tried to understand the key cost drivers behind the supply chain and compare various scenarios (supply chain network configurations). They modeled eight main scenarios, each scenario representing a particular network configuration. The main points of analysis were adding a world-wide distribution center to perform localization tasks currently performed at the regional centers, and the use of air vs surface freight to reduce the amount of time inventory remained in the system. Higher air freight costs might be justified, if it shortened inventory holding time, thus reducing inventory-driven costs.

The results of the initial modeling phase indicated that the best scenario overall consisted of one world-wide distribution center in Asia doing all conversion, localization and distribution, with products shipped by air from the world-wide center to all HP customers. It was reported that the main issue was keeping everyone synched up and working in parallel. HP established "mirror" teams between product generation and manufacturing, and product generation and regions, with team leads, strong high-level sponsorship, and a steering committee (subset of sponsors) that was actively engaged in project reviews and problem solving. Teams made extensive use of e-mail and voicemail to communicate project status to the other teams, and kept key documents on share drives that were visible around the world.

With this project, HP achieved a 90 per cent reduction in supply chain cycle time, from 126 days to eight days and achieved a negative cash-to-cash cycle time by persuading their suppliers to take net 45 instead of net 30 days for payment, in return for preferential supplier status for HP's CD-RW line. They implemented collaborative planning, forecasting and replenishment (CPFR) with their channel partners, which provided timely sell-through information to HP and the supplier. They realized $50m annual savings for HP, resulting from reduced inventory-driven costs, reduced manufacturing overheads, material sourcing benefits. The savings were so great that they recouped all implementation costs in the first month of operation. In addition to the above-described quantifiable benefits, HP also realized intangible benefits from process simplification through the use of the world-wide depot model which outperforms the regional model. During the transition period (September 1999 through May 2000) HP grew its US market share from 27 per cent to 60 per cent and significantly beat revenue and profitability projections.

Many of the re-engineering experiences of the HP are applicable to a library service situation. The points of quick service, global communication and access, team work, quality improvement, cost reduction, etc. are cardinal points to be adopted by a library to provide quality service to their clientele to out perform in education and research in the present competitive environment.

Based on a study in Ramnarain Ruia College Library, Mumbai, Badiger (2001) reported that over and above the user awareness and interest in using automated services, a quantum leap was needed to encourage library staff to exploit the potential of modern technology and bring radical changes to the functioning of the library. Appropriate management of change was also advocated by the study. The observation of Badiger has stressed by Whithead (2001). He states that organizations or senior managers have to persuade their workforce to implement new workflow practices necessary for Business Process Re-engineering (BPR) to succeed. Change should be considered as journey and should incorporate regular measurement and analysis to enable to reach its targets. The starting point and the end should be known.

The Yuan Ze University (YZU), Taiwan has

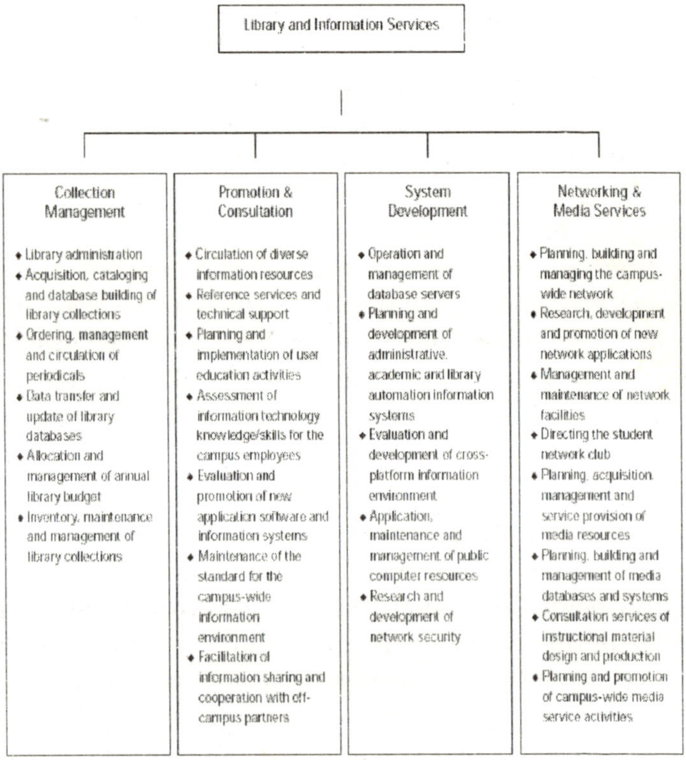

Fig. 2.7.1. Library and Information Service Divisions in YZU Library

Source: Liang (1999)

implemented a project for re-engineering its Library and Information Services (Liang, 1999). The project identified true integration of information activities and information services as the real need of the day. The experience shows that integral use of information technology and information resources could win exemplary results in resource management and service maximization. Re-defining the activities and procedures of conventional divisions of the library has been done along with the re-engineering process. The effort of re-engineering and re-defining was involved significant change for the staff because relocation meant radical change in their work environment, their partners, their job content, and even their professional culture. But, this change was followed by a six-month period of stability which allowed them time to adjust their work routines, pace, and mood. During this period, a more open to change, where people were more self-confident and self-monitoring.

Birth of the integrated organization

The name of the Office of Information Services was changed to the Library and Information Services (LIS) and its head have been designated as the Dean of LIS, and assistant head as the Vice Dean of LIS. The staff of the library and computing center was fully integrated and the LIS Division comprised four divisions: Collection Management, Promotion and Consultation, System Development, and Networking and Media Services as shown in the Figure: 2.7.1.

Liang underlined the following success factors of re-engineering derived from both literature and from YZU's experience:

1. Having a visionary leadership.
2. Making a wide-ranging impact on the target organization.
3. Attending to every crucial aspect of the organization within a short timeframe.
4. Utilizing technology accurately.
5. Creating an organizational learning culture experience.
6. Integrating the organization's mission with that of the parent organization.
7. Understanding the contemporary meaning of "Information Services".

8. Leavening the "S+1" function. "S+1" means a system plus an external force.
9. Providing time for adapting to the new situation.
10. Working on strategic alliances.
11. Making every effort to achieve concrete results.
12. Keeping a balance between ideal and reality.
13. Respecting human factors.
14. Responding proactively to organizational politics.
15. Establishing a solid infrastructure for future development.

Integrating the mission with that of the parent organization

By integrating its mission with the parent organization's technological application, the library and computing center gained wide acclaim at YZU, In order to achieve this ideal, YZU focused its investment not only on the hardware and software, but also on a variety of education and training activities in which LIS played the key role for implementing these tasks. For example, at YZU, every freshman needs to take a general course designed by LIS, "Introduction to Information Society." LIS was the information literacy comprehension test for campus employees. In addition, LIS provided its professional consultation services to set up distance learning and computer conferencing environments.

Making every effort to achieve concrete results

The re-engineering process of LIS concentrated on several target activities such as:

1. Implementing virtual integration (e.g. moving the technical support staff from the computing center to work with reference librarians in the library).
2. Designing customer-oriented services (e.g. visiting

academic units to collect diverse information needs).

3. Holding various information services promotional activities (e.g. holding a homepage design contest and establishing the interactive media center).
4. Advancing technological applications (e.g. developing Web-based OPEC systems).
5. Facilitating cross-universities' resource sharing (e.g. holding academic seminars with other universities).

Politics

Many campus workers, including some teachers, suspected that the real goal of the re-engineering project might be to enlarge the power of the information service organizations. This misunderstanding, plus the democratic environment of higher education, raised various hurdles for the task force to overcome. Such misunderstanding has been resolved smoothly.

Establishing a solid infrastructure for future development

The YZU experience warns that any library should take some basic concepts that must first be translated into actions. These include hardware and software-related issues (e.g. enhancing campus computer and cable networks, improving the ratio of computer/user, and refining information systems) as well as management-related activities (e.g. re-engineering service processes, developing human resources, changing organizational structure, and altering organizational culture). These actions must be parallel planned and executed to establish a solid infrastructure for future development. The National Library Board (NLB) of Singapore has implemented an ambitious plan proposed in the Report of the Library 2000

Review Committee created by the NLB. The NLB has since transformed the libraries by leveraging four building blocks - content, services, people and infrastructure. Through that library development programme, NLB found in each new library site an incubator for innovation. This has spawned a stream of killer applications. To move the organization towards achieving these, NLB has infused the organization with methodologies such as the business process re-engineering (BPR) exercise conducted for the re-design of core business processes. NLB has also harnessed project management methodology to help it develop ideas from inception to implementation. The achievements by NLB since 1995 have not only fulfilled many of the strategies outlined in the Library 2000 Report, but established a firm basis for further development by the NLB into a key player in the nation's national learning enterprise (Chia, 2001).

Christopher Chia gives a detailed account of the integrated library development achieved in Singapore by re-engineering and re-defining the activities and services. Other than a three-tier public library system of regional, community and children's libraries, NLB also manages the majority of junior college libraries; and government department libraries fall under the administration and the management of the NLB. In addition, a few schools have asked the NLB to manage their libraries. The Singapore Management University, Singapore's third university has also outsourced the entire operation of running its library to the NLB since 2000. Hence, NLB enjoyed the advantage that Singapore has an almost common platform for library management.

Infrastructure

Over the last five to six years, the NLB had doubled

the library services and the library sites. A robust supply chain for its materials and an integrated networked infrastructure was needed to support this burgeoning network of libraries. They have moved all their technical services people from a basement in the National Library building in the middle of the city to a warehousing complex about three to four minutes from the airport. This centre purchases on behalf of the national library system about one-and-a-half million books every year. The physical infrastructure of libraries has been augmented by a reliable network infrastructure, which includes local and wide area networks as well as the Singapore ONE broadband infrastructure to allow access to rich content and services anywhere.

Services

One of the key innovations was the rise of a stunning phenomenon – the shopping mall library. These libraries also led the way in the rebranding of Singapore libraries as a lifestyle option, none the least of which was Library@Orchard, an experimentation in 1999 to draw the "missing generation" of young adults who had been lured away from libraries by other attractions. The newest in this line of new-age libraries is the Woodlands Regional Library – Singapore's largest library of 11,000m^2 with more than 4,50,000 items. Opened on 28 April 2001, it was the epitome of all that has worked for NLB's libraries, and then some. The library has become a lifestyle learning mall.

Cinema-going was probably the third most popular lifestyle pursuit in Singapore, with the highest attendances per capita in the world. Yet cinemas have been suffering the attendance decline in these years while people were going back to the libraries. Because of this, every one in two Singaporeans became member of the library. They took more than 30 years to reach millionth member, they took less than six years for the other 8,50,000. But, staffing and budget had not been increased correspondingly. They have re-defined their service paradigms and introduced innovative ways such as electronic library management system (ELiMS), radio frequency identification (RFID) technology, pay library fees and charges using cashcards etc. to avoid long queues and frustrated customers. With ELiMS, stocktaking of books in a shopping mall library which used to take two weeks will take less than a day. The NLB also calculated a savings of 2,000 manpower positions a year due to this Innovation.

One of the most heartening success stories in the NLB's effort to equalize the nation's tech haves and have-nots in the One Learning Place. It had attracted more than 90,000 participants during 1999-2001. This included classes on IT and information literacy skills. Perhaps more heartening than the numbers was that taxi-drivers, housewives and senior citizens were amongst these students. The library provided a nurturing non-threatening environment for them to learn amongst peers – demonstrating the NLB's pivotal role in reaching segments of society on the wrong side of the digital divide. For the convenience of the customers, they have also embraced the Web in a big way to launch electronic services. This was something of double-edged sword since attendance figures in 1994 were not as high and they ran the risk of people not coming to our libraries if they could access it from home. The strangest phenomenon reported was that while their Website figures have climbed steadily, their site attendances have leapt astronomically. Through the Website, they have managed to provide additional convenience for the customers to check their accounts, reserve books, renew, request for deliveries, and recommend books for purchase. This also prevented them from facing the challenge of another three million people coming to their counters for those services.

People

The NLB conducted a business process re-engineering (BPR) exercise between June 1997 and January 1998 with the top 50 people in NLB as participants. The participants of the exercise were tasked with the identification, analysis and re-design of core business processes to remove redundancies – library planning and development, collection development, library operations, and information services. The only guidelines for the participants were that stretch targets for each of these activities should be proposed and met. The stretch targets were, in a word, ambitious. Perhaps as a result of the exponential improvement required to meet the stretch targets, the initiatives spawned by BPR have since become the "killer apps" for NLB. These included the RFID application in libraries. In order to build the library profession further they created an NLB Institute to provide training in the library and information field. The achievements by the NLB since 1995 have not only fulfilled many of the strategies outlined in the Library 2000 Report, but established a firm basis for further development by the NLB into a key player in the nation's national learning enterprise. These phenomenal achievements have been made with minimal increases in recurrent budget and manpower throughout the years.

A survey study by Al-Mashari, Irani and Zairi (2001) revealed that change management, TQM and benchmarking as important tools for organisations aiming to establish the BPR practice. Change management facilitates the insertion of the newly-designed business processes in the working environment. TQM ensures that re-engineering efforts take place when and where they are needed, and secures longer life for the improvements attained. Benchmarking helps shape the strategic direction of the efforts. Yet the findings show that these tools were not highly integrated with BPR. Their findings reveal that organisations were still not competent in integration aspects of BPR.

BPR methodology, techniques and tools

The success of BPR implementation is associated with the use of methodological tools. Yet human resources and change management-related issues are the areas that need to be methodologically addressed by researchers. The study also shows that while diagnosing current processes represents an important stage in BPR, organisations have a difficult task in implementing it. This can be traced directly to the difficulties associated with operationalizing the concept of process orientation and thinking itself, which has been discussed earlier. The study also points to the importance of both ensuring commitment and selecting processes, as two essential initial tasks. It also suggests that both management culture and the degree of formalisation and transparency in management systems can influence the way in which different individual activities may be prioritised. It was revealed that BPR success was associated with the use of techniques, and that organisations tend to use simple techniques and tools. They show that techniques of project planning and management, and process capturing and modelling are highly important in implementing BPR. The results of this study show that features of simplicity and usability by non-technical people, and the ability to enforce consistency in analysis and design are important to consider by software tools developers.

IT Infrastructure role in BPR

This study shows that a socio-technical perspective is the most suitable approach to derive a successful BPR. It also shows that taking a technical perspective to BPR implementation is highly associated with failure. However, BPR success is associated with the level of using supporting technologies. Document management, databases, and communication networks are the most widely used technologies to enable BPR.

A study on effectiveness of BPR by Khong and Richardson (2003) revealed that the acceptance of BPR has been reinforced by the implementation of re-engineering initiatives in many Malaysian banking institutions and the Central Bank of Malaysia, Bank Negara. The study concluded that Critical Success Factors (CSF) of BPR implementation has positive effects on banking and finance enterprises in terms of customer service management and business performance. Detail conclusions are:

i. Since CSFs of BPR implementation process could positively affect customer service management and business performance, BPR is considered a feasible management technique that can improve customer service management and business performance in Malaysian banking and finance companies.

ii. Change of management system and culture has positive effects on business performance of banks and finance companies. However, evidence shows that it has no effect on customer service management.

iii. Management of risk and BPR project management can positively affect customer service management of banks and finance companies. However, evidence shows that it has no effect on business performance.

iv. IT infrastructure has positive effects on customer

service management of banks and finance companies. However, evidence shows that it has no effect on business performance.

v. Customer service management has positive effects on business performance of banks and finance companies.

vi. Change of management system and culture, management of risk and BPR project management and IT infrastructure are highly correlated.

vii. Since CSFs of BPR implementation process could positively affect customer service management and business performance, BPR is considered a feasible management technique that can improve customer service management and business performance in Malaysian banking and finance companies.

The **Information Services Division (ISD), University of Salford, UK implemented a project of** re-engineering its business process re-engineering. As a learning organization, the major areas and focus of the project, CRISP (Customer Resolution and Information Services Project) issues of change management, increasing the effectiveness of customer relationships, etc. The ISD re-engineered its key processes to provide a customer-focused service with resources directed specifically to where they are required. The process has already met challenges, even though its scope was clearly defined. Those challenges include the complexity of the cultures, the threats of loss of momentum due to the need for thoroughness and fairness, and the need for planned communication and change management (Jeal, 2005).

A study by Eden and Bierman (2002), conducted in The New Lied Library at the University of Nevada, Las Vegas, focused on the planning and implementation of technology and change. It proposed for a major departmental re-organization within Lied Library using the concept of Knowledge Access Management (KAS) as

3
ICTs in University Libraries

3.1 INTRODUCTION

The modern ICTs have made radical changes in the conventional system of information processing and its delivery. The flood of information, especially in digital format, has posed lot of issues in the knowledge management scenario. Though the information resources are flooding world over and several technologies have emerged to manage the situation and providing effective information services to its clientele, most of the university libraries in India are not able to exploit these technologies at maximum level. Though all the libraries have automated many of their functions, wide gap prevails between the possible services and provided services. At the same time, there are many good examples world over in the application of ICTs in libraries for the maximization of services and many such libraries have adopted the principles of re-engineering and re-defining as a management strategy. This has posed several questions on how to effectively adopt the modern ICTs in our libraries for maximizing the efficiency of services and whether the principles of re-engineering and re-defining can be adopted for the purpose. On implementation of the recommentations of the National Knowledge Commission, the country is marching ahead to organize all possible infrastructural facilities in order to transform the economy into a knowledge economy. Such implemtation actions are evident in different sectors of the society. For example, the total number of universities in India has reached to 499 during the year 2010 (Association of Indian Universities, 2010). The following tables provide details of this growth.

Table 3.1.1. List of Universities and University level Insittutions in India as per UGC Notification

Sl.No.		*No.*
1	State Universities (including two universities established recently in Kerala veterinary and fisheries sectors)	242
2	Deemed Universities	130
3	Institutions of National Importance	33
4	Private Universities	49
5	Central Universities	40
6	Institutions established under State Legislature Act	05
7	Total	499

Source: Universities Handbook 2010. New Delhi: Association of Indian Universities

Table 3.1.2. Statewise List of Universities and Colleges in India as per UGC Notification

Sl. No.		*No. of Utys.*	*No. of Colleges*
1	Andhra Pradesh	35	448
2	Arunachal Pradesh	02	08
3	Assam	08	217

4	Bihar	18	328
5	Chattisgarh	12	60
6	Goa	01	24
7	Gujarat	27	400
8	Haryana	16	152
9	Himachal Pradesh	07	45
10	Jammu & Kashmir	09	97
11	Jharkand	08	98
12	Karnataka	33	549
13	Kerala (including two universities established recently in veterinary and fisheries sectors)	13	224
14	Madhya Pradesh	19	446
15	Maharashtra	44	839
16	Manipur	02	52
17	Meghalaya	04	19
18	Mizoram	02	18
19	Nagaland	03	15
20	Orissa	14	356
21	Punjab	13	203
22	Rajastan	38	225
23	Sikkim	05	03
24	Tamil Nadu	54	312
25	Tripura	02	16
26	Uttar Pradesh	46	959
27	Uttaranchal	16	37
28	West Bengal	23	362
29	Delhi	20	15
30	Chandigarh	03	16
31	Pondicherry	02	13
	Total	499	6556

Source: Universities Handbook 2010. New Delhi: Association of Indian Universities

3.2 NATURE OF ICT APPLICATION

Re-engineering and re-defing in the context of modern information and communication technologies is not only limited to university libraries but it has direct relevance to all type of libraries, including research and public libraries. But this book mainly focuses on the university libraries, especially in the Indian context. It tries to analyse the present system of functioning of these libraries with the intention to re-define them in the context of modern Information and Communication Technologies (ICTs) and suugests plans for Re-engineering their Business Processes for the purpose of increasing operational efficiency and service effectiveness. The focus is given to the following major ares:

i. To evaluate the existing information resources, personnel resources and other infrastructural facilities available in the university libraries;

ii. To study the prevailing system of library and information services in the university libraries;

iii. To survey the developments in the field of application of ICTs in libraries at the international level;

iv. To identify various management problems faced by the university libraries in the context of modern ICTs;

v. To study the present status of university libraries in terms of application of ICTs, library automation, quality of information services, etc.

vi. To study various manpower issues of university libraries related to the application of modern ICTs.;

vii. To identify the problems in planning the growth and development of libraries, application of ICT and implementation of automation in libraries, quality of information services, etc.;

viii. To identify the requirements of re-defining university libraries in the context of modern ICTs.;

ix. To propose a method for re-engineering library and information services of the university libraries.

A general analysis of the universitry libraries has been done as regards the Universities' profile, mission, vision, courses and functions; resources in terms of budget, staff, infrastructural supports, etc.; collection of books, periodicals, databases and other information resources; use of information and communication technologies and level of automation in libraries for various activities and services; need for re-engineering and re-defining these libraries in the context of modern ICTs., etc.

3.3 PRESENT SCENARIO

The general nature of ICT application in university libraries is as follows:

1. The information resources and ICT facilities of the university libraries are not adequate to meet the education, research and extension activities of their clientele;
2. Even though the Universal Bibliographical Control is ideal for effective information services, the libraries were not able to achieve effective bibliographical control either by self reliance or by effective partnerships and provide document delivery services to the users based on internal as well as external information resources;
3. Though the modern ICTs provide enormous potential for effective library and information services, the libraries are lagging behind in applying and exploiting these technologies, including the latest Web technologies, to the maximum extend possible;
4. Though the university libraries have automated

many of their functions, they were not able to reap maximum benefits of automation, especially in improving the operational efficiency and service efficiency;

5. At the same time, the users are not fully equipped with enough Information Literacy skills for the maximum utilization of information resources, especially that available and accessible in digital format.
6. The management process, including the human resource management system, of the libraries need thorough re-structuring in the context of modern ICTs;
7. The principles of re-engineering can be applied to re-define the activities, functions and service system of the university libraries to achieve maximum efficiency and effectiveness out of the latest ICTs, including the Web technologies;
8. As the development and service set up of the university libraries and their users can not be viewed in isolation, national and state level policies, rules and guidelines are essential to develop the university libraries as part of an integrated national library and information system with the intention to increase the quality of education, research and extension and transform the entire country as a knowledge society.

3.3 SCOPE FOR MANAGEMENT ANALYSIS AND ADAPTATION

Though all the university libraries in India have some sort of similarity and functional uniformity, some sort of structural adjustments may be necessary adopt the technologies in all locations, geographical areas and sociocultural situations. Similarly, while considering the functioning and services of the university libraries, major attention has been given for the service target of the libraries for post graduate and research level programmes of the universities, due consideration should also be given for colleges and undergraduate courses and distance eduction programmes offered by them.

3.5 ICT MANAGEMENT IN LIBRARIES

The management system of the university libraries has been studied using surveys, case studies, observation of working of the libraries, discussions and interviews with the different types of users and staff, review of literature, etc. Personal observation of the organization set up, management practices, functions, facilities, resources, utilization of information resources and facilities by the users, etc. of the libraries have been made. As the concept of re-engineering and re-defining was comparatively new to the library and information field, its applications have been studied in other fields through literature search.

Though the targeted users of the university libraries include affiliated colleges of the university, in the present set up, the services of the university libraries are largely concentrated on the students and faculty of the various teaching and research departments and constituent colleges of the universities. This seems a major limiting factor to cover the library and information services to the entire areas of higher education in the country. Moreover, the services of the university libraries to their distant campuses are also very limited.

4
Analysis of Management Systems of University Libraries

Re-engineering and Re-defining is an important is a tool for effectively managing the University Libraries in the context of modern Information and Communication Technologies by refining their management process and service set up.

4.1 GENERAL PROFILE OF UNIVERSITY LIBRARIES

All universities in India, except few, have separate university libraries. Department and Research Station libraries were also there in many of the universities. The physical facilities, including the structure of building and information resources of libraries, are extremely important in determining the management style and quality of services. Even in the world of powerful ICTs and global access of information resources, physical structure of libraries and its functional design is extremely important for proper use of these resources. Good design is driven by an understanding not only of what users do but also of how they work. The design process involves the active participation of many stakeholders—students, faculty, academic officers, information technologists, librarians—as well as an experienced architect. Good design reflects serious consideration of institutional mission and how space can advance that mission—whether it be learning, knowledge production, or civic engagement. ....The intent of good design is realized, and a library's services are enriched, by staff who are prepared to take on new roles and opportunities. It is space that inspires. ... It enables librarians to devote their time and skills to supporting users in the best way possible, often as teachers or partners in research. And what of the debate over the need for bricks and mortar? To be sure, projects that bring research material online are welcome developments, bringing us one step closer to the ideal of the universal library—as desirable today as it was in the reign of the Ptolemies. But ironically, while the information critical to scholarship and the public good is becoming more accessible than ever in the twenty first century, access alone is rarely enough to serve the needs of scholarship, teaching, learning, and public inquiry today (Council on Library and Information Resources, 2005). Though most of the university libraries have comparatively good buildings, many are facing space crunch to meet their functional their requirements.

As compared to the libraries of the central universities, IITs, IIMs, IISc, etc. in India, the building area of the university libraries are low. Though the student and faculty strength and number of education and research programes of the universities were manifold as compared to that of IITs, IIMs and similar national institutes, only few university libraries have almost comparable space area, infrastructural facilities like central air-conditioning, back up power supply system for the entire library building, modernized reading area and environment, modern audio-visual facilities, etc.

4.2 ICT INFRASTRUCTURE

The ICT infrastructure of the university libraries has improved recently because of the development activities through the INFLIBNET of UGC, NATP of ICAR, etc. Even though, these facilities are far below the actual requirements.

Though almost all libraries have computers, LAN, WAN, Internet connection, barcode facility, OPAC, etc. and many libraries are marching ahead to acquire technologies or facilties like RFID system, LCD projector, WiFi/WiMax, high speed / dedicated Internet connection, WebOPAC, Library Website, digiral library, digital archieving system, full text theses database, etc.

4.3 INFORMATION RESOURCES AND BUDGET

The information resources of any university libraries normally comprised of books, journals, theses, etc. both in print as well as in digital format. Document collection of the libraries may not be adequate to meet all the information requirements of the users. In the context of Indian libraries, availability of resources is far below the requirements. Acquisition of books and subscription to or access to print or digital journals is not adequate, digital libraries of Theses and Dissertations are not developed, etc. Theses information is not easily accessible over the Internet or even in the Intranet level of most of the respective universities, etc.

The vital role of education as a catalyst for national development has been widely recognised. Given the rapidly evolving nature of social and economic trends in today's world, education systems must be able to quickly and effectively respond to these challenges. But the impact of education is also paramount for individuals and households. This is clearly seen in the rising demand for education and the concomitant pressure to improve its relevance and quality. The World Education Indicators (WEI) Programme helps to assess progress towards meeting these demands through the use of international comparisons. While accounting for the conditions which contextualise and shape policies, international comparisons provide a useful benchmark for progress and highlight where and how policies have successfully achieved sought-after results in other parts of the world.

The financing of education constitutes a major concern for policy makers at the national level and, in many cases, at the state and municipal levels. To set realistic objectives for their education systems, policy makers must evaluate the resources required and weigh them against other needs. They also increasingly consider international comparisons to determine whether they are making adequate investments in education and using their financial resources efficiently. These comparisons must be based upon accurate and comparable data from other countries. The national context should be considered, especially when making international comparisons of education funding. The efficiency of the education system will also influence expenditure: less-efficient schools will incur greater costs for the same number of pupils (UNESCO Institute for Statistics, 2006).

For a well planned investment in education sector, proper budgeting processing should be resorted to. Budget generally refers to a list of all planned expenses and revenues. It is an important concept in *microeconomics*, which uses a *budget line* to illustrate the trade-offs between two or more *goods*. As the technology of money and banking continues to make spending easier, individuals, families, companies, and governments need to adopt more effective budgeting methods, strategies, and tools to balance their outflows to their inflows and avoid deficit (or debt-based) spending.

Presently, nearly all large businesses reforecast their original budgets on a quarterly basis. As months pass, the actual income achieved and expenses incurred can be compared to the budget and forecasts. Variances between these financial plans and actual delivery can then be analyzed to provide information that can improve performance. The future sees traditional annual budgets being replaced or complemented by monthly forecasts or rolling forecasts. Monthly forecasts provide fresher and more up-to-date financial plans.

In an appeal to UGC on budget allocation, the SALIS (2006) recommended to allocate exclusive budget head for ICT infrastructure to Library and Information Centres. It also recommended AICTE to provide funds and sanction projects submitted by University/College Libraries and Information Centres to promote research in the area of Library and Information Science.

The university libraries are facing acute shortage of budget allocation and the librarians were of the opinion that budget was one of the important limiting factor in meeting their user requirements. While some libraries did not have enough budget allocation, some others are facing the problem of non-utilization of the allotted fund for want of cash liquidity.

Considering the rate of inflation in effect, the library budgets in general are in a downward trend. This has forced the libraries to deny their user requirements considerably. In order to cope-up with budget constraints, atleast few libraries were resorting to Inter Library Loan and referring users to other libraries. Though limited ad-hoc grants are also sanctioned by UGC, ICAR, Governments and some other agencies in some years, all these are not sufficient to meet the user requirements fully.

In order to overcome the budget constraints, it was underlined the need to strengthen the library cooperation, resource sharing, consortia based procurement of books, journals, centralized processing of documents, development of databases, etc. National, regional or university level programmes of that kind to be strengthened. The UGC Infonet being a marvelous venture towards this direction, more efforts and services like that of OCLC, etc. were proposed. For example, if the National Library would be able to procure in strict sense all the information documents in print and non print published in India and develop comprehensive MARC records and databases in Unicode format, all libraries in India can download required records for individual library catalogue. This database can be utilized for document exchange or resource generation with other countries or libraries as is done by OCLC. Mandatory provisions in Delivery of Books and Publications Act and their strict implementation are required in this line. Otherwise, India will move several decades and centuries as was happened till now.

The modern ICTs are capable and strong enough to support the implementation of such projects. But we need administrative, technical and dynamic leadership of LIS professionals. A national level mechanism with enough administrative and financial powers is essential to coordinate such activities.

4.4 LIBRARY USERS

User is a prncipal component of any library system. The user base of the university libraries may cover researchers, postgraduate and undergraduate students, faculty, administrators, users from business and industry, farmers and even the general public. All facilities, resources, systems and services are targeted towards satisfying the users, that is the clientele of the library. According to Ranganathan, users have to be treated as kings and queens. It is an important question, whether our users are getting due treatment as far as considering their information requirements.

4.5 LIBRARY STAFF

Librarianship as a profession has always been associated with learning and enlightenment. With the growth of popular education, the libraries have emerged as "instruments" of general enlightenment and as "workshops" for advanced research. Libraries are the agencies through which librarians can best serve the noble cause of education. For an individual full of zeal nothing is impossible.

Professor Sharma observed as, "what an irony of fate that the librarians of an ancient country which as early as 2000 B.C. produced the Vedas, gave birth to the first classifier Panini (300 B.C) established libraries earlier than any other country, and contributed substantially to scholarship making thereby deep impact of its culture and civilization upon the people of the work, have been downgraded. What is more painful is that the UGC has acted against its own decision taken and implemented earlier in 1959. The resolution was, the high academic and administrative responsibilities, and practice in the universities all over the world, indicate that the status and the salary scale of the library staff should be the same as that the teaching and research staff. It is further unfortunate that this down-grading of librarians has been done not only contrary to the above decision but also against the recommendations made by the Radhakrishnan Commission Report (India, Radhakrishnan Commission Report, 1949), India, Advisory Committee Report (1959) and the Kothari Commission Report (India, Kothari

Commission Report, 1966). This derogatory decision has been taken when a modern library is considered as sure me+dia of education and indispensable for the successful implementation of a newly schemes of education in India". (Sharma, 1978). Ranganathan (1968) stressed the importance of properly trained staff in libraries as, "the far-seeing Melvil Dewey realized the futility which will characterize free book service for all, unless organized and rendered by librarians with proper professional training. He, therefore, established a professional library school in Albany, USA, as early as 1887. This was the first of its kind. Today, the professional training of library personnel has been taken up by the universities and the library associations in many countries. In the newly developing countries, UNESCO is taking the initiative for the establishment of professional training of the personnel needed to render free book service for all".

The university libraries in India did not have comparable staff strength. The staff in university libraries can be catrgorised in general as follows:

i. Professionals in UGC Cadre;

ii. Professionals in Non-UGC Cadre; and

iii. Non-Professionals

Total number of staff varies library to library in each category. Many libraries running short of staff and this affect the quality and effectiveness of information services. It is essential to re-define the essential minimum departments in a university library and fix the essential minimum staff in each cadre. The agencies like UGC, ICAR, etc. may work out a proper staff formula to suit to the modern ICT context.

Thiough the qualifications and scale of pay of the Librarian, Deputy Librarian and Assistant Librarian were equal to that of the UGC Professor, Reader/Associate

Professor and Lecturer/Assistant Professor respectively. But, disparity prevails regarding the qualifications, scale of pay, etc. other professionals and non-professionals.

At the same time, in some universities, the library professionals in UGC Cadre are categorized in non-teaching cadre, in others they are in teaching cadre. The status of the Librarian in most of the agricultural universities is equal to that of Registrar/ Deans/Directors and he will directly report to the Vice Chancellor and in most of the other universities, the Librarian is reporting to the Registrar.

Though Library Committee prevails in most of the universities to decide on the library policies on procurement, service, plans, etc., their effectiveness to ensure proper development of the library system, facilities, services, etc. are to be improved.

All librarians are vested with some administrative and financial powers for controlling staff, purchase of documents, stationery, etc. But, these powers are limited in matters like deputing library staff for training programmes, courses, conferences, organising programmes, etc.

Professionals have adequate experience in conventional activities such as serials control, classification, cataloguing, acquisition, maintenance, reference, circulation, etc. But, experience in activities and operations like Web hosting, Site Maintenance, software development, Web designing, data security, network administration, etc. are limited to few professionals. Many of them are lacking confidence in handling the operations independently. This is a clear indication that, professionals need rigorous in-service training in modern ICT topics. Thorough re-structuring and frequent revision of LIS curriculum is an immediate need which will help to inject essential ICT skills in the coming generation of professionals.

4.6 LIBRARY HOURS, ORGANISATION OF COLLECTION AND SOFTWARE USED

Even though there are general guidelines by the UGC and many universities to function the university and college libraries minimum 12 hours a day, there is no uniform pattern in the working hours of the libraries in India. Very few libraries or IT Services function round the clock. Many libraries could not extend the working hours even to the most favoured working time of the library from 8 am to 10 pm. At the same time, it is a strong demand of student and faculty users is to extend the working of atleast the computer lab, online division and digital library services to 24 hours.

Library staff also felt the above need because for maximizing the utilization of resources, especially the ICT facilities and digital resources, extending the working hours is the best option. But, the major constraint towards this is shortage of staff. There no uniforminty in shift-in-charge in libraries. It varies from Deputy Librarians to Professional Assistants.

For classification and arrangement of documents, most of the libraries using DDC, and the use of UDC, CC, etc. are limited. While mostly used library automation software is SOUL, many libraies use LIBSYS, ALICE, ADLIB, KOHA, etc.

4.7 LIBRARY SERVICES

All university libraries are providing conventional services such as circulation, reference service, services based journals and CD databases, Internet based services, documentation services; inter library services, user orientation, catalogue search, etc. Though all students as well as teachers are using the library and availaing most of the services, many of them were not satisfied with the present service system of the libraries. But, all were admitted that, the ICTs have improved the speed, quality and effectiveness of the services considerably. Out of the services, most of the libraries have achieved a quantum leap in providing journal services through e-journals. The users of the university libraries were able to access thousands of electronic journals, especially through UGC-Infonet. Moreover, many libraries could digitize the abstracts of theses and dissertations. But, the libraries could not effectively extend these services to distant and out station campuses of the universities and also to the affiliated colleges and institutions under them. In the case of digital archiving and development of digital libraries, only few libraries could do substantial work in this area.

Users prefer to have more online journals and computer terminals; high speed Internet connection, convenient opening hours, more books and journals in print also, convenient location of the library.

Users on the knowledge and use of various services provided by the library reveals that highly acquainted services for both the category of users were E-Mail Service, Photocopying Service and Online Public Access Catalogue. At the same time, the online journals service, inter library loan and institutional membership service, etc. are not known to many users. This indicates the need for re-engineering and re-defining these services with higher quality and effectiveness. Actions are also needed to propagate their use and market these services. The correlation between use and user education / information literacy programmes was also established.

4.8 RE-ENGINEERING AND RE-DEFINING UNIVERSITY LIBRARIES FOR MODERN ICT ENVIRONMENT

Information technology (IT) advances have rapidly changed the ways firms operate their businesses. IT enables organizations to redesign business processes, strengthen their customer relationship management, and develop a new business model. Information-intensive business organizations are utilizing IT to create new knowledge, manage existing knowledge, distribute information, and facilitate inter-and intra-organizational collaboration. While IT helps organizations improve productivity, recent e-commerce development has created highly competitive market environments across all industries. A strategic management to utilize limited resources coupled with proper adoption of ICTs can bring winning results in organizations. Abundant resources alone won't keep an industry giant on top when its hungrier rival practices the strategic discipline of stretch (Hamel and Prahalad, 1993). Veeran (2004) calls for proper organization and administration of university libraries in order to achieve effective utilization of information resources. Salih (2004) also stressed the need for proper application of computer and related technologies for resource management to maximize the effectiveness in services.

Business process redesign is one area where business strategy and IT have played a crucial role (Davenport, 1993; Davenport and Short, 1990; Grover et al., 1995; Hammer, 1990; Irani, Hlupic and Giaglis, 2000). Some firms have reported significant productivity gains by integrating IT into their core business processes.

While a larger body of researchers focus on IT's strategic value or industry-level productivity, practitioners demand rigorous IT evaluation methodologies to financially justify IT investment. Conventional wisdom holds that IT has enormous potential. Many successful IT investment cases indicate that organizational and managerial issues should be addressed when IT investments are made (Lee, 2004). Since IT may fundamentally change the ways in which the business organization interacts with internal and external constituents, business strategy and business processes should be considered in the IT evaluation process. The IT to be evaluated with a comprehensive, flexible, and easy-to-use measurement tool that integrates strategies, business process redesign, and IT design.

Libraries are in the forefront to apply these modern ICTs and they are considered among the leading agencies to transform the society as a knowledge society. To satisfy the users needs and demands most of the libraries have identified the need to implement and promote various kinds of new technologies, but there is still reluctance due to many reasons for libraries and to implement them to the fullest extend and provide the latest technology and services to the clientele (Lihitkar and Rajyalakshmi, 2005).

The management doyen, Peter F. Drucker has remarked that the knowledge in the knowledge society has to be highly specialized to be productive implies two new requirements:

i. Knowledge workers work in *teams*; and

ii. Knowledge workers have to have access to an *organization* which, in most cases, means that knowledge workers have to be *employees* of an organization.

He continued, "*there is a great deal of talk these days about teams and team work. Most of it starts out with the wrong assumption, namely, that we never before worked in teams. Actually, people have always worked in teams very few people ever could work effectively by themselves. The farmer had to have a wife, and the farm wife had to have a husband. The two worked as a team. Both worked as a team with their employees, the hired hands. The craftsman also had to have a wife, with whom he worked as a team he took care of the craft work, she took care of the customers and the business altogether. Both worked as a team with the journeymen and apprentices. The present discussion also assumes that there is only one kind of team. Actually there are quite a few. But until now the emphasis has been on the individual worker and not on the team. With knowledge work being the more effective the more specialized it is, teams become the actual work unit rather than the individual himself.*

The team that is being touted now as the team I call it the jazz combo team is only one kind of team. It is actually the most difficult kind of team, and the team that requires the longest time to gain performance capacity.

We will have to learn to use different kinds of teams for different purposes. We will have to learn to understand teams and this is something to which, so far, very little attention has been paid. The understanding of teams, the performance capacities of different kinds of teams; their strengths; their limitations; the trade-offs between various kinds of teams, thus, increasingly, will become central concerns in the performance of people.

The individual knowledge worker will also have to learn something that today practically no one has learned: how to switch from one kind of team to another; how to integrate ones self into a team; what to expect of a team; and, in turn, what to contribute to a team.

The ability to diagnose what kind of team a certain kind of knowledge work requires for full effectiveness, and the ability, then, to organize such a team and integrate oneself into it, will increasingly become a requirement for effectiveness as a knowledge worker. So far, it is not taught or learned anywhere (except in a few research labs). So far, very few executives in any kind of organization even realize that it is their job, to a large extent, to decide what kind of team is needed for a given job, how to organize it and how to make it effective. We are now in the very early stages of work on teams, their characteristics, their specifications, their performance characteristics and their appraisal.

Equally important is the second implication of the fact that knowledge workers are, of necessity, specialists: the need for them to work as members of an organization. It is only the organization that can provide the basic continuity which knowledge workers need to be effective. It is only the organization that can convert the specialized knowledge of the knowledge worker into performance.

By itself, specialized knowledge yields no performance. The surgeon is not effective unless there is a diagnosis, which, by and large, is not the surgeon s task and not even within the surgeon s competence. Market researchers, by themselves, produce only data. To convert the data into information, let alone to make them effective in knowledge action, requires marketing people, sales people, production people and service people. As a loner in research and writing, the historian can be very effective. However, to produce the education of students, a great many other specialists have to contribute people whose specialty may be literature, mathematics or other areas of history. This requires the specialist to have access to an organization". (Drucker, 1994).

The library and information specialists in India shall adopt this management philosophy of team work to achieve greater goals and efficiency and effectiveness in services. The library management strategies such as pooling and sharing of resources, inter library services, consortia mode of information services, etc. can be re-defined and re-engineered to fit to the technology oriented team work as propounded by Drucker.

Organisational design and ICT

The implementation of process management affects the organizational structure. The reduction of organisational layers and the re-definition of tasks to streamline processes are typical restructuring interventions aimed at improving the alignment of the organisational design and the core processes (Peppard and Rowland, 1995).

With regard to ICT, the interconnection between information technology and the necessity to adopt a process-oriented approach to the organizational innovation is the starting point of the literature on BPR. Several management experts deliberated on the key role of ICT in process management and BPR. ICT plays a complex role in process management that can be described with five components (Davenport, 1993), (Davenport and Short, 1990), (Hyde, 1995), (Saxena and Amal, 1995), (Venkatraman, 1994):

i. Automation of the activities of the process;
ii. Computerisation of the information system of the process;
iii. Support to the control of the process (tracking and informational functions);
iv. Support to the analysis and redesign of the process (when a reengineering intervention is needed); and
v. Support to the project management of the reengineering intervention (when needed).

Susan Longue in an editorial in the Journal, *Information Technology and Libraries*, wrote, "*as technology has become common place in classroom and library instruction, libraries are developing new services and resources. The library is ideally positioned to develop and deliver new services because of its centrality to the overall instructional mission of the institution. These new services often arise out of existing relationships between librarians and teaching faculty that evolved from the need for bibliographic instruction". The paper illustrates a variety of ways that libraries are providing new kinds of instructional technology services to meet changing users' needs. By being keenly aware of changing instructional technology and remaining mindful of pedagogical needs, libraries are redefining their roles in the instructional mission of their institutions*" (Longue, 2003).

4.9 AUTOMATING THE HOUSE KEEPING OPERATIONS AND ACTIVITIES

The ICTs have drastically changed the in-house operations of the libraries. All activities such as acquisition, processing, preservation, services, etc. have changed a lot. Many libraries have introduced either the barcode or RFID technologies for their circulation process, stock verification and document tracking. The National Information Standards Organization (NISO, 2008) has issued *RFID in US Libraries*, containing Recommended Practices to facilitate the use of radio frequency identification in library applications. The scope of the document is limited to item identification – that is, the implementation of RFID for books and other materials – and specifically excludes its use with regard to the identification of people. The NISO recommendations for best practices aim to promote procedures that do the following:

- Allow an RFID tag to be installed at the earliest point and used throughout the lifecycle of the book, from publisher/printer to distributor, jobber, library (shelving, circulating, sorting, reshelving, inventory, and theft deterrence), and interlibrary loan, and continuing on to secondary markets such as secondhand books, returned books, and discarded/recycled books.

- Allow for true interoperability among libraries, where a tag in one library can be used seamlessly by another, even if the libraries have different suppliers for tags, hardware, and software.
- Protect the personal privacy of individuals while supporting the functions that allow users to reap the benefits of this technology.
- Permit the extension of these standards and procedures for global interoperability.
- Remain relevant and functional with evolving technologies.

The NISO Standard RP-6-2008 on RFID in libraries recommended that:

1. RFID tags should comply with the ALA/BISG "Resolution on Radio Frequency Identification (RFID) Technology and Privacy Principles", 1 in particular, ensuring that data relating to individual persons should never be recorded on item tags.
2. In libraries, 13.56 MHz High Frequency (HF) tags should be used.
3. RFID tags for library use should be "passive" (as opposed to "active").
4. The read range of tags for library applications should not be substantially increased in future instances beyond the present range. The typical read range today is 8-20 inches for smaller tags and somewhat higher for larger tags.
5. Only tags including a standardized AFI feature

should be used in libraries.

6. The AFI byte should be coded to define a tag on any loaned item as belonging to the family called "library applications." Furthermore, discharged items in libraries using AFI (Application Family Identifier) for security should be using an AFI code assigned for those items, as described in Section 3.
7. The security recommendations in Section 3.5 should be followed.
8. In order to help ensure interoperability, security implementations for RFID in libraries should not lock a compliant system into any one security possibility, but rather leave security as a place for differentiation between vendors. (See Section 3 for details).
9. RFID tags should be reprogrammable for migration purposes and libraries should ensure that equipment upgrades that can handle both proprietary and standard formats are made before tags are reprogrammed.
10. Data on RFID tags should be encoded according to the Data Model described in Section 2, using encoding described in ISO/IEC 15962 and using relative object IDs specified in an anticipated ISO standard for RFID in Libraries (ISO/NP 28560).

Good libraries world over marching ahead to adopt all possible ICTs towards the better satisfaction of its stakeholders. At the same time, the libraries in India, especially the public libraries and academic libraries were unable to adopt modern technologies with that momentum because of the reasons such as lack of finance, non availability of good library management software, lack of training, less leadership by the librarians, insufficient support from top management, etc. It is an accepted notion that availability of good library automation software at low cost will boost the computerization and automation process of the libraries in India (Francis, 1998b).

Archivists and librarians place great emphasis on preserving content for the long term while ensuring its everyday usability. One of their major challenges is to ensure continuing availability of the digital content in their collections. Another challenge is to keep the medium of storage in a condition as near as possible to the original until the content is no longer needed or until it is migrated to a newer technology as the medium becomes outdated (Byres, 2003). Archiving digital content requires an ongoing technological strategy to ensure access to stored collections over time (Lee et al. 2002). A technological strategy for digital content is increasingly important as more analog content is converted to digital format and as more content is created digitally (born digital). The importance of proper handling of the digital media therefore increases as digital collections grow.

The general view of the users is that many libraries could substantially automate only the operations of OPAC and issue and return functions. They thought that, the operations like reservation and regular watch on documents, remote renewal, inter library loan, e-mail delivery of documents and notices and reminders, etc., were not effectively functioning in the libraries. Though the libraries have adopted barcode technologies, many of them are not using barcode technologies for stock verification. Moreover, only very few libraries could adopt RFID technologies for document tracking and management.

Regarding the provision of digital libraries over WAN also, the libraries are lag in behind. The level of automation of in-house operations was limited to mainly on OPAC and Circulation. That is, only few libraries could achieve automation by effectively integrating all its activities through the library management software for book selection, ordering, supply monitoring, payment release, financial and general management, stock verification, binding, weeding out, serials control, article indexing, etc. The programmes like digital libraries, WebOpac, theses digitization, ILL and network based activities, digital reference service and document delivery etc. were undertaken by many libraries only for name sake.

All libraries were facing problems for training, proper maintenance of hardware systems, availability / adoption of regular updation and newer versions of software, problems in the application of Barcode/RFID, difficulty for WEBOPAC, etc.

4.10 ACQUISITION OF DOCUMENTS IN PRINT

Acquisition of information resources is an important activity in a library which is normally based on a collection development policy. It is a plan, when properly prepared, is the library's master plan for building and maintaining its collections. It becomes a basis for the systematic management of the planning, composition, funding, evaluation and use of library collections over extended periods of time, in order to meet specific institutional objectives.

The major advantages of collection development policy described by professional experts and academicians are summed up as follows:

- It serves as a planning document
- A means for internal and external communication
- Guidance for section of documents and keep away personal biases
- Identify strengths and weaknesses of the collections
- Protects against pressures groups

- Decision-making tool for setting the access vs. ownership issues
- Assists in budgetary planning and funds allocations
- Collection evaluation tool
- Keeps consistency over time and regardless of staff turnover
- Deselection and preservation guidance
- Tool for cooperative plans and consortiums.

A well conceived, planned and precisely written policy should serve as framework to turn the philosophy of a library behind developing and maintaining collections into achievable goals and objectives (Ameen, 2006). The success or failure of a library depends upon the adequacy or inadequacy of its collection... University libraries should have a well-drawn up acquisition policy with the involvement of the users of different categories to build up a really representative collection of the documents or periodicals useful for education and research (Siddiqui, 2002).

It is argued that a written Collection Development Policy and its effective implementation will benefit the users to a large extend. Professionals are pressing this need in the present Electronic Environment also. Search of literature as well as libraries' websites reveal that electronic environment has forced the libraries and librarians to have longer, more explicit, less general, more procedural and better written policies. Along with this notion, several libraries have done efforts to re-define the process of acquisition and collection development of all types of documents in different formats.

A proper collection development policy is essential to re-structure the entire process of information acquisition in the line of ICTs. The library committee is the ideal body to finalise the acquisition policy. While framing policy, it should be keep in mind that the librarian must know the holdings of various libraries of the same university and that of the neighbouring libraries in order to avoid the duplication in the acquisition of materials which can be referred from them. Who should select the documents is a valid point. "*The individual scholar can therefore contribute much to the book selection; but, reliance on his judgment is not enough; there must be continuity in policy and bibliographical expertise of a more general kind*" (University Grants Committee, Great Britain, 1967). Good rapport between the librarian and the faculty is essential in the matter.

It is becoming increasingly clear in many industries that human intermediaries are inefficient for passing information between parties, particularly for relatively structured transactions. IT will reduce the need for vertical integration and lead to increasing use of markets for supply chain coordination. Electronic markets can dramatically reduce buyer search costs. With product and pricing information increasingly available electronically, potential buyers of goods and services can often make faster, lower-cost, better-informed purchasing decisions. And this class of IT can obviate the need for many intermediaries, particularly those functioning as information repositories and brokers. An electronic market system in a differentiated market is likely to promote price competition and reduce the market power of sellers. It may thus create a net welfare gain by lowering the search cost of buyers and also enabling them to locate products better matching their needs. (Nissen, 2001). It has been observed that many IT-based supply chain practices and enabling technologies, electronic catalogs, etc. are available now. At the same time, several challenges are there in the long term preservation of information resources (Gupta, 2007). She stresses the need for any parallel mechanism other than digital to preserve the resources.

The advent of WWW database delivery has forced reform of many odd and disadvantageous pricing schemes that were used in the early days of electronic information products. One often-seen peculiarity was publishers' policies of charging libraries the same subscription fee for every discrete library within a library system using a database. In this scenario, a college library using a database in several branch libraries would have to pay the same subscription fee for each branch utilizing that particular database. This policy had its genesis in the pre-networking days of CD-ROMs. Additional copies of an index or databases had to be purchased at full price or at some usually nominal discount from it. The subsequent introductions of networking, WWW delivery and ultimately remote patron access made this pricing scheme completely untenable. However, many vendors clung to it until forced to knuckle under by the market. Some still insist on structuring their pricing this way, but price additional locations or remote locations very reasonably (Majka, 2000).

1. Due to several reasons, University Librarians prefer paper medium books to acquire. But, in the case of journals, all were favouring electronic medium first. For selection of documents to acquire, the prominent three methods followed by the libraries were publishers' catalogue, books on approval and recommendations of the faculty. Only few libraries adopted the modern practices of online shopping for books and other information resoures successfully. E-mail communication for placing orders, sending reminders, receiving invoices, etc. also not that much popular as compared to conventional communication. This is mainly due to the reasons like government and university rules, audit regulations, lack of

leadership and dynamism on the part of the professional heads, etc.

It is a fact that the process of acquisition of books and other information resources has been considerably changed in all libraries in India. Major change has happened in the case of procurement of journals. Almost all libraries switched from direct subscription to consortia based subscription in the case of foreign journals and databases.

Regarding the collection development policy, many libraries could not even frame a written collection policy or update the existing one and follow the procedure meticulously because of reasons such as budget constraint, irregular flow of liquid fund, purchase rules, unhealthy practices prevailing in the market, etc. Some libraries still following quotation system for the purchase of books.

The users are of the view that the libraries were not properly considering their requests for new books and journals and the delay happening in the procurement of books suggested by them is too much. In the case of procurement of foreign books on specific requests by the users, many libraries are unable to acquire the books during areasonale period. That means, procurement of foreign books is mainly concentrated on what books the suppliers provided.

4.11 ACQUISITION OF THESES AND DISSERTATIONS

All libraries were now collecting theses and dissertations in print and most of the libraries have recently started collecting full text theses and dissertations in digital format also with the intention to develop digital libraries. But, no uniform rules and procedures were prevailing in all universities. Uniform rules and mandatory guidelines should be evolved in India to insist the research students to deposit their theses and dissertations in digital format also. Such documents should be made available as digital documents over the Web for academic and research purposes (Francis, Sushama Devi and Razak, 2007). In India, majority of education and research programmes are funded either by Central or State Governments, the Government of India should enforce this procedure through regulating agencies in education such as UGC, ICAR, AICTE, etc.

Only few universities have made academic regulation to insist the students to deposit their theses and dissertations in digital format also. As there is no effective facility to access the theses of other universities within the country or state, practically, the use of theses and dissertations was limited to the users of that library only.

A large number of scientists and students thought that digitization and web hosting of theses and reports will benefit research activities and it will enhance reference and citation of the work and thus the credibility of the scientists and institutions. They are of the view that the digitization and web hosting have the chance for wider discussion on the research findings and this may indirectly improve the quality of further research as well as the reports and theses produced out of it. Though many scientists and students thought that web hosting may increase the chances of misuse of the documents, others denied such fears as baseless. Hence, as a measure to curb the misuse, the first group suggests limiting the web hosting to extended abstracts with a mechanism to provide desired portion of the document on specific request. In order to get time for proper documentation and publication of research findings and as a measure to limit misuse, scientists and students suggested providing full text theses and reports on the web only after two to three years of its submission. At the same time they favour to make available the digital full text for reference within the respective institutions atleast in the Intranet level.

Students, teachers and library professionals categorically admitted the need for proper legislation, regulations and uniform guidelines for the collection, maintenance and dissemination of theses and reports at university / institution level and also at national level. Library professionals favour to take measures to collect the documents at source in digital format and also to build functional repositories.

The general notion of the users was that library website is a most common and easy vehicle for the delivery of information resources and instruction materials. Yet, library Web pages often fail to serve as a gateway to these resources. Faculty as well as student users have dissatisfaction on the way by which the Indian universities and research institutions providing library and information services through their websites. Most of the users feel that the library websites or webpages or homepages provide inadequate information or guides or navigational tools to the library and information resources.

4.12 CLASSIFICATION, CATALOGUING AND INFORMATION PROCESSING

Though the classification and cataloguing are considered as basic operations of a library, many libraries are failing to do the classification and maintain the catalogue most scientifically and suitably to the users. Modifying the classification scheme according to the need, inadequate information in the catalogue, and delay in removing the cards of weeded out books, etc. are few activities the libraries need to concentrate. There are several reasons for not completing the work effectively. In the case of preparation of union catalogue of all libraries within a university, within a state, etc. any university library could not do much towards this direction. Tadasad and Maheswarappa (2001) reported that many college libraries in Karnataka state could not maintain catalogue. Moreover, libraries follow different forms of catalogue. Shortage of staff, finance, etc. were the major reasons contributed to this situation. If libraries could not maintain even their local catalogue, how they can contribute to union catalogue or database which forms the basis for inter library services.

In this context, the work of classification, cataloguing and processing of information has to be thoroughly re-structured with modern ICTs in order to achieve maximum economy and efficiency in service. Modern libraries can adopt the system of centralized or shared system for bibliographic Processing. This involves:

1. Shared cataloging : When all libraries develop a common catalog database which is updated by the first library receiving a new publication. Subsequently other libraries use the same data record.

2. Cooperative indexing : When multiple libraries of the network receive the same journals and divide the journal titles for indexing and develop a cooperative index for use by all. This component addresses the time and labour saving needs of the networked libraries. This is the first form of resource sharing among the library networks. The emergence of commercial indexing firms like UMI and initiatives like Online Computer Library Center (OCLC) have almost diminished this function from the library networks.

Research Libraries Group (RLG) founded in 1974 and (OCLC), Dublin, Ohio, USA, founded in 1967 — two of the world's largest membership-based information organizations have agreed to come together in 2006 and function as OCLC in order to offer an integrated product and service line to the libraries, archives and museums new leverage in developing services, standards and software that will help them support research and disseminate knowledge online around the globe. OCLC furthering access to the world's information and reducing library costs provides computer-based cataloging, reference, resource sharing, eContent, preservation services and research to more than 57,000 libraries in about 112 countries and territories across. (OCLC, 2006).

CONSER (2007) (Cooperative ONline SERials) is:

i. A cooperative online serials cataloging programme;
ii. A source of high quality bibliographic records for serials;
iii. A source of high quality documentation and training materials for the cataloging of serials and the input of serial records;
iv. A group of serial experts who work together in an atmosphere of collegiality and trust;
v. A promulgator of standards related to serials;
vi. A voice for serials in the library community; and it is also a
vii. A component of the Program for Cooperative Cataloging.

Membership in the CONSER Program includes the national libraries of the United States and Canada, selected university, government, research, special, and public libraries, participants in the United States Newspaper Program (USNP), selected library associations and subscription agencies and abstracting and indexing services. The management of CONSER is carried out through a framework of committees with support from Library of Congress. Overall coordination of CONSER is provided by staff in the Library of Congress' Serial Record Division. The CONSER Coordinator and CONSER

Specialist plan meetings, prepare reports and documentation, and oversee training and quality review.

The CONSER database resides within the OCLC Online Union Catalogue. CONSER members input, authenticate, and modify serial cataloging records on OCLC or contribute original records via FTP. Authentication is the process of approving the bibliographic elements in the record and providing for the record's availability through distribution services and bibliographic products. CONSER's most direct benefit to libraries is the cost savings in having high quality records to use in creating local databases for library public access catalogs, union lists, or serials check-in-files. Its greatest legacy may be the resource it offers the serial world's transition to machine-readable access and delivery of the serial literature.

WorldCat is the world's most comprehensive database of library materials. Updated at a rate of nearly one new record every 10 seconds, WorldCat contains more than 84 million bibliographic records and 1 billion holdings contributed by over 9,000 libraries around the world.

But in such countries, where purchase of facilities like CONCER, WorldCat, etc., for a library is un-affordable and there is no such facility available for indigenously published materials, *shared cataloging* and *cooperative indexing* are still serious options for networked libraries forums. As a country like India has the scope to develop our Indian National Bibliography into a National Catalogue Database from which all Indian Libraries can download the catalogue records for their local catalogue. Compulsory collaboration of all publishers, institutions and content developers in India can be ensured towards this by adding suitable provisions in the Delivery of Books and Publications Act. The bibliographic details of books and other documents published outside the country can be downloaded either on exchange or membership basis through other national or international cataloguing agencies like OCLC. Such a system will ensure uniformity and standardization in cataloguing and can avoid duplication of bibliographic processing.

The Joint Steering Committee (JSC) for Revision of AACR (2007) is working towards a new standard: RDA: Resource Description and Access, scheduled for release in 2009. The new approach of RDA was proposed by the Committee of Principals for AACR and in December 2004 a draft of part I of AACR3 was made available to the constituencies for review. The structure of RDA will now have two parts (parts A and B). Part A will cover Description and Access Elements and part B will cover Authority Control for the form of Access Points. Underlying RDA are the conceptual models FRBR (*Functional Requirements for Bibliographic Records*) and FRAD (*Functional Requirements for Authority Data*). FRBR is the basis for Part A (Description) of RDA, and FRAD is the basis for Part B (Access Point Control). RDA is being developed in line with a set of objectives and principles which are based on the IME ICC draft Statement of International Cataloguing Principles.

The development of RDA and such refinements have direct bearing on cataloguing and search and access facility for the users such as OPAC, WEOPAC, etc. Consequently, the library automation softwares used in the library have to be modified and standardized. Staff and users of the library need orientation and training on the working and use of RDA to reap the benefits of refinement and standardization happened especially to describe the digital resources and ICT based access and use. Challenges of incorporating documents in different languages in the database have made easy by the advent of Unicode. As a universal character code set, Unicode provides a unique number to every character used in modern scripts through out the world... The application of Unicode helps to reduce the relevance of transliteration up to an extent (Veerankutty and Jalaja, 2005).

The professionals working in the university libraries in India are relatively unaware of the latest developments happening in the field of library and information science and technology. Surely, this will have negative bearing in the adoption of such technologies and improving the service system of the libraries.

Moreover, university libraries having any system for shared, centralized or collaborative cataloguing or having membership or tie up with international cataloguing agencies such as OCLC to exchange bibliographic details are very few. This stresses the need for establishing a central agency to coordinate such activities nation wide.

Most of the libraries have developed catalogue records in English. That is, they have transliterated the metadata of documents in other languages. This has several limitations in the use of catalogue as well as resources itself. In order to effectively address the multi lingual problems in cataloguing, adoption of Unicode and enough training for the library staff are essential. Hence, it is time to thought of evolving standards in the line of RDA, FRBR, FRAD, etc. and also to incorporate Indian languages in the OPAC and WEBOPAC.

Though almost all university libraries have claim the existence of OPAC, the search facility is limited to the library builing or to Campus LAN. That means, the OPACs were not searchable from remote locations in the Internet environment. This underlines the need for immediate re-engineering and re-defining the basic service facility of a library by incorporating latest web technologies.

4.13 DEVELOPMENT OF DATABASES

A database is a shared collection of logically related data designed to meet the information needs of an organization. The term originated within the computer industry, but its meaning has been broadened by popular use, to the extent that the *European Database Directive* (which creates intellectual property rights for databases) includes non-electronic databases within its definition. A database is a collection of records stored in a computer in a systematic way, so that a computer program can consult it to answer questions. For better retrieval and sorting, each record is usually organized as a set of data elements (facts). The items retrieved in answer to queries become information that can be used to make decisions. The computer program used to manage and query a database is known as a database management system (DBMS). The properties and design of database systems are included in the study of information science. The content as well as the retrieval mechanism or the search software provided in the DBMS is important for the effective use of the database. There are several digital media in which the database can be made available for the users. The digital media technology also growing fast and recently the technocrats have proclaimed the advent of 16-Layer DVD and Hyper CD-ROM with many promising advantages over the presently popular technologies like DVD, BD, etc. For multilayer optical discs, it has been difficult to obtain clear signals from each recording layer in a stable manner due to crosstalk from adjacent layers and transmission loss It is sure that these technologies will supersede many existing optical as well as other digital storage devices and media.

The 16-Layer DVD would be able to store data upto 40 GB, that is, 25 GBs in each layer. The electronic giants like Pioneer have already announced the success of the technology and feasibility for use at the erliest. The Hyper CD-ROM is a three-dimensional multilayer optical memory, based on the phenomenon of controlled extinction of the fluorescence. It allows the recording of information inside the "shelves" of a glass disk using laser beams. Such a glass disk has a storing capacity of over 10,000 Gigabytes of memory - an amazing size in comparison with those developed by the highest level computer firms and benchmarks - that allows storing of approximately 10 million books of standard format. It is in fact, an "optic three-dimensional multilevel memory" so it can store data in over 10,000 different levels inside a glass disk 10 mm high and 120 mm in diameter. The most attractive aspect is that the support for storage (i.e. fluorescent photosensitive glass) is a very stable in time medium (information can be read during all the life of the glass - estimated to at least 5,000 years). The estimated capacity of this disc is 10TB with extension to 100TB, the average data-transfer rate is 3Mb/s, thermal resistance is up to 550 degree Celsius, stability in time estimated to at least 5,000 years.

The writing / reading of the memory is realized with a system formed by a disk drive having the size doubled compared to the usual disk drives of the desktops PC, which incorporates a confocal microscope. The writing procedure is realized by the irradiation of a selected volume of the optical memory. Following the radiation, there appears an electronic transition at atomic level, and the irradiated areas will present a modified fluorescence compared to the non-irradiated areas.

The field of applications for the Hyper CD-ROM technology is extremely diverse, this device becoming in short period the most secure and stable storage facility in areas like, data archiving systems for large organizations, governmental institutions, banks, insurance companies, hospitals, libraries, museums, TV networks, movie studios, space and military applications, Internet servers, scientific journals and books, etc.

Many other issues such as problems associated with different formats, languages, etc. to be settled while developing bibliographical as well as full text databases. The process of development of databases is specially related to the documentation work of the libraries. In this area, all libraries have to take up the challenge of developing databases of indigenous knowledge and its proven preservation for the posterity.

Though most of the libraries digitized the abstracts of theses and dissertations and started the digital library/ archiving activities in a limited way, digitization of full text theses and other documents was only in the planning stage by many of the libraries. Enough training on technical aspects, financial support for infrastructural development and professional initiative and leadership are need to re-define this area and bring maximum result. Because of this, libraries could not move according to the speed with which the development of the digital technologies happens.

4.14 SERIALS CONTROL AND LIBRARY CONSORTIA FOR ELECTRONIC JOURNALS

Technologically, several experiments, innovations and practices were tested in the field of journal publishing and its access by the libraries. The advent of electronic or digital journals, online journals, magazines, etc. have necessitated a thorough re-defining the serials control system of the libraries. Ezine is a periodic publication distributed by email or posted on a website. Ezines are typically tightly focused on a subject area. In the late 1990s, ezine publishers began adapting to the interactive qualities of the Internet instead of duplicating magazines on the web. An online magazine or journal is delivered in an electronic form. An online periodical may be online-only, or may be the online version of an otherwise print-published magazine or journal. Today, most online magazines or journals are Internet websites.

Information resources in the form of journals occupy pivotal position in any university or research library. Citation analysis of doctoral dissertation in Chemistry reveals that the researchers mainly depend on periodicals for their information use (Srivastava, 2002). Proper control and management of journals is important for meeting the user needs effectively. Two major problems associated with the serials management the libraries facing are the multiplication of number of journals published and the steep increase in their prices. Based on a recent survey on more than 8000 scholarly journals of leading international publishers, Sonya White and Claire Creaser reported that journal prices are estimated to have increased by 39% between 2001 and 2006, while the retail price index has risen by 16% over the same period (White and Creaser, 2007). Some other key findings were:

Median journal prices ranged from £198 to £859 for biomedical titles and £119 to £513 for social science titles in 2006. Increases in the median journal price between 2000 and 2006 varied from 42% to 104% in biomedical titles and 47% to 120% for social science titles.

Such crucial situations coupled with paucity of fund forced the libraries to try several experiments and new practices in the acquisition, management and servicing of journals. Most of these practices have direct application of modern ICTs. Libraries of the University of Nevada, Las Vegas (UNLV), Nevada, USA had re-defined the organizational structure, staff resources and workflow consequent on the movement toward a predominantly electronic journal collection to find the best ways to provide library users with timely and reliable access to electronic resources. Since 1999, the composition of the *Libraries* journal collection has been dramatically changed. The percentage of print-only subscriptions decreased from 59 percent in 1990 to 20 percent in 2004, while electronic journals jumped from 35 percent to 75 percent. The percentage of Libraries materials acquisitions budget spent on electronic resources rose by at least 10 percent each year. The proliferation of electronic resources had a major impact on the acquisitions/serials activities from handling physical objects to initiating and ensuring ongoing access to electronic resources. It has resulted in a workflow that requires ongoing review and change to accommodate the constant technological developments that have impacted the management of information delivered electronically. In order to scientifically move the library from a predominantly print environment to a predominantly electronic environment, the management processes has been re-engineered (*Xiaoyin-Zhang* and *Haslam,* 2005) . According to Vijayakumar and Vijayakumar (2002), though e-journals created several technological and social issues, it provide better facilities in terms of accessibility, speed of distribution and production, subscription cost, multimedia capabilities, etc.

One major collateral blessing to emerge from the rise of online information is the incentives that it offers to libraries to work together for mutual benefit. This can best be seen in the very active effort exerted by many library consortia to obtain group pricing for their members for electronic information products. Vendors have been very receptive to these because it significantly lessens the amount of marketing costs that they would have to bear to make their case in each individual library. The difference between going it alone and buying through a consortium can be huge and is particularly rewarding for libraries that already license a product without such a discount. Those who have not licensed products for cost reasons may well find themselves able to do so. The library economizes in the first case and expands its services in the second; there is an economic benefit to both of these (Majka, 2000). According to UGC (2007), the electronic journals service through UGC Infonet Digital Library Consortium was very popular among scholarly community and was sought after by universities and colleges who do not have benefit of access to e-resources through the programes. The UGC has provided access of more than 4500 electronic journals to more than 125 universities. This programme would be extended to all universities which are under the purview of UGC as well as selected colleges that have required infrastructure to make use of e-resources. Moreover, this will include bibliographic databases and e-books.

As the universities in India are broadly controlled by two agencies like UGC and ICAR, library and information resource management is also performed differently. While the universities under UGC have formed UGC Infonet for consortia mode of journal subscription and services, agricultural universities and agricultural research institutes formed CeRA for journal subscription and services. Moreover, there are several other consortia also in operation in India for institutions under CSIR, DRDO, IITs, IIMs, etc.

In the present system of multi-disciplinary education, research and extension, all the journals are relevant to all universities with varied degree of interest. While subjects like agriculture, veterinary and animal sciences, engineering, economics, banking, management, fisheries, dairy sciences, information technology, remote sensing, biotechnology, etc. are of core interest to agricultural universities, most of these subjects are relevant to other conventional universities also. Consortia based e-journals services of the ICAR (CERA, 2008) intended for the agricultural universities and ICAR institutes in the country were covering only limited journals. In the broader sense, though the areas of interest are similar and the major funding agency for these consortia is Central and State Governments in India, several consortia activities such as for UGC, CSIR, DRDO, DAE, ISRO, ICSSR, ICAR, AICTE, etc. are taking place in the country. This causes duplication of efforts and increases in costs and inefficiency. Libraries outside the stream of agriculture hold very important and otherwise not available information on agriculture, which is original, traditional and sustainable. This will be of great use to agricultural research for developing sustainable methods of farming, animal rearing and fishing (Raman Nair, 2006).

Value of Statewide Consortia

Poter (1997) describes the benefits of statewide consortia for library and information services as follows. "For most academic libraries, statewide cooperation offers distinct advantages and incentives. The state provides a predetermined political and geographical grouping of libraries. There are often common governing agencies for publicly supported institutions of higher education, perhaps a board of regents or a coordinating board for higher education. State government also exercises control over the publicly supported colleges and universities and, of course, provides much of the funding. The extent of direct interest that the governor or legislature takes in the operations of the libraries varies by state, but this interest is always a factor. The fact that a group of libraries shares a common funding source, be it directly through elected officials or through a board of regents or oversight agency, is an important reason to build statewide cooperative systems. There is great appeal in efforts to pool resources and in cooperating to control costs".

On a paper on academic library consortia in Unites States, Bostick (2001) depicts some of the interested consortia activities as Web portals, virtual reference services, digital libraries, hosting distance education classes and programs, and disaster preparedness, etc. He argued that buying power of the libraries for better prices has increased under consortia mode. Francis establishes the importance, necessity and economic feasibility of nation wide library consortia for electronic journals for a country like India (Francis, 2005). As majoriy of research in India is financed by central or state governments and the interest of the students and researchers are interdisciplinary, it is justifiable and economical to establish one nation wide consortia for all educational and research institutions in the country. Though this is the perfect need, the libraries, universities and government agencies could not establish atleast a statewide consortia in the State of Kerala. Based on another study in the libraries in Cochin, Thrissur, Kottayam and Alappuzha districts of Kerala, Francis reported the duplication of journal subscription and poposed to establish networks for resource sharing (Francis, 1993). But, consortia based services and information resources sharing activities for mutual benefit are yet to be gathered momentum in the libraries all over India. The modern ICTs offer immense scope for such programmes. At the same time, consortia based services calls for high level re-engineering and re-defining the present structure and level of operations of the university libraries.

Most of the libraries have the practice of subscribing Indian journals directly from publishers. In the case of foreign journals, consortia based subscription in electronic format is adopted.

4.15 OPEN SOURCE MOVEMENT; AND DEVELOPMENT OF OPEN ARCHIVES AND INSTITUTIONAL REPOSITORIES

The philosophy of open access came during 1990s due to the necessity of facilitating scientific scholarly communication. The Budapest Initiative defines open access as the "*free availability on public internet, permitting any users to read, download, copy, distribute, print, search or link to the full-texts of these articles, crawl them for indexing, pass them as data to software or use them for any other lawful purpose, without financial, legal or technical barriers other than those inseparable from gaining access to the internet itself*" (Budapest Open Access Initiative, 2002). According to Peter Suber, "*Open access to scientific article means online access without charge to readers or libraries. Committing to open access means dispensing with the financial technical and legal barriers that are designed to limit access to scientific research articles to paying customers*" (Suber, 2002). The information documents such as books, journals, theses, reports, etc. may be available through any open access models. According to Sathyanarayana, in the case of Open Access (OA) Journals, the following three models can be considered (Sathyanarayana, 2006):

1. Author pays model : This is like the pre-paid model. The funding agency funds author. He has the freedom to choose the journal. Examples: Biomed Central, Hinawi (Egypt), PLOS, Springer's Open Choice. Author pay model is supported by UK Government. JISC (funding agency) pays to the publisher for author's publication. Similarly in United States, there are funding agencies does for their authors.

2. Sponsor pays model : This model is similar to the Yahoo and Google model. Here, the circulation of scientific literature is considered low compared to popular literature. Hence, the commercial viability of this model is still in doubt. Some publishers have successfully used a mixed media approach, that is, Print plus Electronic, where print generates the required revenue for the sustenance and the electronic version is hosted free for all. Example: MedKnow, Indian Academy of Sciences, etc. A large number of peer-reviewed open access journals are following this model. If the print users completely migrated to online and stop subscribing to print version, this model may suffer a collapse. In such situation, the publishers have to find any alternative.

3. Directly funded by funding agencies : For all practical purpose, such funding agencies has to be the Government of the country. INDMED model may be of this kind. Publishers are not much concerned about revenue loss as their print revenues should be still stable enough. The Brazillian model like SciELO, completely funded by The Government also may be categorized in this group. This type of model will work only if the society/ publisher itself come forward to bear the cost of its publication.

With the advancement of ICT, and its practical application, surely more models will emerge. From a business model perspective, OA domain is still very nebulous and experimental and is still far away from providing an alternative to the traditional scholarly publishing model.

Institutional initiatives to promote open access to the research work carried out by them are witnessed through establishing Institutional Repositories. These are "digital archives of intellectual products created by the faculty, staff and students of an institution accessible to end users both within and without the institution.

As the modern ICTs have increased the volume of generation of information, we could see another face of this situation of increasing the gulf between the haves and have nots of information. Many countries, especially the underdeveloped countries are starving to get access and use latest information. This in turn gives supremacy to such communities in controlling the world and its resources. In order to curb this anti human and lopsided development, universal availability and accessibility of information and knowledge is essential. Development of Institutional Repositories and Open Archives is a practical solution available now. An Institutional Repository may hold various kinds of publications, such as, pre-prints and post-prints of journal articles, conference papers, research reports, theses/dissertations, seminar/working papers, etc.

Stevan Harnad communicated that there are growing demand from US universities for adopting open access institutional archiving. According to him, 115 US university presidents and provosts endorsed the Federal Research Public Access Act (FRPAA) self-archiving mandate proposal. FRPAA of 2006 is a giant step forward for OA. It is an effort to increase taxpayers' access to federally funded research. It will apply to all federal funding agencies above a certain size —including the NIH, NSF, NASA, EPA, and eight Cabinet-level Departments. The bill requires every federal agency with an annual research budget of more than $100 million to implement a public access policy. The policy must ensure that articles generated through research funded by that agency are made available online within six months of publication. It instructs each agency to develop its own policy, under certain guidelines laid down in the bill. Some of those agencies might choose to launch central repositories but others might choose to mandate deposit (for example) in the author's institutional repository. But all must insure OA "*as soon as practicable, but not later than six months after publication in peer-reviewed journals*". (Federal

Research Public Access Act, 2006).

More US university presidents and provosts are signing to support the proposed FRPAA self-archiving mandate. Harnad (2006) recommended for the Immediate Deposit/Optional Access which means authors deposit all their published papers immediately on publication (even if he/she has surrendered the copyright to the journal). If there are no copyright problems the deposited paper could be made available for universal viewing, downloading, etc. immediately. If the journal has an embargo policy, the paper could be released for universal viewing at the end of the embargo period. Subbiah Arunachalam strongly supported this proposal and advised the Universities and research institutions in the developing countries to follow this practice. (Arunachalam, 2006). The Library of the University of Illinois at Urbana-Champaign (UIUC, 2008) has created and implemented a suite of OAI-based on metadata harvesting services, search services, and tools designed to facilitate discovery and retrieval of certain classes of scholarly works, thereby making visible portions of the currently "hidden" Web of scholarly information resources. This work was complementary with and carried on in concert with a related project conducted by the University of Michigan Digital Library Extension Service. This project focused on creating a deep, domain-specific portal designed to search metadata describing selected manuscript archives and digitized cultural heritage information resources. Software developed by this project has been made available under an Open Source Initiative license. This was one of seven metadata harvesting projects funded by the Andrew Mellon Foundation.

Bulu Maharana and others highlights the great importance offered by OAI to the scientists, students, researchers, academicians, librarians, etc., particularly to those in the developing world. They argue that free access to research information from the developed countries have incalculable benefits for local research and the OAI have a key benefit for developing country scientists by participating in research without any further delay (Maharana, 2004).

The developing countries are facing barriers of accessing scholarly literature, as the cost of accessing peer-reviewed journals have increased manifolds over the time. India is no exception, and high impact factor scholarly literature available to the research communities is limited to the elite institutions. Also research publications from developing countries, published in periodicals of developing countries also do not get much attention in international community, as distribution channels of such periodicals in developed nations are very limited. Open access movement makes the dramatic changes in accessibility. As many funding agencies and universities in developed countries support publishing in open access journals and archiving in open access repositories, research literature become easily accessible to the research communities of the world. The importance and usefulness of open access literature have been realized throughout the world. Various nations are taking up the issue seriously. Different open access statements and declarations have been made in various countries in this decade. In India, there are a number of open access initiatives in many forms, such as open access journals, archives of back volumes of journals, institutional repositories, subject-specific repositories, document-specific repositories, open courseware, etc. But, India is not only leading open access movement of the developing countries, but also making developed countries aware of qualitative scholarly literature originated from developing countries. Some sort of declaration and statement is necessary in India as well, which will be a framework for developing open access literature (Ghosh and Das, 2006).

Open Source Software (OSS) is *computer software* whose *source code* is available under a *copyright license* that permits users to study, change, and improve the software, and to redistribute it in modified or unmodified form. It is the most prominent example of *open source* development.

The open source movement (OSM) is a large movement of computer scientists, programmers, and other computer users that advocates unrestricted access to the source code of software. The line between the open source movement and the *free software movement* is somewhat blurry. Both are founded in the *hacker culture*. Mostly, the free software movement is based upon political and philosophical ideals, while open source proponents tend to focus on more pragmatic arguments. *Openness* is a term that has evolved now to refer to projects that are open to anyone and everyone to contribute to, before and/or after the actual programming. Both groups assert that this more open style of licensing allows for a superior software development process (when compared to *closed source*), and therefore that pursuing it is in line with rational self-interest. Free software advocates argue that "freedom" is a paramount merit that one should prefer even in any cases where *proprietary software* has some superior technical features. Proponents of the open source development methodology claim that it is superior in a number of ways to the *closed source* method.

Open source is a term that is applied to the entire concept that the creation and organization of knowledge is best created through open and cooperative efforts - this movement, variously called "open content" or "free culture," has been expressly endorsed by advocates of OSS. The OSM has paved the way for another related development, that is, Open Archive Initiatives (OAI).

Digital repository is either a local, *institutional*, or central (e.g., subject- or discipline-based) digital archive for depositing and providing access to digital contents. The OAI is an attempt to build a "low-barrier interoperability framework" for digital archives containing digital content. It allows people (Service Providers) to harvest metadata (from Data Providers). This metadata is used to provide "value-added services", often by combining different data sets.

The OAI technical infrastructure, specified in the *Open Archives Initiative Protocol for Metadata Harvesting* (OAI-PMH), defines a mechanism for data providers to expose their metadata. This protocol mandates that individual archives map their metadata to the *Dublin Core*, a simple and common metadata set or metadata standard for this purpose.

An Institutional Repository (IR) is an online locus for collecting and preserving - in *digital* form - the intellectual output of an institution, particularly a research institution. For a *university*, this would include materials such as *research journal* articles before (*preprints*) and after (*postprints*) undergoing *peer review*, and digital versions of theses and dissertations, but it might also include other digital assets generated by normal academic life, such as administrative documents, course notes, or learning objects (Wikipedia, 2007).

The two main objectives for having an institutional repository are:

i. To provide *open access* to institutional research output by self-archiving it;

ii. To store and preserve other institutional digital assets, including unpublished or otherwise easily lost ("grey") literature (e.g., theses or technical reports).

IRs are partly linked to the notion of a digital library,

i.e., the collection, classification, curation and preservation of digital content, analogous with the library's conventional function of collecting, classifying, curating and preserving analog content. Several OSS have been developed over the years and many of them can be used for digital archiving and development of IRs. Few of such softwares are DSpace, E-Prints, Fedora (Flexible Extensible Digital Object Repository Architecture), WINISIS, ABCD, NewGenLib, KOHA, etc. Many of these softwares facilitate effective Digital Asset Management (DAM).

Academic Repositories : Many academic libraries are actively involved in building institutional repositories of the institution's books, papers, theses, and other works which can be digitized. Many of these repositories are made available to the academic community or the general public. Institutional repositories are often referred to as digital libraries.

Digital Archives : *Archives* differ from libraries in several ways. Traditionally, archives were defined as: Containing primary sources of information (typically letters and papers directly produced by an individual or organization) rather than the secondary sources found in a library (books, etc);

The technology used to create digital libraries has been more revolutionary for archives. The use of search engines, Optical Character Recognition (OCR) and metadata allow digital copies of individual items to be cataloged, and the ability to remotely access digital copies has removed the necessity of physically going to a particular archive to find a particular set of records.

Cornell University and the Wisconsin Historical Society are considered as leaders in the field of digital archive creation and management. The Library of the University of Illinois at Urbana-Champaign (UIUC) has created and implemented a suite of Open Archives

Initiative (OAI)-based metadata harvesting services, search services, and tools designed to facilitate discovery and retrieval of certain classes of scholarly works, thereby making visible portions of the currently "hidden" Web of scholarly information resources. This work is complementary with and carried on in concert with a related project conducted by the University of Michigan Digital Library Extension Service. The OAI Metadata Harvesting Project at Illinois focused on creating a deep, domain-specific portal designed to search metadata describing selected manuscript archives and digitized cultural heritage information resources. Software developed by this project has been made available under an Open Source Initiative license. This is one of seven metadata harvesting projects funded by the Andrew Mellon Foundation (UIUC, 2008).

As per a webometric ranking of world universities by the Cybermetrics Lab, a research group belonging to the Consejo Superior de Investigaciones Científicas (CSIC), the largest public research body in Spain, the first rank goes to Massachusetts Institute of Technology and the first Indian university included in the list is Indian Institute of Technology, Mumbai with 559th position (CSIC, 2008a). In a similar ranking of world's open access repositories, the first rank goes to "arXiv.org E-Print Archive". In their latest version of 300 top repositories, only four are from India. Indian Institute of Science is placed at 36th rank. Openmed of NIC is at 111, Indian Institute of Astrophysics is at 228 and National Institute of Oceanography is at 231. (CSIC, 2008b).

The university libraries have initiated actions in the area of Open Archives and Institutional Repositories. But, the problems of lack of infrastructural facilities, inadequate training, funding, leadership, etc. curtail the possible development of these activities. The Open Source

Movement and Development of Open Archives and Institutional Repositories have necessitated re-defining the role of the modern libraries because presently many documents were left out of proper documentation. These actually creating serious hindrances in the process of patenting and settlement of issues related to intellectual property rights.

In order to do proper documentation of publications, the UGC had sanctioned the posts of Documentation Officers to the University Libraries. But, due to several reasons the actual achievement of the goal set was still out of reach. At the same time, the possibilities of open source movement and IR are best tools to undertake the documentation activities by the university libraries efficiently. The development of institutional repositories of documents like theses, reports, documents containing local and indigenous knowledge, etc. will help the users in a great way. Moreover, such databases will pave the way for strengthening the marketing approach of the libraries.

4.16 DEVELOPMENT OF DIGITAL LIBRARIES

Digital libraries are libraries without walls, though they do need boundaries – we argue that the very notion of a collection implies a boundary (Witten, 2001). A digital library may or may not function as part of conventional library. The digital content may be locally held or accessed remotely via computer networks. In libraries, the process of *digitization* began with the catalogue, moved to periodical indexes and abstracting services, then to periodicals and large reference works, and finally to book publishing. Prof. Rema Devi highlighted the importance of Digital Library in E-Learning programmes. No single institution can effectively manage and provide access to more than small portion of the information universe (Rema Devi, 2005). While developing digital libraries, availability and familiarity of good software packages is a major issue. Several software packages are available now to develop digital libraries. "Greenstone", "E-Print", etc., available for free use for digital library programmes.

Types of Digital Libraries

The term Digital Library is diffuse enough to be applicable to a wide range of digital entities. Divisions can be made between libraries that have some physical presence where patrons are able to access physical holdings as well as digital holdings and libraries where collections are almost completely digital. *Project Gutenberg*, the *Internet Archive*, etc are examples of this later case.

Advantages

1. Benefits in storage : Traditional libraries are limited by storage space; digital libraries have the potential to store much more information, simply because digital information requires very little physical space to contain it. As such, the cost of maintaining a digital library is much lower than that of a traditional library. A traditional library must spend large sums of money paying for staff, book maintenance, rent, and additional books. Digital libraries do away with these fees.

2. Easy adoption of latest technologies : Digital libraries can immediately adopt innovations in technology providing users with improvements in electronic and audio book technology as well as presenting new forms of communication such as wikis and blogs.

3. No physical boundary : The user of a digital library need not to go to the library physically; people from all over the world can gain access to the same information, as long as an Internet connection is available.

4. Round the clock availability : A major advantage of digital libraries is that people can gain access to the information at any time, night or day.

5. Multiple accesses : The same resources can be used at the same time by a number of users.

6. Structured approach : Digital libraries provide access to much richer content in a more structured manner, i.e. we can easily move from the catalog to the particular book then to a particular chapter and so on.

7. Information retrieval : The user is able to use any search term bellowing to the word or phrase of the entire collection. Digital libraries can provide very user-friendly interfaces, giving clickable access to its resources.

8. Preservation and conservation : An exact copy of the original can be made any number of times without any degradation in quality.

9. Space : Whereas traditional libraries are limited by storage space, digital libraries have the potential to store much more information, simply because digital information requires very little physical space to contain them. When a library has no space for extension digitization is the only solution.

10. Networking : A particular digital library can provide a link to any other resources of other digital libraries very easily; thus a seamlessly integrated resource sharing can be achieved.

11. Cost : In theory, the cost of maintaining a digital library is lower than that of a traditional library. A traditional library must spend large sums of money paying for staff, book maintenance, rent, and additional books. Although digital libraries do away with these fees, it has since been found that digital libraries can be no less expensive in their own way to operate. Digital libraries can and do incur large costs for the conversion of print materials into digital format, for the technical skills of staff to maintain them, and for the costs of maintaining online access (i.e servers, bandwidth costs, etc.). Also, the information in a digital library must often be "migrated" every few years to the latest digital media. This process can incur very large costs in hardware and skilled personnel.

Disadvantages

Some people have criticized that digital libraries are hampered by copyright law, because works cannot be shared over different periods of time in the manner of a traditional library. The content is, in many cases, public domain or self-generated content only. Some digital libraries, such as Project Gutenberg, work to digitize out-of-copyright works and make them freely available to the public. An estimate of the number of distinct books still existent in library catalogues from 2000B.C. to 1960, has been made.

Other digital libraries (more specifically, digital collections, which may be acquired by libraries) accommodate copyright concerns by licensing content and distributing it on a commercial basis, which allows for better management of the content's reproduction and the payment (if required) of royalties.

Digital libraries cannot reproduce the environment of a traditional library. Many people also find reading printed material to be easier than reading material on a computer screen although this depends heavily on presentation as well as personal preferences. Also, due to technological developments, a digital library can see some of its content become out-of-date and its data may become unaccessible.

The faculty, students and researchers in the academic and research institutions are the main producers of primary research. Publishing the result of their research and sharing it with the peers is the most challenging issue for most of the researchers. Traditionally, the scholarly publishers and academic libraries have been playing complementary roles to facilitate the scholarly communication cycle; from publishing and distribution (by publisher) to management and archival preservation (by institutional libraries). Due to several factors, the publisher-library market relationships have begun to shift to the institutional digital libraries. The digital library technology can compliment to the existing scholarly publishing model with an innovative publishing structure with faster online distribution facility as well as the systematic documents management and long-term preservation. The digital collections which capture and preserve the intellectual output of a single or multiple institution or organization, are called online Institutional Repositories or digital libraries. Digital libraries are rapidly emerging as an essential component of the scholarly communication and information sharing systems for distribution and sharing of information resources of the institutions and organizations (Jaswal, 2006).

Collection Digitization

Numerous libraries have embarked upon in-house efforts to digitize particular collections of documents or works in order to provide convenient access to them. There are many innovative and attractive sites that provide WWW-based access to such material. A well-crafted digital collection can be a source of pride and prestige as well as a benefit to scholarship. Such conversions are quite labor-intensive and therefore expensive; and most archival quality efforts require sophisticated and expensive scanning equipment. Personnel have to be trained or hired to scan the material and to proof read and correct the resulting files. The digital collection must be formatted for display and arrangements made for secure data storage, backup and retrieval. Some libraries have opted to use outside contractors for such projects because of the need to employ unfamiliar equipment and skills.

World Summit on the Information Society, 2005 has underlined the increased role of libraries and the essential adaptation required for them in the modern ICT environment as follows:

"Encourage research on the Information Society, including on innovative forms of networking, adaptation of ICT infrastructure, tools and applications that facilitate accessibility of ICTs for all, and disadvantaged groups in particular. Support the creation and development of a digital public library and archive services, adapted to the Information Society, including reviewing national library strategies and legislation, developing a global understanding of the need for "hybrid libraries", and fostering worldwide cooperation between libraries. Encourage initiatives to facilitate access, including free and affordable access to open access journals and books, and open archives for scientific information". (WSIS, 2005).

One of the greatest attractions of a digital library is its multimedia resources humans can use for information retrieval to knowledge discovery and information integration. A problem of multimedia researchers is to find a so-called killer-Apps which can demonstrate well the potentials of research topics such as video summarization, semantic annotation, multimedia cross indexing and retrieval, etc. Deeper research and wider applications of digital libraries revealed their indispensable role as test bed for multimedia technologies (Zhuang, 2005).

Kuny and Cleveland (1998) had rejected Internet as Digital Library. They regarded it a myth to consider it digital library. As a bookstore cannot be called a Library in the same manner Internet providing access to huge information resources cannot considered as a Library. "Finding information is difficult, the quality of the information is quite variable, and reliable, professional assistance for the confused and lost is lacking". In a Report on Mass Digitization, NCLIS, U.S. has identified and listed the following nine issues to have potential impact on national information policy (NCLIS, 2006):

i. Copyright—fair use, orphan works, opt-in vs. opt-out models—be handled in digitization projects.

ii. Quality: quality of OCR good enough quality of content and authentication.

iii. Roles and priorities for libraries in the digital age.

iv. Long-term ownership of books and journals and other media.

 Long-term preservation of books and journals and other media, and preserving the public record.

v. Standardization and interoperability.

vi. Roles of publishers and booksellers in the digital age.

vii. Business models are needed in the era of mass digitization –Pay-Per-View open access model & its movement affect the economics of digitization.

viii. Information literacy.

ix. Assessment - digitization and electronic access are meeting people's needs.

Access to digital libraries and their collections is dependent upon a stable information technology infrastructure (power, computers, communications links etc.). Hence, despite the egalitarian potential of the digital library, many of those who could most benefit from its global reach (for instance in the *Third World*) are not able to do so.

Searching

Most digital libraries provide a search interface which allows resources to be found. These resources are typically *deep web* (or invisible web) resources since they frequently cannot be located by *search engine crawlers*. Some digital libraries create special pages or *sitemaps* to allow search engines to find all their resources. Digital libraries frequently use the *Open Archives Initiative Protocol for Metadata Harvesting* (OAI-PMH) to expose their metadata to other digital libraries, and search engines like *Google* can also use OAI-PMH to find these deep web resources.

There are two general strategies for searching a federation of digital libraries:

(i). *Distributed searching*; and (ii). *Searching previously harvested metadata*.

Distributed searching typically involves a client sending multiple search requests in parallel to a number of servers in the federation. The results are gathered, duplicates or eliminated or clustered, and the remaining items are sorted and presented back to the client. Scalability and performance issues tend to plague distributed searching for large federations of digital libraries. Protocols like *Z39.50* are frequently used in distributed searching. Searching over previously harvested metadata requires the pooling of metadata collected from every digital library in the federation. This solution scales better than distributed search, but it introduces the problem of data freshness; digital libraries need to be re-harvested on a periodic basis to discover new and updated resources. *OAI-PMH* is frequently used by digital libraries for harvesting metadata.

In the preset days, everybody is telling about the digital libraries. But, very few earnest attempts were taken by the libraries at national level and state level. Though the leading role and achievements of the institutions like the National Centre for Science Information (NCSI),

Indian Institute of management (IIM), Kozhikode, M.S. Swaminathan Foundation, Chennai, etc. were remarkable in this respect, most of libraries in the country were moving very slowly. Though several free digital library/IR softwares are available now and the ICT tools and Internet are powerful enough to provide unlimited potential for documentation and pooling and sharing of information resources, effective and sound programmes were limited towards this. Leadership on the part of University Librarians was also lacking in this respect. The post of University Librarian in many universities in India is vacant for long period and their library systems are managed by in-charge officers. This system management of the libraries would normally lack leadership and enthusiasm. In order to re-engineer and re-define the digitization and development of digital libraries several factors such as lack of professional and technical leadership, inadequacy of finance, copyright issues, etc. have to be addressed properly.

All university libraries mainly depend on the available or accessible documents for information service. The areas like documentation services, information and knowledge management, etc. were largely untouched by the libraries in the context of modern ICTs also. Though digital library software like Greenstone, E-PRINT, D-SPACE, etc. are freely available and UNESCO, IISc, IIM, NISCAIR, and many other agencies are involved in imparting training and manpower development, the libraries could not lead digital library programmes as desired.

4.17 INFORMATION SERVICES

One interesting positive side effect of ICT and web based information delivery is the reforms in pricing practices of digital resources and the libraries have been able to provide the same set of information resources to all of their patrons, regardless of location. This possibility some way leads to a sort of equitable access to information. It was not uncommon for either networking limitations or simple economics to preclude a library from offering an identical set of products to its patrons at each of its locations. The advent of location-indifferent pricing, better networking technologies and the standardization of user interfaces have eliminated this consideration from all but the most technologically disadvantaged libraries. The resulting increase in patron productivity and convenience is again unquantifiable yet undeniable. Re-defining the nature of information services and re-engineering its processes became an urgent necessity to cope up with the situations warranted by the modern ICT. The study reveals that all libraries covered under the study have to move forward to effectively extend their services to their remote locations and affiliated colleges. Actually, their present services were centred on the main campuses. The NAAC (2006) reported the best practice of the Mangalore University in this line. They could extend the library services to 108 affiliated colleges under the university by providing membership and services for them. As service refinement process and marketing strategy, in turn, they could earn a couple of lacks earnings also to the library.

Almost all service areas of the libraries need to be re-defined in the latest ICT environment. In the case of circulation service itself, several IT based experiments have introduced during the last several years. Barcode technologies, RFID, Smart Cards, etc. are few of them. Among these, RFID is the latest and superior, though the cost is comparatively very high.

RFID technology can be used, amongst other things, for keeping track of things. The system comprises two parts, RFID Tags and RFID Reader. The tags are small radio transmitters/responders (transponders) which include a miniature antenna that can be attached to pallets and cases of the individual products. The tag is programmed with information to track the item. RFID reader is needed to make the tags divulge the information programmed into them. An RFID reader is a transceiver, which sends out a query via a radio signal that is then answered by an RFID tag. The reader emits radio waves in ranges of anywhere from one inch to 100 feet or more, depending upon its power output and the radio frequency used. When an RFID tag passes through the electromagnetic zone, it detects the reader's activation signal. The reader decodes the data encoded in the tag's integrated circuit (silicon chip) and the data is passed to the host computer for processing (Association for Automatic Identification and Mobility, 2007). In libraries, the use of RFID reduces the amount of time required to perform circulation operations. It also helps librarians to eliminate valuable staff time spent for scanning barcodes while checking out and checking in borrowed items. For the users, RFID speeds up the borrowing and return procedures. Library employees are released for more productive and interesting duties. Staff is relieved further when readers are installed in book drops. Some RFID systems have an interface between the exit sensors and the circulation software to identify the items moving out of the library. Were a library user to leave the library and not be caught, the library would at least know what had been stolen. If the user card also has an RFID tag, the library will also be able to determine who removed the items without properly charging them (Shahid, 2005).

The university libraries have achieved very good progress in providing information services through journals. The subscription or access of journals enhanced from hundreds to thousands. But, in the case of other services, a thorough re-engineering is warranted in all libraries. Though the ICTs would be able to extend the resources and information services to all students, teachers and even to other people, irrespective of the universities, states or country, the libraries were not able to absorb these potentials to the maximum extend. Radical re-structuring of the Web based activities was needed in order to increase the effectiveness of the existing services and also to incorporate new services.

Though the libraries provide digital access to resources, these facility could not be effectively extended to the users at their door step. Even the faculty users have limited access to these resources at their cabin. The IFLA/FAIFE (2005) World Report on Libraries, National Security, Freedom of Information Laws and Social Responsibilities, 2005 underlines that the lack of access to the Internet deprives library users of a core information resource in the 21st century.

The available or accessible digital resources could not be effectively extended to the distant users or to the cabin or laptos of the users. This indicates the need for strengthening of computer network of the campuses by using latest computer technologies like WiFi, WiMax, etc. and with high speed Internet connection. The Web based application of RRID can extend library counter servies to distant campuses of the universities. At present the information services in India are mainly available on the physical opening and working hours of the respective libraries. Several western libraries and some Indian libraries could provide the Web and digital library services beyond the opening hours of the libraries by adopting latest wireless technologies. All the libraries have 24 hours dedicated/leased line Internet connectivity. As the working hours of the libraries were limited, the Internet and e-journal facility kept idle several hours a day.

4.18 DIGITAL REFERENCE SERVICE

People have become increasingly comfortable utilizing and, indeed, relying on digital services as part of their way of life. For example, many people are now shopping, banking, ticket reservation and paying their bills online. They also communicate with others in their personal and business lives by using email or real time services such as online chat, instant message services, or video conferencing. People are also beginning to expect their libraries to provide some type of digital service. These services include access to the online catalogue, the ability to place requests online, access to electronic resources and, of course, the provision of some type of digital reference service.

One of the fastest growing and most innovative services being developed by libraries today is digital reference. Such services refer to a network of expertise, intermediation and resources put at the disposal of a user seeking answers in an online/networked environment. A digital reference transaction occurs when a question is received electronically and responded to electronically (Bertot, McClure, & Ryan, 2000, p. 12). Many libraries are now providing digital reference service, either as an integrated component of their regular reference service, as a separate service, or as part of a collaborative consortium. Many other libraries are thinking about or are about to implement such services. Additionally, an increasing number of digital reference services ("AskA") have been developed in the commercial, educational and non-profit sectors that are not directly affiliated with any specific library (e.g., AskJeeves, Internet Public Library, AskERIC). The focus of both library and non-library affiliated digital reference service has been to provide information to the user via electronic means.

The provision of digital reference service can take many forms and has developed in a variety of ways. In many cases, digital reference service, as provided by libraries of every type, has evolved naturally and does not exist separately from traditional reference service. Here, reference staff answer questions received both in traditional ways (face-to-face at the reference desk or via the phone) and digitally (most often via email or chat). They often also respond via a combination of traditional and electronic (digital) methods. In such situations, even a single reference transaction can be comprised of a combination of both traditional and digital methods of communication and response (including the provision of the answer). In these cases, the reference staff members are not specifically designated as either traditional or digital reference librarians. In other library situations, a separate digital reference service has been developed and is offered to users. In such situations, the digital reference service has been designed to function as a separate service from the provision of traditional reference service. Personnel are often assigned to the digital reference service or a completely separate staff exists to provide strictly digital reference service. In many cases, the digital reference service is advertised and promoted as a separate library service, and the points of access to the service are not tied to the physical library facility.

These points of access can include a separate digital reference web page within the library's website, a separate email address, or the capacity for online chat, interactive video, or voice over IP sessions (which may also be accessed through the library's digital reference website). Additionally, these digital library services are often available to the user during times when the physical library is not open. And of course these services can be provided regardless of the user's physical location. Indeed, one of the main reasons that a library develops a separate digital reference service is to help meet a user's needs, which may not match the library's ability to provide reference service in a traditional way.

While the development and implementation of digital reference services has received wide attention during the last several years, only limited attention has been given to the assessment of digital reference services. Many see the provision of digital reference service as a way of increasing access to library services in a manner that is not dependent on physical visits to the library (McClure, 2002). Another recent study led by the investigator on the Content Management for Digital Delivery of Agricultural Information revealed that the acceptance and use of digital libraries were heavily depend on user centered digital libraries. The use of ETDs increased when the digital library software and tools for accessing, retrieving, printing, downloading, etc. had been modified. It was also reiterated that the revolutionary shift from paper to digital documents and the changed pattern of content management and information delivery has made the library websites as an urgent necessity for effective reference and information services (Francis, Sushama Devi and Razak, 2007).

The figure 4.18.1 reveals the trend of development Websites during 1995-2008.

The technocrats predict that future digital reference and content management services will be based on many new generation technologies and standards such as "Broadband media", Digital Subscriber Lines (DSL), Very High Bit-Rate Digital Subscriber Line (VDSL), Virtual Private Network (VPN), Internet Protocol Version 6 (IPv4), MPEG–4, etc. Moving Pictures Expert Group (MPEG) is a digital video and audio compression format that was defined as part of the International Standards

Organization (ISO). Broadband media sometimes called "streaming media", because the services or "content" that is delivered via broadband networks is digitized, and received by users of the content in continuous real-time "streams". In fact, high-speed IP access through Digital Subscriber Lines that utilize existing voice lines for high-speed transmissions is the foundation of the broadband media services network. DSL is a group of increasingly high-speed technologies that enables fast Internet access in homes and businesses. DSL "always on" connections will also form the basis of the sophisticated broadband media services networks of tomorrow (International Engineering Consortium, 2007).

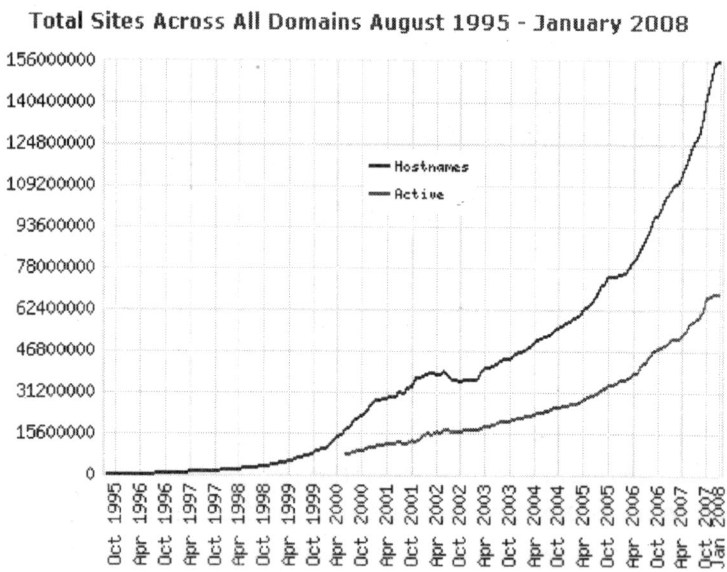

Fig. 4.18.1. Websites developed during 1995-2008

In Streaming Media, there is simultaneous transfer of digital media (video, voice, and data) that is received as a continuous real-time stream. A streamed file is simultaneously downloaded and viewed. Very high bit-rate DSL (VDSL) is a technology for transmitting very high-speed digital information over short reaches of an existing phone line to homes and businesses. A Virtual Private Network (VPN) uses encryption and other security methods to prevent information from being intercepted and guarantees that only authorized users can access the network.

Fast Internet access combined in broadband media services will connect people and businesses around the world like never before. Broadband media services will put the consumer in total control by enabling personal, custom, on-demand viewing of entertainment, e-learning, video games, and other types of content. Users will choose what they want to hear, see, or be entertained by on their own, and people will no longer have to plan around preconceived broadcast schedules for home entertainment. Furthermore, broadband media services will allow individuals to easily create their own content, personalize it, and distribute it for viewing on TVs, PCs, remote laptops, and mobile phones and other wireless devices around the world, instantly.

The proliferation of high-speed broadband IP access and broadband media services will require content creators to distribute large amounts of rich media to a global audience of high-speed users with increasingly greater demand for access to specific services. The challenges for broadband media development include understanding true consumer wants and needs for services and perfecting the technology standards behind the high data rates and significant bandwidth required for seamless delivery of high-quality multimedia services.

The power of the Internet is taken to a new level with broadband media services, in that individuals can create their own content and distribute it to electronic devices around the world (televisions, wireless phones, laptop computers, etc.) at the click of a button. Just as the Internet will continue to bring people together and provide individualized services like never before, the IP network technology that enables broadband media services is rapidly improving and becoming more powerful. Different types of networks will evolve in this context. In a truly mobile information society, mobility, traditional fixed and mobile-network services, value-added services, and the Internet are all combined to offer seamless services for end-users.

The evolution of the broadband media services network can be characterized by transitions like: dial-up-like circuit-switched network to a data-oriented network, connectivity to service-creation platforms, copper-based network towards an all-optical network, convergence of mobile and fixed networks, etc.

With the IP access network as a foundation, broadband media services–specific network enhancements are required. Essentially, broadband media services allow consumers to customize their viewing via network control devices. Specific standards such as MPEG, specific services, such as voice on demand (VOD), etc. to be considered.

Video encoders are devices that create digital video. Input to the encoders can be analogue video or a Digital Video Broadcasting Group (DVB) multiplex. Both are required because some video content will be statically loaded from video tapes and some content will be captured from a satellite (DVB) multiplex. Video encoders that are used to deliver broadband media services most often allow for the creation of MPEG content and have the ability to support IP multicast at varying bit rates, as well as the ability to decrypt video streams to remove conditional access. The new IP will replace the current version, IP version 4 (IPv4). IPv6 has been designed to meet the challenges of the growing Internet and includes several improvements over IPv4. The main benefits of IPv6 include a larger address space, integrated security, support for auto-configuration of terminals, and support for mobility.

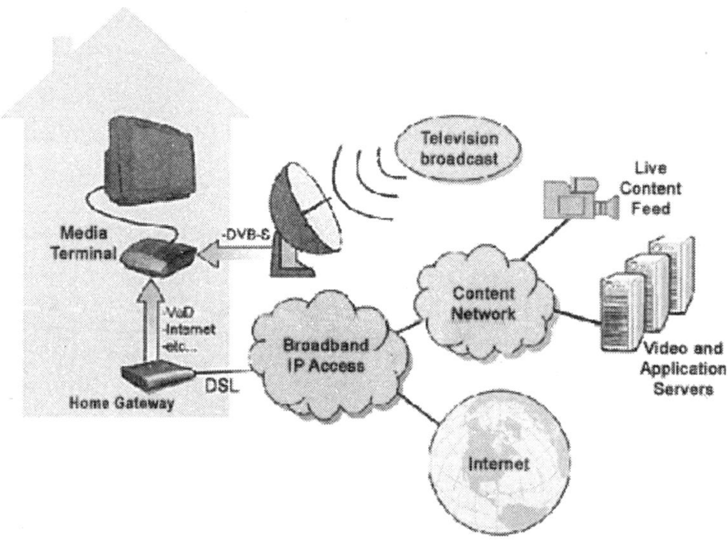

Fig. 4.18.2: Broadband Media Services for the home

The MPEG–4 stream encoding rate range is wider (5 kbps–60 Mbps). It allows interactive objects in the stream, making it more multimedia ready. Moreover, MPEG–4 aims to pave the way toward a uniform, high-quality encoding and decoding standard that would replace the many proprietary streaming technologies in use on the Internet today. MPEG–4 is also designed for low bit-rate communications devices, such as wireless mobile devices that can display video. It supports scalable content, which means content is encoded once and automatically played back and transmitted at different rates depending on the available network connection.

The university libraries are yet to exploit the potential of digital reference service. The technologies and tools like VPN, streaming video, etc. can be used for providing digital reference service based on the documents like theses and reports and other documents to be provided with restriction or limited access provisions.

The digital reference service has the potential to extend the services beyond the physical working hours and man management of the services. The Artificial Intelligence and Expert Systems can monitor the services even to the remote users. The users' demand for strengthening the Web based reference services is increasing. As most of the universities in India are basically affiliating universities, the libraries of these universities have the responsibility to offer services to their affiliated colleges and institutions. But, within the present set up, they were totally unable to think of such dynamic extensions. The libraries can re-engineer their websites by incorporating Content Management System for digital delivery of information and documents.

Development of digital content is another area all our libraries should focus special attention targeting the global users/clientele. These services call for the tapping of the potential of latest mobile technologies.

4.19 INFORMATION SERVICE FOR DISTANCE EDUCATION AND LIFELONG LEARNING

Distance learning can be defined, in the most general terms, as a method of education that involves an instructor and student(s), who are separated geographically and must rely on one or more methods of long-distance communication. It is the direct descendant of correspondence and home study courses, which were developed in the nineteenth century. The telecommunications and telematics options available today facilitated the provision of high-tech educational environment and the enlargement of the potential user base.

Bargellini and Bordoni (2001) stressed the predominant and central role of libraries in education, learning, and vocational training in support of increasing knowledge especially in distance learning scenario. The rapid evolution of information and communication technology in the learning field imposes supports and stimulates the re-engineering of the library. World Summit on the Information Society (WSIS), 2005 has stressed the role of continuous and life long education as follows:

"Continuous and adult education, re-training, life-long learning, distance learning and other special services, such as telemedicine, can make an essential contribution to employability and help people benefit from the new opportunities offered by ICTs for traditional jobs, self-employment and new professions. Awareness and literacy in ICTs are an essential foundation in this regard. Content creators, publishers, and producers, as well as teachers, trainers, archivists, librarians and learners, should play an active role in promoting the Information Society, particularly in the least developed countries.

To achieve a sustainable development of the Information Society, national capability in ICT research and development should be enhanced. Furthermore, partnerships, in particular between and among developed and developing countries, including countries with economies in transition, in research and development, technology transfer, manufacturing and utilization of ICT products and services are crucial for promoting capacity building and global participation in the Information Society. The manufacture of ICTs presents a significant opportunity for creation of wealth.

The attainment of our shared aspirations, in particular for developing countries and countries with economies in transition, to become fully-fledged members of the Information Society, and their positive integration into the knowledge economy, depend largely on increased capacity building in the areas of education, technology know-how and access to information, which are major factors in determining development and competitiveness" (WSIS, 2005).

Most universities offer courses in their multiple campuses and also through their affiliated or recognized colleges / institutions. In many universities, courses are extensively being offered in distance education mode also. Academic libraries have begun to build impressive portfolios of online services and programs for remote users. Yet as libraries develop new services for their remote users, little notice is paid to whether or not the initiatives are useful, successful, or whether targeted users are even aware of their availability. Additionally, although the ACRL Guidelines for Distance Learning Library Services (ACRL, 2004) state that, "Members of the distance learning community are entitled to library services and resources equivalent to those provided for students and faculty in traditional campus settings". Some institutions have not ensured that they are fully serving remote students. ACRL is in the process of revising the earlier guidelines. Many librarians, including those in charge of distance library services, lack awareness about accessibility-related issues. But, this is often not the case with regard to accessibility. The actual requirement is effective access to adequate library services and resources to all. The library network and the online resources also should be made mandatory to the off-campus users also. It is argued that the Guidelines for Distance Learning Library Services need to explicitly spell out the importance of an accessible online infrastructure, which serves the needs of all off-campus students, including those with disabilities. The education resources must be designed to afford students with disability, maximum access, 'anytime, anywhere', without the need for outside assistance. The paramount issues of importance exist for academic libraries serving students are:

i. Whether the information resources and services provided to students are sufficient to meet their education and research needs?

ii. Whether the services and collections provided to remote students are equivalent to those offered to on-campus users.

iii. Which services and resources are most used and /or most needed by the users and why?

Recent developments in technology, Internet, and World Wide Web have created many new opportunities allowing consumers to buy products and use services from the sanctuary of their homes. E-learning is one of the many manifestations resulting from convergence of new technologies and emergence of the web. E-learning is referred to by several other names like online learning, virtual learning, distributed learning, distance learning, etc. Technology-based instruction has the broadest meaning and refers to training through any media other than the traditional classroom. Many countries and societies are striving to utilize modern technologies in this regard. Efforts to promote e-learning by the Singapore government and the National Library Board (NLB) was reported by Chaudhry (2006). It was remarked that E-learning is strategic to Singapore because of the recognition that lifelong learning is important if the economy and people are to keep up with the rapid pace of change. E-Learning is likely to make skills upgrading more practical for adults and economically viable for companies to provide to workers.

Much has been said and written about the promises of distance education. It is clear that, for it to succeed, students' access to and effective use of information resources to support their learning is essential. Supporting their own institution's distance learners has become a core activity for a growing number of academic libraries. In addition many national and local governments are expecting the public library network to engage more effectively in fulfilling its role as a provider of support for lifelong learning. It is important, therefore, that libraries review the response that they are making to meet the needs of learners who may be restricted or no means of gaining access to print-based collections. In traditional distance education, rudimentary efforts were made by the teaching institutions to ensure that collections of core texts and journals were accessible to registered students through, for example, postal loan services. Otherwise the student was dependent on buying textbooks (sometimes without an effective bookseller or postal service to assist them to acquire books from national or international sources), or using any relevant materials or services provided by a local public or academic library. However, the world we live in has changed significantly.

A key enabling factor is new ICTs. Increasingly distance education is utilising e-mail and web-based facilities to deliver teaching materials and provide interactive tutorial support across the Internet in both the industrialised and developing world. Similarly, to meet the needs of distance learners, library services now include not only a traditional postal loan service, but also off-campus access to Internet databases, and online access to the full-text of electronic journals or specially digitised book chapters. However, such technologies can only be applied effectively if there is a clearly developed rationale and well-defined strategy which addresses the issues that libraries must engage with in order to best serve the needs of distance learners (Johnson, Reid and Newton, 2002).

The university libraries have negligible consideration to address the needs of distant users for their information requirements. As the public libraries in India mainly concentrating on entertainment and general books and information materials, the users' requirements for academic information could be seldom catered by them.

4.20 RE-ENGINEERING PARTNERSHIPS AND INTER LIBRARY SERVICES

It is an accepted reality that no library in the world is self reliant in itself. Close collaboration and active partnership are the order of the day to win maximum. There are several good partnerships in LIS field. AgNIC, the Agriculture Network Information Center, stands as one of NAL's strongest and broadest partnerships. Founded in 1995 by five institutions, this alliance has swelled to 59 members around the world, with NAL providing the AgNIC secretariat, managing the Web portal and contributing some funds for projects. Today, with technology rapidly advancing and budgets shrinking almost as fast, these partnerships are more important than ever. They provide a range of cost savings, including leveraging resources, sharing skills and collaborating on projects. In addition, partners' diverse perspectives open new vistas, while the communities the partners represent supply readymade channels for marketing services. Partnerships are, in the end, the ultimate win-win. Every partner brings something to the table, and every partner benefits from the outcome (National Agricultural Library, 2008).

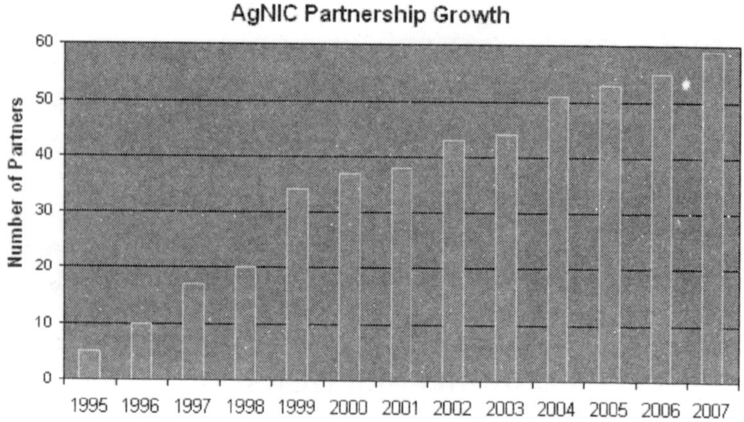

Fig. 4.20.1. Growth of Partnership in AgNIC (Source: NAL, 2008)

Inter Library Loan, also known as, document delivery, or document supply etc, is a service whereby a user of one library can borrow books, videos, DVDs, sound recordings, microfilms, or receive photocopies of articles in magazines that are owned by another library. Sometimes for a small fee, or possibly for no cost, a library that has the item will loan or copy it, and the item is transported to the requestor's library to be checked out or just used within the library. Without interlibrary loans, if a library patron found an item they wanted, they would have to travel to that library, and apply for a local library card if eligible, or present a reciprocal card in order to borrow the item. By taking advantage of interlibrary loan, in comparison, the library staff can search large numbers of libraries at once, transport the item from several miles to thousands of miles away, and allow a patron to borrow the item using his or her local library card. Interlibrary loan and resource sharing have a variety of systems and workflow, often based on the scale of service, regional networks, and library systems. Loans between branch libraries in the same system may take one or two days, while loans between library systems may take a week or more to be delivered. If an item is rare or difficult to find, this may be the easiest way to gain access to it. Books may be posted by courier and photocopies may be faxed or scanned and sent electronically. Additional fees may be charged for urgent service.

Resource sharing networks

Since the mid-1980s, searching for books located at other libraries has become easier, as many libraries have allowed library users to search their *online catalogs* at the library or over the *Internet*. Libraries have formed voluntary associations with each other to provide an online union catalogue of all the items held by all member libraries. Whenever a library adds a new item to its catalogue, a copy of the record is sent to update the union list. This allows libraries to quickly find out what other libraries hold an item, and software can facilitate the requesting and supplying of interlibrary loans. In the U.S., *OCLC* (Online Computer Library Center) is usually used by public and academic libraries, and *RLIN* (Research Libraries Information Network) is used primarily by academic libraries, although some libraries are members of both. Australia and New Zealand use *Libraries Australia* and Te Puna respectively, the national bibliographic networks of those countries.

Libraries that do not belong to a network can participate in interlibrary loan by making the arrangements by postal mail, fax, email or phone. Libraries may also have reciprocal arrangements with each other in order to supply loans and copies for free. The OCLC First Search WorldCat Database is the best place to look for Interlibrary Loan items, and libraries have online catalogues and "order form" to use to obtain the items.

A rare book may be hard to obtain in physical form. But, digitization will help to provide such documents in full or part of it. In order to refine the inter library loan process; the present libraries need to employ the techniques of process improvement to manage change (Nozero and Vaughan, 2000). According to them, library re-engineering and process improvement, change management, etc. have reaped benefits in improving the Inter library Loan services of the Dickinson Library at the University of Nevada in Las Vegas, University of Nevada, Las Vegas, Nevada, USA.

Schafer and Thornton, (1999) stresses the importance of paradigm shift from ownership to access of information resources in providing the inter library loan services. This has a far reaching impact on acquisition and collection development policies of the libraries. In the context of information explosion and proliferation of literature, it is practical to argue for access than acquire the information resources. The modern ICT and web technologies have practically enabled effective access of information irrespective of its location. This has necessitated re-defining the inter library loan services and re-engineering its process.

As university libraries have memberships in Library Consortia and Library Networks and they claim the provision for inter library loan services, only small percentage of the users have knowledge about this service. This establishes the need for re-engineering and re-defining the partnerships between libraries and strengthen inter library loan services. Institutional tie ups with other libraries and networks, intensified user education and training programmes and adoption of latest ICTs and Web technologies for digital document delivery will help to strengthen the service.

4.21 LIBRARY WEBSITE AS A CLEARING CENTRE OF INFORMATION

A website is a collection of web pages, typically common to a particular domain name or sub-domain on the World Wide Web on the Internet. A web page is a document, written in HTML / XHTML, which is almost always accessible via HTTP, a protocol that transfers information from the website's server to display in the user's web browser. The modern ICTs have made lot of radical changes in the conventional system of information processing and its delivery. Most universities offer courses in their multiple campuses and also through their affiliated or recognized colleges / institutions. In many universities, courses are extensively being offered in distance education mode also. Academic libraries have begun to build impressive portfolios of online services and programs for remote users. Yet as libraries develop new services for their remote users, little notice is paid to whether or not the initiatives are useful, successful, or whether targeted users are even aware of their availability. Additionally, although the ACRL Guidelines for Distance Learning Library Services (ACRL, 2004) state that, "*Members of the distance learning community are entitled to library services and resources equivalent to those provided for students and faculty in traditional campus settings*". Some institutions have not ensured that they are fully serving remote students. The actual requirement is effective access to adequate library services and resources to all. The library network and the online resources also should be made mandatory to the off-campus users also.

Indian Universities constitute one of the largest higher education systems in the world. With 294 universities / institutions, 13150 affiliated colleges, 88.21 lakh students and 4.27 lakh teachers; it is a great challenge to ensure effective coordination and communication (UGC,

2006). Several programmes have already started in India to provide seamless supply of information by way of course materials, access to journal and databases, etc. in electronic format to the academic and research community. The UGC, AICTE, etc. have done leading role in this respect. The National Programme on Technology Enhanced Learning (NPTEL) is a joint venture of seven Indian Institute of Technologies (IIT) and Indian Institute of Science (IISc) to provide study materials in engineering sciences and technology. This project has formally launched in September 2006 and is funded by the Ministry of Human Resources Development, Government of India. (NPTEL, 2006).

One of UNESCO's priorities is to promote universal access to information and to strengthen communication capacities at the local level (UNESCO, 2005). It stresses the importance of websites for effective access of information resources available world over. Several universities and libraries have already adopted website as an important tool for information delivery. Library users also prefer to avail information services through the library websites.

As websites becoming important means for information services, it is essential to design the websites with utmost care and effectiveness. Hence, many libraries have changed their websites into content management system. Library websites should employ technical skills to transform them as a proper clearing centre of information. Among those skills are creating clear, concise and readable information and establishing procedures that ensure the site is kept up to date and remains high in search engine rankings. It must also be copyright-compliant and data protection-compliant. In this role, the librarian has to function as Web content manager.

Based on the experience of Library Website of the Imperial College, London, Corcoran, observed that, "There are a number of elements that can be used to enhance your writing and ensure that a user remains at your website. In the academic library environment we may be inclined to think that we have a captive audience of students, academics and staff. However, we must remember that the library spends a huge amount of money on resources, and if a user has difficulty in accessing them and as a result does not use them, the money has been wasted. . . . . In academic libraries we are dealing with various types of users, from undergraduate and postgraduate students to academic and administrative staff, as well as visiting members of the public. Our content should be written with all of them in mind. . . . Usability studies have shown that web users scan a page for information. . . . . A website that is obviously out of date loses its credibility. Users will return only if they know that it is updated regularly. If the site is updated regularly, existing users will be aware of this and return, and if the pages are written with high search engine rankings in mind, new users will be made aware of your site. A content management system makes it easier for library staff with little technical expertise to edit web pages, but we need to learn these new techniques in order to take the best advantage of the technology that we now have" (Corcoran, 2006).

Lebowitz notes that, "Although many consider the library to be the heart of the university, the use of the library is often not incorporated into courses being prepared for distance delivery .... as academic institutions extend their educational offerings beyond the campus, to rural, suburban, and urban locations, they need to consider... the role that the library plays in the educational process" (Lebowitz, 1997). She recommends that librarians convince fellow educators and administrators that as they are expanding their institutions' educational offerings beyond the campus boundaries, they need to provide their students with access to library services, which include among others, instruction in use of resources, document delivery, and communication facility between the students and librarian.

Stephen H. Dew reports a survey conducted at the University of Iowa, on their off-campus students, he emphasizes the need for librarians to understand their students and what they want in order to have successful programs for off-campus students. Dew states that, "librarians tend to focus on disseminating the information that we think our students need. We talk at length to students about library services; we give presentations to them about all kinds of information resources, and we develop Web pages full of information just for them occasionally we need to reverse roles, listen instead of talk, and let the students tell us a few things" (Dew, 2001). This survey was one way in which librarians at the University of Iowa "listened" to what their off-campus students are saying. The students were asked to rank various library services on the basis of importance. The following services were ranked highest: Web and / or e-mail reference 71.3 percent, remote access to full-text databases 65.1 percent, home delivery of books and articles 60.7 percent. The survey revealed that reference services, electronic services and document delivery were ranked high, while user education services were ranked lowest.

Another study in the libraries in Kerala State reveals that several issues have to be addressed by the libraries in order to meet the information needs of the users in the main campuses as well as in distant campuses. Among these issues are: the need to have more library and information resources available in full-text online, including electronic journals, full-text and secondary databases, etc. that can be accessed remotely. The need to have effective and expedient inter library and document delivery services are justified. Strengthening of Information Literacy Programs with stress on topics and areas like information technology equipments, retrieval software, was also advocated by the study (Francis and Kabir, 2008b).

The library users generally view that the library services available through Websites are not effective. Though some information is available through library websites, it is a fact that provision for online interaction through the websites is rare. Universities having separate website for their libraries are also limited. That itself has limited provisions for information services.

While comparing these websites with that of western countries, websites of the Indian universities / libraries have to be improved considerably. While immense scope is available for information services through websites, the libraries can exploit this technology, especially for delivering services to the off-campus users and also to the users of affiliated institutions.

4.22 ADOPTION OF LATEST WEB TECHNOLOGIES

Websites and web based information services occupy paramount importance in the present context. Hence, web designing, incorporating information resources in the web, their updation, etc. are extremely important. There is tremendous amount of information and resources on the Web. But the precision in the retrieval of relevant information is more important than getting all junk of information. . The crux of every retrieval system worth its name has always been how good the representation system it depends on (Prasad, 2007). Proper management of content and semantic web technologies offers immense scope to transform the Web into a meaningful system. Website of the Cornel University Library (2007) provides some important hints in evaluating a library website. It stressed the context in which the library and website provides service. The User context and Web context have been taken as primary factors as follows:

1. The User Context : The most important factor when evaluating Web sites is the search needs. What for the websites has to be used?. Using the Web for: Entertainment? Academic work? Hobbies or a vocational interests?, etc. Scholarly sources are traditionally very strongly text-based. Compare the appearance and the content of an academic journal with a popular magazine.

2. The Web Context : Some of the visual distinctions that signal the nature of content in print sources hold true on the Web as well, although, because the Web encourages wider use of graphics, Web versions of printed works usually contain more graphics and more color than their print counterparts. Color graphics appeared on the New York Times Web site before they appeared in the printed New York Times, for instance.

The website of the Cornel University provides the following criteria or eight-point checklist for the evaluation of library websites or web pages:

i. What can the URL tell you? .
ii. Who wrote the page? Is he, she, or the authoring institution a qualified authority?
iii. Is it dated? Current, timely?
iv. Is information cited authentic?
v. Does the page have overall integrity and reliability as a source?
vi. What's the bias?

vii. Could the page or site be ironic, like a satire or a spoof?

viii. If you have questions or reservations, how can you satisfy them?

Kini (2002) argues that in order to obtain good results in information search from distributed systems, modelling of information elements can be employed and such models should be capable to clearly and explicitly translate the intention of the user to the retrieval system. Dynamic and explosive changes and developments are happening in the web environment and web technologies to maximize the search efficiency. The changing concept of Web as **"Web 2.0"** will have substantial implications for libraries, and recognizes that while these implications keep very close to the history and mission of libraries, they still necessitate a new paradigm for librarianship (Maness, 2006). The term, Web 2.0 is now widely used and interpreted, but Web 2.0, essentially, is not a web of textual publication, but a web of multi-sensory communication. It is a matrix of dialogues, not a collection of monologues. It is a user-centered Web in ways it has not been thus far. Related to this, Casey and Savastinuk (2006) has coined the term, "Library 2.0" and Maness further defined this concept as "the application of interactive, collaborative, and multi-media web-based technologies to web-based library services and collections". He explained this theory and its practical implication in libraries. A theory for Library 2.0 could be understood to have these four essential elements:

It is user-centered : Users participate in the creation of the content and services they view within the library's web-presence, OPAC, etc. The consumption and creation of content is dynamic, and thus the roles of librarian and user are not always clear.

It provides a multi-media experience : Both the

collections and services of Library 2.0 contain video and audio components.

It is socially rich : The library's web-presence includes users' presences. There are both synchronous (e.g. IM: instant messaging) and asynchronous (e.g. wikis) ways for users to communicate with one another and with librarians.

It is communally innovative : This is perhaps the single most important aspect of Library 2.0. It rests on the foundation of libraries as a community service, but understands that as communities change, libraries must not only change with them, they must allow users to change the library. It seeks to continually change its services, to find new ways to allow communities, not just individuals to seek, find, and utilize information.

Library 2.0 : Library 2.0 is a user-centered virtual community. It is a socially rich, often egalitarian electronic space. While Librarian 2.0 might act as a facilitator and provide support, he or she is not necessarily primarily responsible for the creation of the content. Users interact with and create resources with one another and with librarians. In some ways, it is a virtual reality for libraries, a Web manifestation of the library as place. A library's presence on the Web in Library 2.0 includes the presence of that library's constituency and utilizes the same applications and technologies as its community, a concept *Habib* (2006) recognizes in a very useful model for Library 2.0 in regards to academic libraries. The phenomenon of colossal growth of Websites is also confronted with continuous emergence of variety and powerful search tools. Keyword or metadata based retrieval was the prevailing common strategy for locating text, data or image, etc., from a database or Website. But, the development of Computer Vision Research Technology now became the basis for image searching. It has made use of the Polar Rose

Principle of geometry for comparative analysis and searching of images. The software, "Polar Rose" was made available as a plug in that can be used in the search engine, Fire Fox (Polar Rose, 2008).

Web 3.0 : Web 3.0 technologies intended to provide much more advanced and user friendly facilities for information search as well as information preparation. The user will be able to do all activities such as word processing, painting, calculation, teaching, publishing, database administration, etc. through Web. The user can do all digital operations on Web without using any other software. That means, all the required software will be incorporated on the Web for ready use with a computer and Internet connection. The recently emerged Web portal, "Zecubes" is built up on semantic enabled Web 3.0 technologies (Zecubes, 2008).

Such ever developing technologies, search engines and tools put heavy pressure on the library and information professionals. In order to provide information services, regular absorption of such technologies by the library professionals became a must now than ever before. Maness provided the details of how the applications so common to Web 2.0 will continue to evolve, and how libraries might utilize and leverage them for their patrons, are inherently hidden—they are wholly about innovation. But the conceptual reinforcement of a library's web-presence and how it must evolve into a multi-media presence that allows users to be present as well, both with the library or librarian and with one another, are clearly in need of development. He argued that there are enough scope for close relationship between the evolving Web and the evolving library and as a consequence, this will facilitate innovation and experimentation in library electronic services. Few of such services are:

Synchronous Messaging : More widely this is known as instant messaging (IM), it allows real-time text communication between individuals. Libraries have begun employing it to provide "chat reference" services, where patrons can synchronously communicate with librarians much as they would in a face-to-face reference context. Libraries may do well to continue adopting this technology as it evolves, as it allows reference services in an online media.

Streaming Media : Library instruction delivered online has begun incorporating more interactive, media-rich facets. The static, text-based explanation coupled with a handout to be downloaded is being supplanted by more experiential tutorials. The ACRL's Instruction Section provided a database of tutorials, many of which were Web 2.0 in their nature, called Peer Reviewed Instructional Materials Online (PRIMO). Many of these tutorials used Flash programming, screen-cast software, or streaming audio or video, and couple the media presentation with interactive quizzing; users respond to questions and the system responds in kind. This has the potential for the continued development of these tutorials. These could take the form of multi-media chat rooms or wikis, and users would be able to interact with one another and the learning object at hand, much as they would in a classroom or instruction lab.

Blogs and Wikis : Blogs and wikis enable the rapid production and consumption of Web-based publications. In some ways, the copying of printed material is to web-pages as the printing press is to blogs. A blog is a "*portmanteau*" word invented by combining parts of the words, web and log. It is a website where entries are commonly displayed in reverse chronological order. "Blog" can also be used as a verb, meaning to maintain or add content to a blog. Blogs are HTML for the masses. Contents of blogs are also known as the "blogosphere". The most obvious implication of blogs for libraries is that they are another form of publication and need to be treated as such. They lack editorial governance and the security this provides, but many are nonetheless integral productions in a body of knowledge, and the absence of them in a library collection could soon become unthinkable. This will, of course, greatly complicate collection development processes, and the librarian will need to exercise a great deal of expertise and fastidiousness when adding a blog to a collection. Or, perhaps the very notions of "reliable" and "authoritative", so important to collection development, will need to be rethought in the wake of this innovation. Realising the dynamic role of blogging various institutions, academic bodies, professional bodies, etc. are planning to have full-fledged course on subjective study at different levels of standards. This tool gives an upper hand to library and information professionals to disseminate and share in faster and in an innovative way, which is not possible through other conventional methods (Gupta, Singh and Gopal, 2006). *"Technorati"*, *"blogdigger"*, *"Feedster"*, etc. are examples of blog search engines. As of December 2007, *"Technorati"*, was tracking more than 112 million blogs. Before blogging became popular, digital communities took many forms such as "Usenet", "CompuServe", "e-mail lists", "Bulletin Board Systems", etc.

A wiki is a type of website that allows users to easily add content and is especially suited for collaborative writing. The word "Wiki" comes from the Hawaiian word "wiki" meaning quick or fast. In essence, wiki is a simplification of the process of creating HTML web pages combined with a system that records each individual change that occurs over time, so that at any time, a page can be reverted to any of its previous states. A wiki system may also provide various tools that allow the user community to easily monitor the constantly changing state of the wiki and discuss the issues that emerge in trying to achieve a general consensus about wiki content. Wiki content can also be misleading as users may add incorrect information to the Wiki page (IFLA/UNESCO, 2006).

Wikis are essentially open web-pages, where anyone registered with the wiki can publish to it, amend it, and change it. Much as blogs, they are not of the same reliability as traditional resources. This complicates collection development and information literacy instruction. The lack of peer review and editorship is a challenge to librarians. Social Networks:- Social networks enable messaging, blogging, streaming media, and tagging. *MySpace*, *FaceBook*, *Del.icio.us*, *Frappr*, *Flickr*, *LibraryThing*, etc. are example with their service features. *LibraryThing* enables users to catalog their books and view what other users share those books.

Podcast : Podcast is a collection of digital media files which is distributed over the Internet using syndication feeds for playback on portable media players and personal computers. The term "podcast" is a portmanteau of the acronym "Pod" – standing for "Portable on Demand" – and "broadcast". The term, *iPod* was coined with Pod, prefixed with the "i" commonly used by Apple for its products and services. Some established audio players, such as *AmaroK*, *Winamp* and *Mediamonkey* also offer poscasting functionality. Podcast listeners can listen in one of two ways: through a specialized hardware device called an MP3 player or on a computer using media player software. Podcasting's initial appeal was to allow individuals to distribute their own radio-style shows, but the system quickly became used in a wide variety of other ways, including distribution of school lessons, official and unofficial audio tours of museums, conference meeting alerts and updates, and by police departments to distribute public safety messages. Is is becoming increasingly popular in education. Podcasts enable students and teachers to share information with anyone at anytime. An absent student can download the podcast of the recorded lesson. It can be a tool for teachers or administrators to communicate curriculum, assignments and other information with parents and the community. Teachers can record book discussions, vocabulary or foreign language lessons, international pen pal letters, music performance, interviews, and debates. Podcasting can be a publishing tool for student oral presentations. *Video podcasts* can be used in all these ways as well (Wikipedia, 2007).

Tagging : Tagging essentially enables users to create subject headings for the object at hand. It allows users to add and change not only content (data), but content describing content (metadata). In Flickr, users tag pictures. In LibraryThing, they tag books. In Library 2.0, users could tag the library's collection and thereby participate in the cataloguing process. Tagging simply makes lateral searching easier.

RSS feeds : RSS is used in Web terminology for Really Simple Syndication or Rich Sites Summary or RDF Site Summary or Real-time Simple Syndication. *RSS feeds* and other related technologies provide users a way to syndicate and republish content on the Web. It is a family of Web feed formats, specified in XML and used for Web syndication. Web feeds provide web content or summaries of web content together with links to the full versions of the content and other metadata. Users republish content from other sites or blogs on their sites or blogs, aggregate content on other sites in a single place, and ostensibly distill the Web for their personal use. Such syndication of content is another Web 2.0 application that is already having an impact on libraries, and could continue to do so in remarkable ways.

Already libraries are creating RSS feeds for users to subscribe to, including updates on new items in a collection, new services, and new content in subscription databases. They are also republishing content on their sites. *"Atom"* is the name of a specific *web feed* format. Web feeds, from a user's perspective, allow Internet users to subscribe to websites that change or add content regularly.

YouTube is another latest Web facility. It is a video sharing website where users can upload, view and share video clips. YouTube was created in mid-February 2005 to display a wide variety of video content, including movie and TV clips and music videos. In October 2006, Google Inc. acquired this technology. Unregistered users can watch most videos on the site, while registered users are permitted to upload an unlimited number of videos free of charge according to their social policy and related terms and conditions (YouTube, 2008).

Villanova University's Falvey Memorial Library has harnessed the power of contemporary Web search technology to develop an open-source resource discovery portal "*VuFind*" that enables users to query and browse the library's resources in a simple yet sophisticated manner. VuFind is a next generation catalog that empowers users by supporting personalization and social networking services such as tagging and peer-to-peer comment sharing. Interesting features are the facets to refine search results, the tagging system, the possibility to add reviews and notes to the records and cite them, the availability infos inside the record itself and the similar items (VuFind, 2007). The goal of VuFind is to enable users to search and browse through all of library's resources by replacing the traditional OPAC to include: Catalog Records, Digital Library Items, Institutional Repository, Institutional Bibliography; and Other Library Collections and Resources.

Though the Government of India had declared 2007 as the 'Broadband year', many other actions are needed to transform the passive users to active users for the effective utilization of Internet. I-Cube, IMRB International and IAMAI (2007) reports that awareness, content, access and technology are the four pillars which help to achieve this goal. Tha has been described as follows:

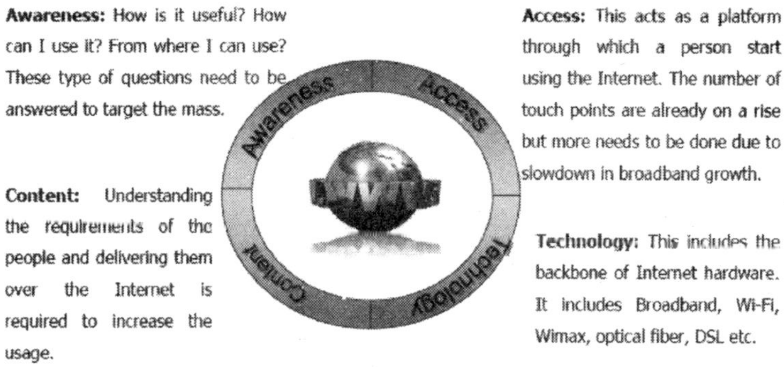

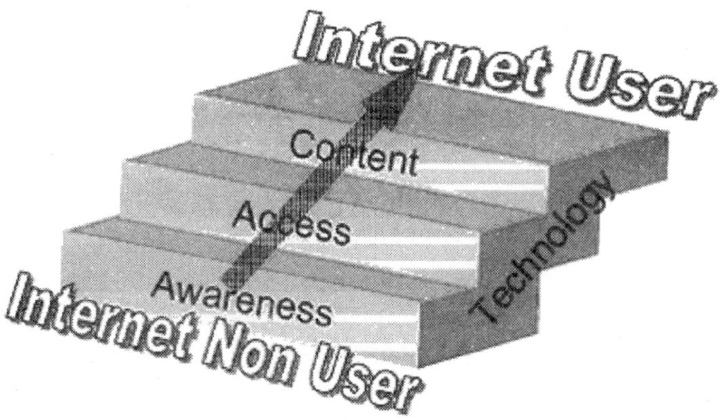

The latest Web technologies and facilities discussed above provide immense potential for the libraries and librarians to reach their clientele spread over the world.

But, the libraries in India could not hit these technologies and facilities to the maximum for extending information services. The only noteworthy advancement achieved in this direction is e-journals services. The credit of this mainly goes to the actions of the UGC and Inflibnet than the individual efforts and technological or professional leadership of the concerned libraries. If such advancement in services has been implemented, the libraries could extend the services based on e-journals to users of distant campuses and affiliated colleges either by library websites, responding to e-mail requests, etc. It was evident that the libraries were lagging to provide enough user education on web based services, web technologies and even to give wide publicity on the available information resources and services.

It is a fact that there are student and faculty users have not yet seriously or effectively started using the Internet and digital information search. Number of such users is comparatively more in lingustics and social sciences than in technology and science subjects. This indicates the essentiality for re-engineering information literacy and user education programmes. The adoption of latest web technologies, especially the semantic web technologies by the database developers, search engines, librarians, library users, etc. will help to improve the recall and relevance in searching.

As substantial number of users could not retrieve relevant information even from the normal Web, it would be necessary to provide regular orientation and training programmes for retrieving information from the deep Web or Invisible Web. Adoption of Semantic technologies and Content Management System also would help the users in this direction.

In adopting latest ICT or Web technologies, the libraries, especially academic and public libraries are lagging. Many users and library professionals have only theoretical idea on many of the latest technologies like Blogs, Wikis, Podcasting, RSS feeds, Streaming media, etc. But, in application level, the universities and libraries have to go further to take advantage of them.

4.23 INFORMATION LITERACY AND USER EDUCATION

Information literacy (IL) is described in the Alexandria Proclamation of 2005, as essential for individuals to achieve personal, social, occupational and educational goals. IL skills are necessary for people to be effective lifelong learners and to contribute in knowledge societies. This is why IL was endorsed by UNESCO's Information for All Programme (IFAP) as a basic human right. (UNESCO, 2008). Information literacy is a key component of, and contributor to, lifelong learning (ACRL, 2000). Information literacy is generally defined as having the ability to recognize when information is needed, then to be able to locate and evaluate appropriate information and use it effectively (ALA, 1989). The recommendations, guidelines and standards formulated by ALA on Information Literacy Programmes (ILP) are noteworthy.

The teaching of library use or information skills is not only to provide students with the specific skills to complete their education but also to prepare them to be lifelong learners in the workplace and their general lives. The normal contents of information literacy are regarding the use of catalogues, information sources, etc. They also deal with methods and techniques of information retrieval from databases, online or on CD-ROM, including search strategy development. Practical sessions should be included to ensure that the users become familiar with the characteristics of each database relevant to their research topics. It also should cover aspects of the thesis or report writing such as format, style and layout. Recommended citation styles are also taught in detail. Subject specific information retrieval tools, databases and other information resources should be demonstrated according to the subject interest of the students.

The ideal method for enabling students to develop their information literacy skills, as often mooted by many practitioners, is embedding the information literacy activity into a student's course materials. This method allows information literacy to be delivered in the context of the subject they are studying, to attract marks and to be devised on the basis of collaboration between library staff and academic colleagues (Hosein, 2006). The ILP integrated with the course curriculum have its own benefits.

IFLA/UNESCO (2006) Internet Manifesto Guidelines 2006 has categorically depicted the increased need for user training and information literacy programmes in the present context of ICTs and Internet by stating that the libraries and information services have a responsibility to facilitate and promote public access to quality information and communication. Users should be assisted with the necessary skills and a suitable environment in which to use their chosen information sources and services freely and confidently. In addition to the many valuable resources available on the Internet, some are incorrect, misleading and may be offensive. Librarians should provide the information and resources for library users to learn to use the Internet and electronic information efficiently and effectively. They should proactively promote and facilitate responsible access to quality networked information for all their users, including children and young people. Nandi and Panigrahi (2005) argues that the Library and Information Centres may be utilized as a very good platform for rendering Information

Literacy Programmes relating to cyber crimes, but at the same time users should change their behaviour and attitude towards the usage of computer.

Most of the agricultural universities and many of the conventional universities in India have examples of embedded system of ILP in their curriculum. A recent study on ILP in Kerala Agricultural University revealed that there is a strong relationship between the user orientation and use of information resources, particularly the digital resources. It was also realised that many of the problems created by the transition of information documents from print to electronic medium could be better managed with the help of proper user education courses with stress on ICTs. Because of this, the teachers and students have shown special interest to absorb knowledge on modern methods of information retrieval. Academic courses as part of the curriculum will add weight and importance to such programmes. The library and information science professionals were also opined that such programmes will help in re-engineering and re-defining the Library and Information System for the modern era. Their involvement as teachers and trainers will have an over all impact in improving the performance of the libraries and ultimately the user satisfaction (Francis, Razak and Kabir, 2006).

On User Education and Information Literacy, the SALIS (2006) appealed the UGC, and AICTE to introduce a paper on 'Library Science Education' in the curriculum of UG courses. It also recommended the Government of Tamil Nadu to introduce library hours compulsory for all the classes. Another recommendation submitted was to change the nomenclature of Library into 'Department of Library and Information Services'. These recommendations were justified on the ground that this move will convert the 'teacher-centred learning' into 'student-centered learning'.

In the present context, the ILP can also be given as an e-learning module either through CD Databases or through library websites. This will benefit the universities having multi campus locations and distance education programmes. A recent study by WebJunction (2006), an OCLC Support Service, indicated the benefits such as *Convenience for learners, Ability to reach more learners, Cost effectiveness of e-learning; and the freedom e-learning provides learners to direct their own learning.*

The online ILP, "**SAFARI**" (Skills in Accessing, Finding, and Reviewing Information) developed by Open University, UK was an important model of that type (Open University Library, 2001). University of Botswana Library has been offering orientation to its first year students, and bibliographic instructions, to senior students. It used the content management system, WebCT, for e-learning and ILP first in 2003. Their experience revealed that if implemented properly, online or Web delivery of ILP with good content management systems like WebCT has several advantages over the conventional the conventional systems (Lumande, Ojedokun and Fidzani, 2006).

Table 4.23.1. Few Course modules provided for ILP using WebCT by University of Botswana Library in 2003 (Source: Lumande, Ojedokun and Fidzani, 2006).

Week	*Face to face Lecture*	*Laboratory Sessions*	*Independent Learning Time (Library workstations)*
4	Information Skills 1 Unit 1: Concept of Information		
5	Information Skills 2 Unit 2: Organization of	Lab 1: WebCT orientation class	WebCT content & self-tests for

	Information Unit 3: Finding Information		unit 1, 2 & 3
6		Lab 2: Online Public Access catalogue (OPAC)	
14	Information Skills 3 Unit 4: Reference Sources	Lab 3: Reference sources	WebCT content and self-test for unit 4
			Final Assignment to be submitted electronically

Fig. 4.23.1. WebCT, for e-learning and ILP, University of Botswana Library experience (Source: Lumande, Ojedokun and Fidzani, 2006).

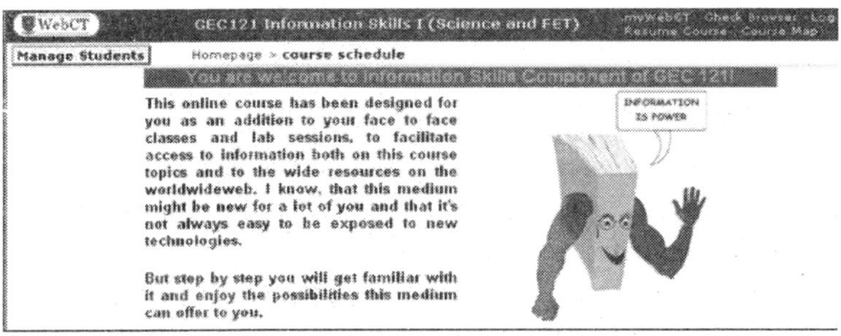

Fig. 4.23.2. WebCT, for e-learning and ILP, University of Botswana Library experience: Middle section of Homepage (Source: Lumande, Ojedokun and Fidzani, 2006).

Murdock (1995) establishes that the bibliographic instruction and ILP need to be re-defined in the changed context of information technologies and supports the processes of re-designing and *re*-engineering the library and information systems to transform them as computer- and user-friendly libraries.

It is a fact on university and college libraries in India that the user education or information literacy programmes offered to student as well as faculty users are not at all effective. Though both student and faculty users are really demanding for effective ILPs with sress on modern ICTs, many universities did not have proper provisions for this and at the same time many libraries and library professionals are not capable to handle such programmes. Only few university libraries in India started the practice of online or Web delivery or e-learning provision on ILP. At the same time majority of the students and teachers suggest offering ILP as part of the course curriculum.

In this case, agricultural universities are far better as compared to conventional universities. All agricultural universities in India having one paper, named, Library and Information Services, in their post graduate curriculum for their MSc, MVSc, MTech and PhD courses. But, such courses are not introduced by many universities at the undergraduate level.

4.24 INFORMATION MARKETING

The Chartered Institute of Marketing has defined marketing as, "*the management process responsible for identifying, anticipating, and satisfying consumer's requirements profitably*". Marketing includes analysis of customers, both current and potential; analysis of competitors and competitive forces; and analysis of the company or institution itself, of its strengths, weaknesses, culture and partnerships. Once that analysis has been done, and only then, can one move on to deciding on a course of action, determining whom to target and what to emphasize, and then carrying out that plan. As the library is considered as non-profit organization, it is better to group its marketing strategies under the category of societal marketing. The doyen of marketing management Philip Kotler defined the concepts of Societal Marketing as, "*the Societal Marketing concepts holds that the organization's task is to determine the needs, wants, and interest of target markets and to deliver the desired satisfaction more effectively and efficiently than competitors in a way that preserves or enhances the consumer's and society's well-being*" (Kotler, 1999). This approach of marketing is more appropriate to libraries because it is stressing the needs of the users by increasing the efficiency and effectiveness of services with the ultimate goal of society's well-being. The National Agricultural Library (2008), USA stresses that the marketing in libraries must target the right people the right way at the right time, ensuring efficiency, effectiveness and good Stewardship.

The marketing aspect of information is highly relates to its value and quality. According to Hendriks and Wooler (2006), there are four main headings in the structure of information or knowledge: quality; character; management style; and shelf life. He concluded that added value via the establishment of the Return of Investment (ROI) must be a top priority for information services in any organization. Information management should align its goals with organizational strategies. Active information services will find themselves positioned at the heart of the intellectual capital of their organizations, namely at the cross-point of knowledge and information flows, where intellectual capital depends on the dynamics of knowledge and information. The information professional should have a high level of understanding of the core processes of the client, and a general understanding of who the client's client is. A good communication plan is the last but crucial step in the ROI. The ROI will be based on an information map, placing the information department and its services at the centre, and showing different relations with information end-users with different types of added value, based on different information flows. Risk management will provide information managers with a good understanding of the reduction of risks that will take place when decision makers and key knowledge workers are provided with the right knowledge and information. Research activities undertaken by the information department will result in the understanding necessary to establish the ROI, but will also greatly enhance the understanding by end-users in the organization of the information and knowledge services available to them. The result of an ROI study is a shortlist of added values, expressed in the different units of 'money', time' and 'quality'. Finally, all three expressions must be converted to money so that, despite the variety of inputs, one figure represents the entire return on efforts in information and knowledge services.

As in the case of all other organizations, the factors like emergence of modern technologies, globalization, competition for quality products and services, etc. have changed the library's relationship to its clients and its internal organization.

Based on a study of the role of the library in the context of American Commercial Society, Ed D'Angelo observed that whereas before, clients were expected to adhere to the bureaucratic rules and procedures of the library, today they are increasingly viewed as customers in a marketplace. Features of a bureaucracy include impartiality, comprehensive written rules and procedures, and impersonality. Rules are objectively defined and applied impartially to all members and clients of the organization. But in a market all terms of service are negotiable at the point of transaction. Thus, under a market model, if a customer owes the library a fine, he can negotiate with the library to reduce or eliminate his fine. In the interest of "good customer service" and preserving its relationship with the customer the library may agree to reduce the fines owed by some customers who aggressively negotiate lower fines, while others pay the standard fine. The library might even choose to overlook stolen material if on balance it gains by doing so. Indeed since public libraries receive funding from third parties there is little incentive to do otherwise. This same laissez-faire attitude applies to all the rules of the market-oriented public library. .... The basic principle of New Economy management theory is to replace bureaucratic structures with market mechanisms. The market-oriented library prefers that its employees relate to one another as they would in the marketplace. Full time permanent employees are encouraged to view one another as "customers." But according to him the market-oriented library has several disadvantages.

He continued that during the New Economy era most changes were attributed to information technology. But machines don't manage change. People in positions of power do. Machines, even computers, do only what they are told to do. Most of the changes we experienced during the New Economy era were due to aggressive market-oriented management policies, not to technology alone. Technology merely gives management the tools to carry out its policies. .... The greatest reduction of in-house labor during the New Economy era was due to outsourcing, re-engineered work routines, removing layers of management and supervision, and downsizing; not to automation. Most technological innovations such as web-based catalogs improved the quality of service but did little to reduce labor needs. ..... Outsourcing allows an organization to replace an internal bureaucratic relationship to its employees with a market relationship to an outside vendor. Outsourcing of cataloguing and telephone or web based reference services can be introduced. ..... Librarian work routines have been re-engineered by eliminating their role as gatekeepers of the culture (D'Angelo, 2004). Information manager should know that in marketing main focus is on the clientele and the goal is clientele satisfaction. He should also know that supply crates demand. He should adapt to changing environment of users (Shah, 2005).

In the area of information marketing also, the university libraries had done negligible progress. The approach towards marketing will improve the quality of services and its standardization. Though institutions like NISCAIR, DELNET, etc. have done some contribution towards information marketing, university libraries are yet to frame policies and programmes towards this direction. At present, the university libraries are mainly collecting revenues as library fees, membership fees, overdue charges, charges for photocopying, printing, downloading records from databases, etc. The receipts collected by these methods were negligible. Towards this goal, all the libraries need to make marketing plan with quality consciousness.

The prevailing gulf in the availability of information resources between the universities and colleges provides enormous scope for marketing. The recent declaration of UGC (2007) on the proposed strengthening of the UGC Infonet Digital Library Consortia indicates that the teachers and students of the colleges in the country have to wait several years more to get accessibility of the e-journals. This consortium provides libraries unlimited market potential. But, the libraries need to re-define and re-engineer their service set up with leadership, quality consciousness and value addition. Several institutions, libraries and librarians are struggling now to get proper advice, training, consultancy, etc. on various aspects such as library automation, software development and maintenance, personnel management, database development, OPAC, development of digital libraries and archives, documentation, web technologies, etc. These areas also provide substantial scope for marketing as both the selling and buying libraries will reap the benefit mutually.

As the marketing of information products and services is directly linked with quality, the librarians generally felt that the service system of the libraries is not upto that level. As the inter library services also had direct bearing on quality, the libraries should be able to intensify efforts both on ILL and marketing in a complementary nature. Shortage of staff, lack of infrastructural facilities, attitude of the staff on providing services, lack of professional leadership, etc. are few reasons that hindering effective marketing by the libraries.

4.25 RE-DEFINING DIVISIONS OF THE LIBRARY

In the modern age of globalization and competition, new technologies and management processes are used as a means to improve the efficiency and effectiveness of the organizations by eliminating wastage in processes and reducing cost. Several strategies and management methods were developed over the years to suit the requirements. Six Sigma is such a method used to improve the management processes. It has been considered as a management strategy that employs a well structured business improvement methodology to tackle process variability and drive out waste from the business processes with the application of statistical tools and techniques in a scrupulous manner.

Technically, six sigma means 3.4 Defects Per Million Opportunities (DPMO) where sigma is a term used to represent the variation about the average of any process. It is a business improvement strategy used to improve profitability, to drive out waste, to reduce quality costs and improve the effectiveness and efficiency of all operations processes that meet or even exceed customers' need and expectations (Antony and Banuelas, 2001). Six sigma has the potential of reducing variability from processes and products by using either a continuous improvement methodology or a design/re-design approach, also known as design for six sigma (DFSS). General Electric (GE) claims to be the first in applying and developing DFSS concepts. With the application of DFSS, the GE Medical systems could reduce the scanning time from three minutes to 20 seconds in full body scans. This resulted in important savings in hospital personnel (Antony and Banuelas, 2002).

Libraries, whether they are big or small, considered as institutions within institutions. That means, all the processes and complexities of managing a service organization are applicable to the libraries. In this context, the management processes of the libraries have to be planned independently. As the modern technologies, especially the ICTs, have scrupulously changed the in-house operations and service processes of the present libraries, there is a great need for re-defining its divisions in order to attain reduction in quality costs and improve the effectiveness and efficiency of all operations and processes that meet users' need and expectations.

The information outburst has completely revolutionized the management system of libraries. The traditional divisions of the university libraries are not suitable as such in the current context. The operations starting from acquisition to services call for re-engineering and re-defining. A single change of the numbering system of International Standard Book Number (ISBN) itself has necessitated changes in several activities of the library. From 2007 onwards, all ISBNs have to be 13 digits long instead of the earlier system of 10 digits. To cope up with this change, all existing ISBN-10s have to be translated into ISBN-13s by adding 978 at the beginning, using the first nine digits of the ISBN-10 with appropriate hyphens, and re-calculating the final check digit. That is, corresponding number of ISBN-10: **1-55853-234-**X in ISBN-13 is : 978-**1-55853-234**-2. Conversely, ISBN-13s beginning with 978 can be recalculated to ISBN-10s. Once the supply of 978-prefix ISBNs is depleted, publishers will begin assigning ISBNs with a 979 prefix, thus effectively doubling the pool of available numbers. The new ISBN-13 is precisely the same number as the 13 digit European Article Numbering – Uniform Code Council (EAN-UCC) system.

The transition from ISBN-10 to ISBN-13 is another Y2K problem for librarians, software people and system administrators (Breaux and Dawson, 2006). It raises plenty of other questions to vendors in accepting orders for books, supply chain management, online delivery, barcode systems, etc. In libraries, ever occurring changes of this type will affect it's a to z operations like acquisition, cataloging records, inter library loan, printing of bibliographies, OPAC, searching of database, interoperability of databases, etc. All these changes are necessitated mainly because of the development and application of modern ICTs and these technologies have to be managed by the libraries in an integrated way, instead of approaching them in conventional division settings.

The functional divisions or sections most common in university libraries in India are: Acquisition, Technical processing, Maintenance, Reference, Circulation, Periodicals, Documentation/Information Services, etc.

As majority of the library professionals consider that they were not able to effectively utilize the new skills acquired by them, changes are needed in the organization structure of the libraries which will help to increase the efficiency in work flow by integrating all activities of the library in an automated system. Though computers were used for several operations of the libraries, most of the activities were carried out without proper integration. Effective network administration is essential to improve the whole process in a perfect integrated environment.

The advancement of ICTs has necessitated paradigm shift in library operations and a thorough re-organization of its functions. The following table gives a clear picture of the process of that functional shift required in the present context:

Table 4.25.1. Divisions proposed for the University Libraries

Divisions Proposed	*Activities may be organized in each Division*
1. *Information Acquisition*	Acquisition of all print and non-print documents such as books, journals, theses, patents, reports, etc.
2. *Information Processing*	Classification, cataloguing, database development, metadata activities, development of digital libraries and Institutional repositories or archives, etc. of all types of documents
3. *Information Maintenance*	Maintenance activities of all documents in print and non-print such as shelf management, stock verification, binding, maintenance of documents in micro form, CD, DVD, BD, HDD, etc.
4. *Information Services*	Membership activities, Circulation, Information Literacy and User Education, Inter library

Adminis-tration	services, Documentation services, web delivery of information services, etc.
5. ***Network***	Acquisition and maintenance of all hardware and software systems such as computers, servers, web servers, power systems, etc., Arrangements for hosting and decentralized maintenance of library website and web pages, etc.

4.26 NETWORKING AND RESOURCE SHARING

Libraries are now being compelled by the prevailing circumstances to form a united front that would make it possible to provide adequate solutions to common problems such as:

- budget cuts;
- response time for services;
- obsolete equipment;
- untrained personnel;
- out-of-date collections; and
- generally, weakened services.

Networking in library and information systems provides a wider access to the information resources improves public and technical services and enhances operations by sharing resources, reducing duplication and offering more cost-effective services. These are but some of the benefits that participating institutions may derive from networking. Other benefits are: sharing experiences; creating sources for resources: developing strategic alliances; facilitating and promoting collaboration and co-operation so that libraries can improve and expand access and distribution to information resources; and training and development of professional librarians.

The appropriate legal framework, relevant and clearly defined common objectives, policies, procedures, adequate staffing, funding, motivation to co-operate and commitment on the part of all the players, and in recent times the state of the information and communication technology, determine the success of any networking process. Effective communication is important in the business of sharing. Participants must know from which point in the network they are likely to get what information. The availability of union catalogues and common serial lists is equally important. All participants are expected to make a contribution from which others can benefit. Trust, will, professionalism, effective teamwork and the existence of team spirit are additional factors that determine the success of networking. Lack of institutional support and a lack of interest on the part of participants can derail the sharing process (Martey, 2002). According to Jebaraj and Devadoss (2004), a network may fail in the early stages if there is no proper planning or if adequate funds are not available. Moreover, a common memorandum of agreement signed by the participating libraries at the institutional level is essential for the success of a network venture. On a more practical level, catalogue data must be in a standard, machine readable form for it to be shared and exchanged. And, finally, a continuous flow of external assistance is crucial for the network's survival.

Library Resource-Sharing in the Online Digital Information Environment

Bushra Almas Jaswal strongly opined that the time of traditional library resource sharing networks is now over and in the current age surrounded by the new developments of information technology; the Internet, e-mail, high-speed data networks, web catalogs, Blogs and digital libraries, the networks like LABELNET, DIEVINSA, etc. seems like white elephants (Jaswal, 2006). The mandatory objective of the Inflibnet is to establish an effective resource sharing network by the automation and networking of all types of libraries in India. But, even after several years of its functioning, it could not achieve this target. In order to fulfill this goal, it was suggested to implement the project with the compulsory leadership and participation of the universities in the respective geographical regions (Francis, 1997a). Active involvement and leadership of all types of academic, research and public libraries was strongly advocated for the establishment and effective functioning of integrated information system in any region or country (Francis, 1998a).

Re-defined Digital Collection Development

The impact of the resource sharing efforts in the digital information age posed several issues to the libraries in their management process. The fact that more and more information is now available in the digital form, which is accessible online in extensive amount, easily retrievable through powerful online search engines and shared with users located over long distances through high speed networks in virtually real time has introduced new forms of resource sharing among the libraries. Information produced or acquired in the digital format by one institution, in an electronically connected environment, can be easily shared with other institutions. This fact has created a fear for economic survival among the publishers and producers of digital resources. So, the publishers impose a number of restrictions on sharing of their information. In certain cases the libraries only buy access to the resources but not the ownership. This has given way to special form of Library Consortia where libraries get together to negotiate better terms from the publishers at a lower cost to each sharing institution.

The advancements and recent developments in the areas like online journals, e-journals consortia, digital libraries, digital archives, etc. have opened unlimited possibilities for resource sharing and inter library services. Now the university libraries mainly concentrate to provide services to the users coming to their campuses. As a value addition, the available e-journals could be made usable to the outstation users of the university and also to the users from affiliated colleges, government departments, industrial houses, farmers, etc. As there may be business restrictions to make accessible the journals to the outstation users by user name and password, the libraries can provide article services using the rich collection available or accessible in the libraries. The models of DELNET and similar other networks and libraries can be adopted to provide such services. In order to make the services efficient and more effective, marketing approach and strategies on internal resource generation can be employed by the libraries.

Among the university libraries in India or within a State, there is no specific agreement or formal or functional relationship prevails for sharing their resources mutually. At the same time, these libraries were starving for information resources, technical manpower, other facilities, finance, etc. What the libraries performing on resource sharing was mainly due to the individual interest and informal relationship prevailing among the professionals. Thus, this system exhibits many weaknesses and inconsistencies. So, it is imperative to win maximum fruits of networking and resource sharing that the libraries should frame formal policies, guidelines, norms and agreements because the availability and accessibility of information highly determines the quality of education and research programmes of the universities. The UGC, State and Central Governments, Higher Education Council, etc. can play active roles in this respect.

Since the libraries were mainly concentrated on conventional services based on the resources available or accessible within the libraries, the users also could not raise their demands for external resources. In order to cater to the needs of the clientele, libraries should re-define the network based services by applying ICT based tools for document delivery services. Since this is a labour intensive activity, highly motivated and trained professionals with maximum leadership are needed to offer such services effectively.

4.27 HUMAN RESOURCES AND TRANSFORMATION OF MANAGEMENT PROCESS OF LIBRARIES

Even with all necessary resources, in order to win the game, we need proper management. Hamel and Prahalad (1993) underlined that management can leverage its resources, financial and non-financial, in five basic ways: (i) by concentrating them more effectively on key strategic goals; (ii) by accumulating them more efficiently; (iii) by complementing one kind of resource with another to create higher order value; (iv) by conserving resources wherever possible; and (v) by recovering them from the market place in the shortest possible time.

Information management research has underlined the importance of information exchange in connection with problem identification. Collective responsibility and an overall perspective for decision-making in an organization are important. The holistic viewpoint is also important in a wider perspective. Information management activities cannot be isolated processes, and information and knowledge management should consider both human and system factors. This can be summarized in the Figure: 4.27.1, which is based on information culture research in Finnish insurance companies (Widén-Wulff, 2001).

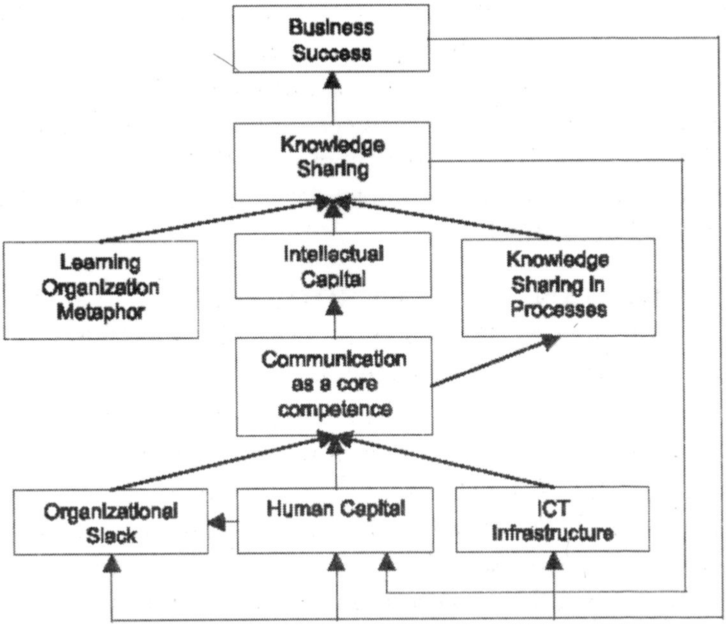

Fig. 4.27.1. Knowledge Management System, a Finnish Model
Source: Widén-Wulff and Ginman, 2004.

In this study it was concluded that knowledge sharing is more effective in environments where the learning process is emphasized and implemented in the organization. Intellectual capital is important and it is born in the process of communication, which needs to be a core competence in a knowledge sharing organization. Communication as a core competence exists when there is enough personal knowledge, human capital, an Information and Communications Technology (ICT) infrastructure to support the communication process, and sufficient organizational slack (Widén-Wulff and Ginman, 2004).

Several studies show that automation without considering human factors might be counter productive.

A higher level of automation may not necessarily improve the overall productivity of an organizational team. It involves a number of important human issues that may not be evident to an application developer. Recently there have been some interesting developments in the area of Computer Supported Cooperative Work (CSCW) that provide a binding between organizational business processes and emerging communication technologies (Rodden, 1996). Successful development of management applications requires a good understanding of management processes (Ray and Fry, 1993). A study in Kerala reveals that librarians consider I.T. not as a means to reduce their workload, but as a device to render effective information service to patrons. It stresses the need for participatory style of management to achieve maximum benefit out of the application of IT in libraries (Somanathan Nair, 1997). If people who are associated with automation – either who operate technology or who are served with it, respond badly to it, the anticipated effectiveness of using technology will not be achieved. The attitudes people hold towards a proposed technological change determine their response to the change. Failure to take these attitudes into account and deal with them appropriately leads very often to catastrophe and even organizational collapse (Somanathan Nair, 1998).

As library organizations become more complex and face the need for significant transformation in the way they are organized, more managers and administrators applied several managerial experiments to cope up with the situation. Many of them seek to understand the principles and practices of organization development (OD), a program of organizational improvement with strategic planning. Most libraries have a strategic plan, and many are in the regular practice of keeping the plan up to date (Sullivan, 2004). A second-generation OD comprised of organizational transformation; the learning organization; a focus on teams as a significant means for work accomplishment; total quality management; visioning and future search conferences; re-defining and *re-engineering*; work re-design, etc. There are a number of libraries-academic, public, and special-that have employed one or more of these programs when faced with the need for significant improvement of the organization.

4.28 ROLE AND STATUS OF LIBRARIANS

It is a generally accepted notion that the work of library and information science professionals are teaching in nature and hence universally they have been considered as teachers/faculty in schools/colleges/universities and scientists in research institutions. Many eminent educationists considered the task of librarians as even related to the teaching of teachers or training of trainers. All advanced nations have accepted this principle and implemented it. But, in some states in India, including Kerala, the reverse situation prevails. The following remark made by Soundararajan (1979) reflects its gravity: *"Though the term 'College Librarian' means the head of the library and an important person in the educational hierarchy in foreign countries, it is tragic that the same word, in our land of paradoxes, means a clerk. Our educational administrators consider librarians as mere custodians (and not educators) perhaps due to ignorance or because of the fact that clerks were in charge of libraries some decades back. To erase this obsolete idea from the minds of all concerned, it is absolutely essential to re-designate the qualified librarians as Professors and Assistant Professors".*

In the present context, though it seems to be an extreme remark, more or less similar situations still prevail in many colleges and institutions in the country.

Though many college librarians are in the UGC Scale or similar higher scale than the Office Superintendent, in many cases the librarians are being controlled by the Office staff because they are classified by the UGC or Governments, as non-teaching staff and hence no department status for the libraries and academic or faculty status to the librarians. So, in practical, the reporting officer or controlling officer of the librarian is normally the Office Superintendent.

In order to study the problems of college libraries, the Government of Kerala appointed an expert Committee, headed by V.P. Joy, IAS as the convener. The Committee has made several valid recommendations to revamp the libraries in Kerala (Kerala, Expert Committee on College Libraries, 1994). Onc of the relevant recommendations on the status of the librarian was as follows:

"The Committee considers it desirable to give the college librarians, academic status (non-vocation) and bring librarian also under the definition of 'teacher' as done in Madurai, Madras and other University Acts. ... Librarianship is a highly complex profession warranting specialized and technical knowledge of various sorts like personnel administration / financial management and different bibliographical techniques. Librarians also require higher academic qualifications like other heads of the departments of the college as recommended by the UGC".

Even with such clear cut recommendations, the Government of Kerala or the universities have not implemented many of the valid recommendations. At the same time, Government of India, many state governments and national regulatory bodies in education, like UGC, ICAR, AICTE, NCERT, etc. have already recognized the teaching and scientific role of librarians. Most of the national research organizations in India like DRDO, CSIR,

ISRO, etc. have given the job title for librarians as "***Scientist***". Some universities also have the job title similar to that of their teachers, such as "***Assistant Professor***", "***Associate Professor***", "***Professor***", etc. The Government of Andhra Pradesh has issued orders to classify the university and college librarians as stated before (Andhra Pradesh, 2003). The Karnataka State College Librarian's Association has reported that the Karnataka State Government Cabinet has passed a resolution on 21st July 2006 deciding that the Librarians as Teachers (Karnataka State College Librarian's Association, 2006). In India, large number of national research and development organisations and institutions has given same designations to library and information professionals on par with their colleague, scientists or teachers. In the light of the above facts and keeping in view the changing scenario and new responsibilities it was requested UGC to re-designate the LIS professionals in universities and colleges as Professor, Associate Professor, Assistant Professor and Lecturer (Indian Academic Library Association, 2008).

All agricultural universities and many of the conventional universities in India have the system of involvement of librarians in direct teaching. They teach curriculum based topics such research methodology, information sources, information retrieval techniques, ICT, search engines, style and format of writing articles, books, theses, etc. A recent study in KAU re-iterated the need and effectiveness of teaching-training role of librarians. It revealed the prevalence of strong relationship between the user orientation and use of information resources, particularly in the case of digital resources. Because of this, the teachers and students have shown special interest to absorb knowledge on modern methods of information retrieval. The involvement of librarians as teachers and trainers helped to create over all impact in improving the performance of the libraries and library services (Francis, Razak and Kabir, 2006). Other related studies also stressed the need for thorough restructuring of the human resource management of the university libraries in the context of modern ICTs. (Francis, 1997b) (Francis and Kabir, 2008a).

In order to perform the librarian efficiently and effectively, certain administrative powers and social status are needed. But what is the present status of the librarians in the educational institutions such as schools, colleges and universities in many states?. It is a general notion in Kerala that librarians are social service persons who work for literacy. Such librarians, we find in public libraries, are common every where in the state and their standing number is more than ten thousand. Since their service is generally part time and honourary, it is quite natural that they will leave the sector generally on receiving a fruitful employment after a few months or years service. So, if we count the number of persons served so far as the so called public librarians in the state are several thousands. Such librarians did not need any minimum qualifications and they are getting only an honorarium. But, actually, they are not professionals. On literacy movement and social service angle the role of honorary public librarians are invaluable. But, it is unscientific to consider them at par with professional librarians.

Even after the implementation of UGC Scale to the librarians, common people think that librarians are low paid professionals and they did not have any major qualifications. Another reason to this notion is that, in colleges and government departments, promotion to the cadre of librarians is prevailing from the peons, attenders, and other Class IV staff. Even though this promotion is made as Librarian Grade IV, most people believe them almost at par with Librarians in universities. Recently, the Government of Kerala (2006) has reduced the qualifications of Librarian Grade III from BLISc to CLISc for internal candidates. Such actions and the predominant system of honourary librarians in Kerala have established a different social status. So, measures are urgently needed to identify, classify and establish due status to each category of library professionals working in different sectors. Otherwise, the librarians ranging from honourary public librarians to the librarians in universities can not impact effectively in their respective institutions in particular and the society in general. In a positive move to implement UGC qualifications and scales to Librarians in private colleges in Kerala, the government has issued an order by which all colleges will have one UGC Cadre Librarian and in future these posts will be filled with incumbents having the qualifications prescribed by the UGC (Kerala, 2008). This has to be implemented properly and such move is essential for all colleges including medical, engineering, nursing, pharmacy, education, management, poly techniques, etc.

Few state governments and universities in the country have not officially approved the important academic role of librarians. All central government controlled and internationally reputed IITs, IIMs and IISc and central universities have given academic and faculty status for their librarians and the research institutions like CSIR, ISRO, DRDO, etc. have designated librarians as 'scientists'. But, it is contrary that in one of its order, the UGC itself has described the librarians as administrative personnel. Though the librarians in the UGC Cadre get salary at par with teachers, their impact and efficient functioning in the society will be reduced because of these reasons. The Fifth Pay Commission Report of the Government of India says "it is in recognition of the importance of information in policy formulation, planning, decision making, and administration that libraries have been established . . . the libraries may be covered by a computer network". The Commission has also recommended the creation of an All India Library Service, revision of categorization of formula and staffing pattern in each category of library. It also proposes to give more weightage to the activities that are related to dissemination of information. The Report of the Pay Commission of the Government of Kerala, 2004 has recommended providing UGC Scale to Librarians in colleges receiving financial assistance from UGC. But, on implementation stage, lot of hurdles had put by the administrative machinery. The National Knowledge Commission headed by Dr. Sam Pitroda has come with proactive recommendations and actions in identifying the value of libraries and role of librarians in the modern society.

Confusing Designations and Status of Librarians

The designations, qualifications, scale of pay, status, etc. of library professionals and semi-professionals in different government departments, institutions, agencies, etc. in Kerala State are not comparable. Hence, utter confusion and misunderstanding prevail among administrators, academics, teachers and students of schools, colleges and universities, government officials and the general public. This is adversely affecting the library system and its service effectiveness.

Table 4.28.1. Comparison of designations, qualifications,scale of pay, etc. of library professionals in Kerala State

Designations	*Scale of Pay**	*Qualifications, Experience required and mode of appointment*
Librarian (UGC) (in Universities)	16400-22400	As per UGC Scheme. 18 years experience as University Assistant Librarian or College Librarian in UGC Cadre. MLISc 55 % and outstanding academic performance. PhD, NET, Publications, etc. desirable.
Librarian (UGC) (in Colleges)	8000-13500	MLISc 55 % and NETPromotion and also by direct recruitment
Librarian Gr. I (in Colleges)	7200-11400	MLISc 55 % and NETPromotion and also by direct recruitment
Librarian Gr. I (in Govt. Depts..)	7200-11400	BLISc and seniority based promotion and also by direct recruitment
Librarian Gr. II (in Colleges)	5800 – 9425	BLISc and seniority based promotion and also by direct recruitment
Librarian Gr. II (in Govt. Depts.)	5800 – 9425	BLISc and seniority based promotion and also by direct recruitment
Librarian Gr. III (in Colleges)	5000 – 8150	BLISc; Seniority based promotion and also by direct recruitment
Librarian Gr. IV (in Colleges)	3590 – 5400	CLISc; Appointment by promotion and also by direct recruitment
Librarian Gr. IV (in Govt. Depts.)	3590 – 5400	CLISc; Appointment by promotion and also by direct recruitment
Librarian (in Village Libraries under the Kerala State Library Council)	Honorarium Rs. 500/- to Rs. 750/-	No minimum qualifications. Training in Library and Information science desirable

Deputy Librarian (UGC) (in Universities)	12000-18300	As per UGC Scheme. 5 years experience as University Assistant Librarian or College Librarian in UGC Cadre and outstanding academic performance for direct recruitment or 11 years for Promotion by Career Advancement MLISc 55%, + PhDNET, Publications, etc. are desirableDirect recruitment/ Career Advancement
Assistant Librarian Sel. Gr. (UGC) (in Universities)	12000-18300	As per UGC Scheme. 5 years experience as University Assistant Librarian Senior Scale in UGC scale and attended Refresher Courses and other academic achievementsCareer Advancement
Assistant Librarian Sr. Gr. (UGC) (in Universities)	10000-15200	As per UGC Scheme. 6 years experience as University Assistant Librarian in UGC scale and attended Refresher Courses and other academic achievements Career Advancement
Assistant Librarian (UGC) (in Universities)	8000-13500	MLISc 55 % and NET
Assistant Librarian Gr. II (in Universities)	6675-10550	Degree + BLIScSeniority based promotion
Assistant Librarian (in some agencies/ govt.)	3590 – 5400	CLISc and seniority based promotion and also by direct recruitment
Junior Librarian (in Universities)	7200-11400	Degree + BLIScSeniority based promotion
Reference Assistant (in Universities)	6675-10550	Degree + BLIScSeniority based promotion

Technical Assistant (in Universities)	5800 – 9425	Degree + BLIScSeniority based promotion
Library Assistant (in Universities)	5000 – 8150	Degree + BLIScDirect recruitment
Library Assistant (in Colleges)	2610 – 3680	VIIth Standard

* For easy understanding and comparison, pre-revised scales are given for the posts both in UGC and Non-UGC Cadres

The number of library professionals in the UGC Cadre (in colleges/universities) and in the Non-UGC Cadre (in colleges/ universities/ government depts.) in the entire State of Kerala is less than 100 (one hundred) and 1,000 (one thousand) respectively. At the same time, more than 10,000 (ten thousand) librarians without any minimum qualifications and scale of pay are working in the public libraries here. This situation has crated a false understanding among most of the general public and even among many of the persons working in universities/ colleges that no qualifications are required for librarians and they don't have any substantial income. The result of this is that the social status of librarians are very less and in many colleges and universities they are treated less than lower division clerks or office assistants. Hence, though it is highly essential for the society, it is very difficult and hard in Kerala to influence and guide the students, academicians and the general public by the librarians. Since the schools, even the higher secondary schools, coming under the regulation and control of Government of Kerala did not have any qualified librarians and the school libraries are managed by other subject teachers. Hence, functioning of the library is dependent on the extra time and willingness of the other Subject Teacher in-Charge of the Library. This system could not provide even essential services to students and teachers and hence students are not able to inculcate reading habit from the childhood and understand the importance of libraries and role of librarians. Ultimately, this adversely affects the quality not only of school education but also the higher education and research.

Since the librarians in Central/State government research institutions are designated as "Scientist" or "Technical Officer" or "Scientist Assistant" or "Technical Assistant", people consider them as different group from librarians. Though the librarians in colleges/universities/ government are highly qualified and equally paid, the society could not be able to exploit their potential to the maximum.

The library professionals in the universities in Kerala are categorized as Non-Teaching Staff. Even the professionals in the UGC Cadre are categorized as Non-Teaching and Non-Academic personnel. The guidelines of UGC also not clear in this respect. The Education Commission headed by Dr. S. Radhakrishnan envisaged that in research institutes and universities, the libraries were considered as higher than class rooms and as such the role of librarians.

Based on the order of the Kerala (1999) Government, the Kerala State Council for Science, Technology and Environment (KSCSTE) has given the scientific status for the librarians under its research institutes. Hence, the librarians are governed by the same rules for scientists. But, in universities in Kerala, the librarians even in the UGC Cadre are governed by the rules for non-teaching staff. This is purely unscientific.

Though the term, "teacher" is used in all educational institutions, varied designations are existing in different types of educational institutions. That is, designations like lecturer, assistant professor, reader, associate professor, professor, principal, dean, etc. are prevailing in colleges and universities and UP/LP School assistant, high school assistant, higher secondary teacher, vocational teacher, headmaster, etc. are used in schools. But, in the case of library professionals, the term, "librarian" is used for in all libraries starting from part time voluntary rural librarian to the librarian in the universities.

This system gives utter confusion among the students, teachers, general public, academicians, administrators, politicians and even the library professionals. Hence, the confusion in the society will continue till clear designations would be provided to differentiate each cadre as in the case teachers.

Hence, all library professionals in the UGC Cadre in the universities should be re-designated as prevailing in all research institutes under Governments of India and State Governments. In order to have a uniform and comparable staff pattern and also to clear the confusion prevailing in the society, the designations of the library professionals may be re-designated as listed in table: 4.28.2 below:

Table 4.28.2: Proposed designations, scale of pay, etc. for the library professionals in Colleges and, Universities

Designations / Scale of Pay

Existing	*Proposed*	*Scale of Pay (Pre-revised)*	*Institution*
Non-UGC Cadre			
Librarian Grade IV	Junior Technical Asst. (JTA)	3590 - 5400	Colleges
Librarian Grade III	Technical Asst. (TA)	5000 - 8150	Colleges
Librarian Grade II	Senior Technical Asst. (STA)	5800 - 9425	Colleges
Librarian Grade I	Technical Officer II (TO-II)	7200-11400	Colleges

Senior Librarian	Technical Officer I (TO-I)	7800-12975	Colleges
Library / Profl. Asst.	Technical Asst. (TA)	5000 - 8150	All Utys.
Technical / Profl Asst. II	Senior Technical Asst. (STA)	5800 - 9425	All Utys.
Reference Asst./ Jr. Librarian	Technical Officer II (TO-II)	7200-11400	All Utys.
Asst. Librarian Gr. II / Reference Asst (Hr.Gr.)	Technical Officer I (TO-I)	7800-12975	All Utys.
Asst. Librarian Gr. I	Senior Technical Officer (STO)	10000-15150	All Utys.
UGC Cadre			
Assistant Librarian	Asst. Professor / Asst. Librarian	8000-13500	Uni./ Colleges
Deputy Librarian	Assoc. Professor / Dy. Librarian	12000-18300	Uni./ Colleges
University Librarian	Professor / Librarian	16400-22400	Uni./ Colleges

Suitable qualifications, mode of appointment and scheme of promotion, etc. are given in table 4.28.3.

Table 4.28.3. Suitable qualifications, mode of appointment and promotionfor the library professionals in Colleges and Universities

Qualifications :

1. Qualifications for JTA should be SSLC + CLISc, that for TA / STA, Degree + BLISc and for TO/STO, Degree + MLISc.
2. PhD should be made as the compulsory qualification for Associate Professor / Deputy Librarian and also for Professor / Librarian. The NET should be a compulsory qualification for recruitment to the Asst. Professor/Assistant Librarian in the UGC Cadre. Publications, experience in project coordination, leadership in library automation, etc. should be given weightage.
3. The experience for the post of Professor / Librarian should be amended as 18 years in any professional or semi-professional cadre in university or research libraries of equivalent status and the candidate applying for the post should be in the UGC

Cadre of Senior Asst. Librarian / College Librarian with scale of pay 10000-15200 or higher.

Mode of Recruitment

The recruitment to the Non-UGC Cadre may be done by direct appointment to JTA for Colleges and to TA for universities.

Promotion and Career Advancement

1. Instead of the prevailing system of vacancy based / ratio based promotion, it should be time bound promotion on completing some specified in-service training courses.
2. The residency period may be fixed as 5/6 years in each cadre. So, the incumbent recruited as JTA will become TO-I after 20/24 years of service, if he acquires MLISc degree. Similarly, the incumbent recruited as TA will become STO after 20/24 years of service. Here, no chance for luck or personal influence in the promotion and everybody will get equal opportunity and justice.
3. The incumbents in the TO/STO cadre may be given age relaxation for direct recruitment to the UGC Cadre.
4. Assessment based encouragement in the form of good service entry, cash award, special allowance not linked to increment, etc. may be instituted for the staff instead of the prevailing systems based on seniority, availability of vacancy or flexible complimenting scheme because all such systems have lot of demerits and create complexities in administration and dissatisfaction among employees.

4.29 LIBRARY PERSONNEL

The personnel in university libraries can be classified into three categories as follows:

1. Professionals;
2. Semi-Professionals; and
3. Non-Professionals

1. Professionals : After the implementation of UGC Scheme in universities and colleges in India, as in the case of other academic staff, three cadres of professionals, that is, University Librarians, Deputy Librarians and Assistant Librarians, are provided for university libraries. The qualifications, status, scale of pay, nature of recruitment, career advancement, etc. of these posts are as provided in the UGC Scheme.

2. Semi-Professionals : Four types of semi-professionals, that is, Library/ Professional Assistants II, Technical/ Professional Assistants I, Reference Assistants/ Junior Librarian and Assistant Librarian Grade II, are available in the libraries. The status and scale of pay of these posts are given in Table: 4.29.1.

3. Non-Professionals : There is no uniformity in the case of non-professionals available in the university libraries. The designations of such positions are, Assistant Registrar, Administrative officer, Administrative Assistant, Section Officer, Assistant, Office Superintendent, Stenographer, Typist, Clerical Assistant, Photostat Operator, Artist, Library Attender, Library Assistant, Library Boy, Library Girl, Gardner, Library Cleaner, Security Guard, Sweeper, Cleaner, Peon, Class IV, etc.

Table 4.29.1. Status and scale of pay of Library Professionals in UGC Cadre in University Libraries

Designation	*Comparable posts in Agricultural universities*	*Comparable posts in other universities*	*Scale of pay(Pre-revised)*
University Librarian	Deans / Directors	Professor	16400-22400
Deputy Librarian	Asso. Professor	Reader	12000-18300
Asst.Librarian Sel. Scale	Asst.Professor Sel. Scale	Lecturer Sel. Scale	12000-18300
Asst.Librarian Sr. Scale	Asst. Professor Sr. Scale	Lecturer Sr. Scale	10000-15200
Asst.Librarian	Asst. Professor	Lecturer	8000-13500

Table 4.29.2. Qualifications and Scale of Pay of Library Semi-Professionals in Non-UGC Cadre in University Libraries

Designation	*Quali-fications*	*Scale of Pay (Pre-revised)*	*Nature of Recruitment*
Professional/Library Assistant II	Degree+BLISc	5000 - 8150	Direct Recruitment
Professional/Technical Assistant I	Degree+BLISc	5800 - 9425	By promotion from LA
Reference Assistant/ Jr. Librarian	Degree+BLISc	7200-11400	By promotion from TA
Assistant Librarian (Non UGC)	Degree+BLISc	7800-12975	By promotion from RA

The qualifications and recruitment procedure for library professionals in UGC Cadre universities in Inida are same, there are differences in designations. Some conventional universities and most of the agricultural universities categorized them in teaching/faculty cadre and others treated them as non-teaching staff. At the same time there is no similarity in the qualifications, recruitment procedure, promotion system, etc. of the library staff in the Non-UGC Cadre.

Professionals show much enthusiasm for acquiring higher qualifications by enrolling for different types of courses for the reasons such as to meet statutory requirement for promotion, quest for acquiring new knowledge and skills, professional dignity, etc. As continuous academic and skills development of professionals has been identified as one of the important aspect for better services, it is ideal to encourage all professionals to acquire such skills. PhD should be made as the compulsory qualification for Associate Professor/ Deputy Librarian and also for Professor/University

Librarian. The experience criteria for the post of Professor/ University Librarian should be amended as 18 years in any professional or semi-professional cadre in university or research libraries of equivalent status.

4.30 QUANTUM OF STAFF

A scientific formula was not prevailing in the universities to calculate the total staff requirements in each category of staff, including library professionals. The process of sanctioning staff was highly affected by the personal influence and cadre pressures of the staff. Since the promotion in Non-UGC cadres is mainly based on the availability of posts in each cadre, such a pressure is being exercised regularly by the trade unions and service organizations to achieve promotion by creating more posts, especially in the top positions. This tends to form the shape of the staff structure with widened top and narrowed bottom. Another drawback of this system of promotion was that more number of posts would be created in the influential groups and at the same time shortage of staff was usually occurred in other cadres. Because of this, too much time and effort of staff is being wasted for the unending process of post creation. Though the promotion seems to be given on the basis of seniority, in the present set up, most times it will be purely based on chance and not even on merit. This has resulted discontentment among staff, including those availing speedy promotions.

High rigidity in the institutions as a whole is another consequence of the above staffing pattern. And hence, methods like works study, re-engineering, change management, etc. will not be effective in such a system.

Another major problem experienced is that the posts of University Librarian in Universities are vacant for several years. Major reason for this situation was attributed towards the attitude and actions of the university and government authorities. Another reason was the non-availability of librarians with the required experience as specified by the UGC. 18 years experience in the UGC cadre of the College Librarians/University Assistant Librarians was essential for this post. Since two third or even more candidates are entering the UGC Cadre of librarians after a long period of service in the cadres of Junior Librarian/Junior Lecturer, Technical/ Professional Assistant, and College Librarians Grades I, II and III, etc., to get candidates having the required experience as specified by UGC is difficult at present. Though many universities had advertised for the post of University Librarian and they find it difficult to get qualified candidates.

The KAU Expert Committee on Library Staff Pattern has recommended a scientific formula for deriving the professional staff of the University Library. It has classified the departments of the university library into Service Departments and Non-Service Departments and recommended to provide one UGC Cadre professional in each Non-Service Department and two such staff in each Service Departments as they have to work at least in two shifts. It was also recommended for the minimum number of professionals in Non-UGC Cadre as two in each Non-Service Departments and three in each Service Departments and the total number of Non-UGC Cadre posts should be calculated based on a mathematical formula (Kerala Agricultural University, Report of the Expert Committee on Staff Pattern for KAULIS, 1999).

It is a fact that unscientific staffing pattern, methods and rules are prevailing not only in libraries but also in the whole university system in the country. As there was no common or scientific policy or pattern or formula for the allotment of required number of staff for the libraries, uneven staff structure prevails in different libraries.

Though many libraries are suffering from severe shortage of staff, some others are having surplus staff without enough work to effectively allot for them. Lack of scientific approach based on work study for the deployment of staff in each division practically results either under staffing or over staffing. So a scientific policy on staff and mandatory provisions to meticulously implement that policy is essential to re-define the personnel management system of the libraries and provide optimum number of staff.

A formula given in figure 4.30.1 is proposed to derive the total number of library professionals in UGC and Non-UGC Cadres with minimum one UGC Cadre professional in each Non-Service Department and minimum two such staff in each Service Departments according to the number of shifts the library functions. Minimum number of professionals in Non-UGC Cadre also should be one in each Non-Service Department and two in each Service Departments for the functioning of one shift of the library. That is, four Non-UGC professionals are needed for a service department of the library which functions in two shifts (12 hours a day).

Similarly, all colleges and poly techniques in the country should have one Librarian in the UGC Cadre with enough number of supporting professional staff. The number of UGC Cadre posts has to be increased based on a formula depending upon the number of courses, students and documents, in each college as done for the staffing of other teaching departments in the colleges.

Formula for deriving the Quantum of Library Professionals required for the University Libraries

$$S = \frac{U + 5(P) + 10\,(R + S)}{500} + \frac{PD}{15000} + \frac{ED \times C}{15000} + \frac{PJ}{150} + \frac{EJ}{1000}$$

In which,

U = Number of Under Graduate students in the university

P = Number of Post Graduate students in the university

R = Number of Research Scholars in the University

S = Number of Scientists/Teachers in the University

PD = Number of Printed Documents held in the University Library

ED = Number of Electronic Documents held in the University Library

C = Total Content Size of the NPD in Megabytes

PJ = Number of Printed Journals subscribed (based on the average of last years' subscription)

EJ = Number of Electronic Journals Accessed (based on the average of last years' subscription/consortia based access)

Note: Formula adopted from the Report of the KAU Expert Committee on KAULIS, 1999 and modified to suit the present situation.

4.31 RECRUITMENT AND PROMOTION

Motivation and morale of personnel largely depend on the policies and practices followed by the institutions in their recruitment and promotion. In government sector, the prevailing policies were more or less argumentative, based on chance and not on performance or service length. Hence, different categories get separate deal or chance for promotion. In universities in Kerala, when some categories have more than seven assured promotions during the service of 30 years, few categories hardly get three promotions. Similar situations prevail in most of the universities in India. This causes deep discontentment not only among staff having low promotion but also among the staff with higher promotions. As there is no scientific formula for the promotion of library staff, especially to those in the Non-UGC cadre, promotion given based on availability of vacancy in higher cadres and also based on some ratio.

This system was prevailing not only to the library staff but also applicable to almost all other staff, except to teachers in schools, colleges and universities in government departments and educational institutions. Because of this, the staff is not satisfied with the promotion system and exists high rigidity in the entire government sector, including universities. The change in number of sanctioned posts and retirement of staff immediately affect the promotion. Hence, all categories of staff like to exercise informal powers to get sanctioned more number of posts. While vacancy dependent or retirement based promotion provide irregular opportunities, merit / performance based promotion create lot of problems in assessing the merit/ performance.

4.32 KNOWLEDGE LEVEL AND PROFESSIONAL DEVELOPMENT OF STAFF

The knowledge level of professionals is extremely important in rendering quality service to the users. Library and Information Managers are these days deluged with advice as to know to acquire and organize learning resources and satisfy the complex and ever increasing information needs of the users. However, to achieve their goal, the question of a resource constrained regime has to be kept in mind without sacrificing the interests of the users (Raina, 2004). Changes in library tasks, policies and practices call for a new knowledge base and skills among the professionals. These include, technology handling abilities, managerial skills and a better understanding of copyright and legal issues (Parekh, 2003). Universities, professional bodies and agencies are striving hard to impart all sorts of knowledge and technical expertise to LIS professionals. Online Programmes for All Libraries OPAL (2008) is such an international collaborative effort founded in 2003 by libraries and other organizations to provide web-based programs and training for library users and library staff members. These live events are held in online rooms where participants can interact via voice-over-IP, text chatting, synchronized browsing, and other functions. Libraries and other organizations are encouraged to become OPAL institutional members. Examples of OPAL public online programs include book discussion programs, interviews, special events, library training, memoir writing workshops, and virtual tours of special digital library collections. OPAL is administered by *TAP Information Services*, a small company that helps libraries and other organizations innovate. Many international organizations like ALA have become members of OPAL.

It is a fact that many professionals are unaware of the latest developments happening in the field, especially the practical acquaintance and conceptual knowledge on latest ICT developments and systems. This gives a strong indication to the need for strengthening the In-Service Training Programmes for the library professionals, especially those in Non-UGC Cadre. The UGC Orientation/ Refresher courses should be re-defined and streamlined by timely incorporating latest technologies and also to provide more practical insight and capability to actual library management and service. The HRM policies and practices of the libraries found inadequate right from the beginning of induction of the newly recruited staff and this situation continues till the end of their service.

Though almost all library professionals have enough operational knowledge on computers, photocopier, etc. they are having least operational knowledge on technologies like V-SAT, RFID, Optical Fibre, Video conferencing and Web Hosting, bandwidth, broadband/leased line connection, IP address, digital camera, LCD projector, computer server, network management, etc.

The main reasons for this backwardness is mainly attributed to the inadequate provision for training programmes, especially for staff in non-UGC Cadre, lack of facilities and experienced faculty to conduct training in high end areas, etc. The top position in the hierarchy of training needs of the library professionals occupies the aspects, *Digital library*, *Web designing*, *Database Development*, *Hardware maintenance*, *Web hosting and maintenance*, *Institutional Repositories* and *Network Administration*, *Internet and Online Search*, *Library Automation*, etc. *Teaching techniques, Information Literacy skills*, *Personnel / General management*, *Communication and Inter Personal skills*, *Public relations*, etc. are also needed for the successful library practice.

It is clear that professional development programmes have to be intensified in order to build operational level knowledge and ICT competency among the staff. The booming phenomena of digital libraries and the essential need for services based on digital information resources warrants the acquisition of thorough theoretical as well as practical knowledge on digital processing, storage and transmission of information and latest Web technologies by the library professionals.

4.33 HUMAN RESOURCE REQUIREMENTS OF MODERN LIBRARIES

Rapid technological changes and advances require an ever more adaptive and sophisticated workforce. There is a pressing need to cultivate a new workforce of electronic resources librarians, information managers, system integrators, and the training and education providers to conceive, build, and implement a wide array of user-oriented applications using innovative information technology. Development of Information Technology and its application to information management has influenced the whole process, and led to development of Information systems and services. Other areas which have great influence on Information Management are the wide application of modern management principles and information ideas developed in business schools and public sector organizations. These have resulted in the acceptance of concepts like strategic planning, cost benefit analysis, resource management and marketing (Rajyalakshmi, 2004). Information technology solutions will only be successful if the libraries focus on the work force, which is expected to satisfy the critical information needs of the users. The library professionals and other staff of the library should be provided with consistent and comprehensive training in electronic technical skills, instructional delivery and design, managerial supervisory skills, and continuing education. There is also a need to increase collaboration among library units. The team concept should be revisited and reemphasized. To be successful in the 21st century, academic libraries need to be more proactive and more customer service oriented (Konnur and Bhandi, 2004). The profession demands for leaders who are not only doers, but also effective communicators (Sornam and Nagarajan, 2004). Dubey (2003) stated that in the ever changing technological environment, especially one in which library services could be expected to become increasingly 'digital', it is extremely important for librarians to keep themselves well informed concerning new products and new developments in the field. He also underlined that the libraries and professionals need to focus on studying the impact of the new technologies on the creation, storage and distribution of knowledge.

The IFLA/FAIFE World Report 2005 points out that as library Internet use increases the types of information that users access becomes more varied. However, at the same time as access to increasing numbers of information resources is opened up, there is also the possibility that material deemed to be less appropriate is accessed by users. This type of material differs according to perception - it could be pornographic, it could be political or it could be religious in nature. As could be expected, the type of material deemed 'dangerous', 'offensive' or 'subversive' differs from country to country and region to region. Regardless of its content, its appearance on Internet screens inevitably leads to calls for the filtering of Internet access – especially in libraries where children are active users. How libraries choose to deal with calls for filtering is best decided on a local level but guidance from a national library association can play a decisive role (especially if professional values and policies such as the IFLA Internet Manifesto are adopted) - as can interference from governments, local or national. In order to exercise effective control mechanism of this type for the integral benefit of the users, the modern librarians should develop skills and competencies not only in content management but also in ICT aspects like Internet protocols and control software, filtering tools, etc. Moreover, the librarians should be able to develop essential competencies to the users also through user education and information literacy programmes.

In an appeal on staff development, SALIS (2006) submitted the following recommendation to the National Assessment and Accreditation Council (NAAC) for its consideration and implementation: "*Any quality initiative is a continuum. In consonance with this endeavour, it is utmost essential to have a Continuous Professional*

Development (CDP) programme for the library professionals as in vogue in R&D institutions such as CSIR, DRDO, ISRO etc., it is requested that NAAC should insist CDP for Library Professionals".

General Competencies & Technical Competencies

In order to service their clientele effectively, the library and information professionals acquire several types of competencies. Competencies have been defined as the interplay of knowledge, understanding, skills and attitudes required to do a job effectively from the point of view of both the performer and the observer (Murphy, 1991). The unique competencies of a university librarian include in-depth knowledge of print and electronic information resources in subject areas of interest to the university and the design and management of information services that meet the strategic information needs of the individual or group being served.

According to the Special Libraries Association (SLA), as we move towards the millennium, library and information professionals are facing at least three major paradigm shifts (SLA, 2003).

- The first shift is the "***transition from paper to electronic media***" as the dominant form of information storage and retrieval. Linked to this transition is the convergence of previously separate media, such as text, graphics, and sound, into multimedia resources.
- The second shift relates to the "***increasing demand for accountability***", including a focus on customers, performance measurement, bench marking and continuous improvement. All of this is taking place in an era when the financial resources available for providing library and information services are shrinking.

- The third shift comes from "***new forms of work organization***" such as end-user computing, work teams, management delayering, job sharing, telework, outsourcing, downsizing and re-engineering.

All three of these shifts are related to a combination of factors such as global competition, new computing and communications technologies, and the perceived need to measure the productivity of knowledge and service workers. In the information age, university librarians provide the information edge for the knowledge-based organization to their critical information needs. In order to fulfill this key information role, librarians require two main types of competencies:

i. ***Professional competencies*** relate to the special librarian's knowledge in the areas of information resources, information access, technology, management and research and the ability to use these areas of knowledge as a basis for providing library and information services.

ii. ***Personal competencies*** represent a set of skills, attitudes and values that enable librarians to work efficiently; be good communicators; focus on continuing learning throughout their careers; demonstrate the value-added nature of their contributions; and survive in the new world of work.

The SLA has listed the following competencies essential for special librarians. Since the university librarians are dealt with higher education and research and the nature of service and the information resources and documents to be managed by them are similar, all these competencies are relevant to the university librarians also.

I. Professional Competencies

i. Expert knowledge of the content of information resources, including the ability to critically evaluate and filter them.

ii. Specialized subject knowledge appropriate to the business of the organization or client.

iii. Develops and manages convenient, accessible and cost-effective information services that are aligned with the strategic directions of the organization.

iv. Provides excellent instruction and support for library and information service users.

v. Assesses information needs and designs and markets value-added information services and products to meet identified needs.

vi. Uses appropriate information technology to acquire, organize and disseminate information.

vii. Uses appropriate business and management approaches to communicate the importance of information services to senior management.

viii. Develops specialized information products for use inside or outside the organization or by individual clients.

ix. Evaluates the outcomes of information use and conducts research related to the solution of information management problems.

x. Continually improves information services in response to the changing needs.

xi. Effective member of the senior management team and a consultant to the organization on information issues.

II. Personal Competencies

i. Committed to service excellence.

ii. Seeks out challenges and sees new opportunities both

inside and outside the library.

iii. Sees the big picture:- Sees the library and its information services as part of the bigger process of making informed decisions.

iv. Looks for partnerships and alliances:- Provides leadership on the information management team. Forms partnerships with other libraries or information services inside or outside the organization to optimize resource sharing.

v. Creates an environment of mutual respect and trust.

vi. Have effective communications skills.

vii. Works well with others in a team.

viii. Provides leadership.

ix. Plans, prioritizes and focuses on what is critical.

x. Committed to lifelong learning and personal career planning.

xi. Acquire personal business skills and creates new opportunities.

xii. Recognizes the value of professional networking and solidarity.

xiii. Flexible and positive in a time of continuing change.

Lot of technological advances which have affected libraries and student learning over the last decade: wider access to the Internet, availability of multimedia learning materials, the rise of electronic journals, convergence between libraries, IT and other support services. These are the kinds of developments that libraries have welcomed as opportunities to improve the support they offer to the academic community. In order to maximize the effectiveness of these technologies, Morgan (2001) explains that the interpersonal skills for library professionals will be crucial in providing the added value in support of students in using the library technology. He stresses the increasing importance of university library staff in an age of continuous (mainly) technological change and suggests a greater involvement of staff in the change process including the use of management-related skills by all staff (rather than exclusively by managers), wider participation in decision making and a greater degree of strategic awareness. Gadre and Satalkar (1997) opined that psychological and behavioural techniques like Transactional Analysis (TA) may be used in the libraries to explain why users, professionals and administrators behave in specific patterns. It enables people to identify patterns of transactions between themselves and others. Ultimately, it can help to determine which egostate is most heavily influencing our behaviour and the behaviour of other people. The requirement of positive administration having harmonious interpersonal relations is to have parallel transactions by giving right kind of stimulus depending upon the Ego State and Personality of the workers (Saha, 1998).

4.34 RESTRUCTURING THE LIBRARY AND INFORMATION SCIENCE EDUCATION

Any serious project or programme requires adequate human and financial resources, facilities and equipment. In many developing countries while information technology offers a more efficient and effective means of information handling, there are problems, namely, lack of expertise needed to effectively and efficiently us IT; and some disturbing features of IT. International and regional information systems/programmes have of necessity helped to train in short courses and workshops persons to utilize IT and methodologies specific to the respective systems. While this has been useful, it covers only a small proportion of the countries' requirements of trained information manpower in order to advance rapidly such that the networks can be more optimally utilized by the participating entities. Library and information schools in developing countries need to revise their curricula acquire and develop appropriate training facilities and teaching expertise in IT methods of information management in the changing context (Neelameghan, 1993).

In order to identify important knowledge and skill components required for library and information professionals, the International Federation of Library Associations and Institutions (IFLA) has reviewed the library and information coursework based on the educational policy statements issued by government or professional associations such as the Institute of Information Science (UK), the Library Association (UK), the Special Libraries Association (US), the Medical Library Association (US), the Association of Library Service to Children (US), the Australian Library and Information Association, etc. As per this, the core elements of the course should include the followings modules;

i. The Information Environment, Information Policy and Ethics, the History of the Field.
ii. Information Generation, Communication and Use.
iii. Assessing Information Needs and Designing Responsive Services.
iv. The Information Transfer Process.
v. Organization, Retrieval, Preservation and Conservation of Information.
vi. Research, Analysis and Interpretation of Information.
vii. Applications of Information and Communication Technologies to Library and Information Products and Services.
viii. Information Resource Management and Knowledge

Management

ix. Management of Information Agencies.

x. Quantitative and Qualitative Evaluation of Outcomes of Information and Library Use.

The programme should incorporate appropriate means by internship and field work to allow students to appreciate the interplay between professional theories and their application in professional practice. Methods of teaching and assessment should be designed to develop or enhance students' interpersonal communication skills, ability to work in teams, and time and task management skills. At the professional level, emphasis should be placed on developing students' analytical and problem-solving skills.

In order to assist practicing librarians and information specialists to maintain competence in a changing society and to keep educators aware of issues and trends in practice, the programme should either conduct suitable workshops and short courses for the benefit of practicing librarians and information specialists or partner with other agencies in doing so. If distance learning methods of course delivery are used, the quality of the educational experience should be comparable to similar experiences offered on site. Chikate and Gadge-Chikate (2007) reported successful 30 years of one month post course internship system prevailing for the BLISc students of the RTM Nagpur University, Nagpur.

Course Design, Curriculum and Accreditation

On a review of the present skills imparted by the LIS courses, it was observed that there is a wide gap between the needed competencies and those imparted through the courses. Most of the library professionals are failing to efficiently undertake the challenges posed by the modern ICTs in information management. In this context, the LIS courses have to be thoroughly updated in order to cater to the needs of the modern libraries. The professionals strongly demanded the inclusion of more ICT based modules such as hardware and software, network administration, communication technologies, web programming, web designing, web hosting, digital libraries, etc. in the LIS courses. General modules such as education psychology, communication and public relations, etc. are also needed by the librarians. Dissemination service is part of the work of public relation. It consists of arresting the attention of the public to the commodities or services offered. This is done through special write-ups produced for the purpose in a style and with a flair that can convert the public to a mood of acceptance of the commodities and services (Ranganathan, 1957b).

A process of formal curriculum review should take place on a regular basis. This review should incorporate inputs from employers, practitioners and professional associations, as well as students and faculty. Earlier universities were offering courses under Arts Faculty and the degrees were awarded as Bachelor of Arts (BA) or Master of Arts (MA) in Mathematics, Physics, History, Literature, etc. Consequent on the expansion of subjects, several new faculties were formed in universities and separate degrees like BA/MA, BSc/MSc, BEd/MEd, BPEd/MPEd, MBBS/MD, LLB/LLM, BLISc/MLISc, etc. were awarded. Several years back, the then existing nomenclature of BLibSc and MLibSc have been changed to BLISc and MLISc. Kuvempu University, Madras University, etc. are offering courses as MSc (Library and Information Science) and DRTC and NISCAIR are offering courses as Associateship in Documentation and Information Science.

This difference is creating some confusion among the policy makers, administrators and even the general public.

For example, the DRDO has approved any MSc or MTech degrees for their recruitment as scientist. But, MLISc or ADIS or any other non-science/technology faculty degrees will not be considered for this purpose. At the same time, most of the papers and modules of the LIS and Documentation courses are having pure science or applied science orientation. Moreover, a modern librarian should have in-depth knowledge in subjects like computer science, ICT, digital libraries, mathematics, statistics, management, psychology, etc. The revised curricula of many of the universities show the inclusion of majority of topics in ICT for BLISc/MLISc (Osmania University, 2006). Wider discussions are going on regarding the change of nomenclature of the degrees awarded in LIS. While most of the veteran and very senior librarians are favouring the continuation of conventional names, middle level or young professionals do favour the change into MSc/MTech in LIS or Documentation or at least to offer the LIS courses under the faculty of science or technology. A discussion happened in LIS Forum indicates such an interest (Srinivasulu, 2006). In another discussion through LIS forum, Prof. P.B. Mangala proposed the change of the LIS course as Library and Information Management.

SALIS (2006) appealed to introduce accreditation system either by AICTE or NCTE for courses such as BLISc and MLISc. Prof. Varalakshmi (2006) proposed accreditation of LIS courses in India by the Indian Library Association (ILA).

Library professionals in general are of the opinion that curriculum and structure of LIS courses should be re-designed to the tune of present requirements and giving more stress on the topics of IT. Inclusion of compulsory project work and internship in LIS courses will give more benefit. An accreditation body, named, Library Council of India (LCI) or so, may be established to monitor quality and standardization aspects. Till the formation of LCI, the work of accreditation may be done by AICTE or NCTE.

4.35 RE-ENGINEERING THE HUMAN RESOURCE

The vision for re-engineered HR in the future is that all human resource services should be available instantaneously, on demand, at the place most convenient to an employee: his or her own workstation, anywhere in the world with radical redesign of workflow processes, using information systems technology, networked with the help of computers and allied technology and with people competent and empowered to do the whole job for their customers (or themselves) at their first point of contact with a customer (or the information system), to achieve dramatic results for improvements in quality and productivity (Gaur, 2003). In terms of recruitment and selection it is important to consider carrying out a thorough *job analysis* to determine the level of skills/technical abilities, competencies, flexibility of the employee required etc. At this point it is important to consider both the internal and external factors that can have an impact on the recruitment of employees. The external factors are those out-with the powers of the organisation and include issues such as current and future trends of the labour market e.g. skills, education level, government investment into industries etc. On the other hand internal influences are easier to control, predict and monitor, for example management styles or even the *organisational culture*.

Though human resources have been part of business and organizations since the first days of agriculture, the modern concept of human resources began in reaction to the efficiency focus of *Taylorism* in the early 1900s. By 1920, psychologists and employment experts in the *United States* started the *human relations* movement, which viewed workers in terms of their *psychology* and fit with companies, rather than as interchangeable parts. This movement grew throughout the middle of the 20th century, placing emphasis on how *leadership*, cohesion, and loyalty played important roles in organizational success. Although this view was increasingly challenged by more quantitatively rigorous and less "soft" management techniques in the 1960s and beyond, human resources had gained a permanent role within the firm.

Facing problems of mankind, it is opportune to mobilize as many intellectual resources as possible in order to resolve the emerging troubles. The students have to be trained to construct pertinent knowledge together (for example using the method, Learning by Teaching). Students can be trained in constructing knowledge outside the classroom too. Cakar et al (2003) has presented a HRM process model consists of the following three sub-processes:

(i) Make HRM Strategy;

(ii) Implement HRM Strategy;

(iii) Monitor Impact on Business Results.

Each of these sub-processes consists of a number of activities.

Cleeve (1995) establishes that proper emphasis on human resource management is highly crucial in the handling the process of change in a library. The reactions of the people in an organization are key determinants of success in *re-engineering* the library and information services.

The management experts strongly argue that the participation in decision making will lead to increase in performance and efficiency. But many universities and authorities in India fail to maintain effective involvement in the management of university libraries.

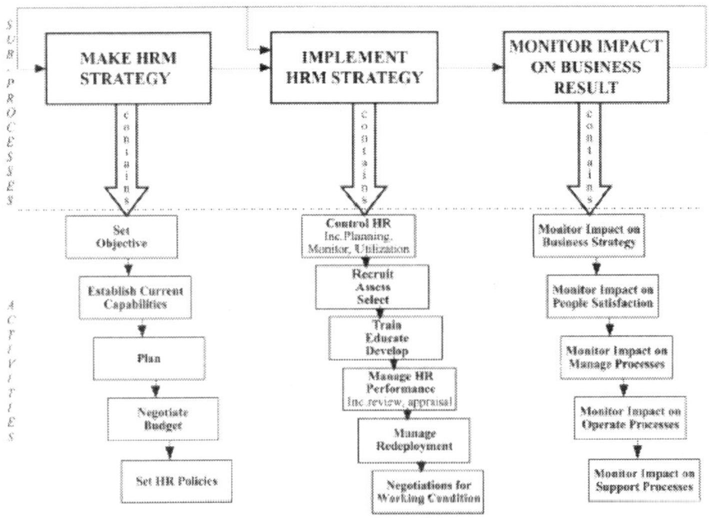

Fig. 4.35.1. HRM Process Model by Cakar, Figen et al (2003)
Source: Cakar, Figen (2003)

4.36 RE-ENGINEERING AND RE-DEFINING FRAMEWORK FOR UNIVERSITY LIBRARIES

The Library and Information System not only in the country but also world over are facing unprecedented changes. The modern ICTs have contributed much towards this situation. The proliferation of information resources and the modern ICT based tools to manage the information services have anchored the libraries on new styles of management approaches. The increasing cost of information resources coupled with shrinking budget provisions have forced the libraries to experiment these management styles as a means for the survival of the fittest. The need for re-defining libraries and re-engineering the business operations have to be addressed with this target in mind for increasing efficiency and effectiveness of services. The modern librarians are working under heavy pressure to deliver greater results with fewer resources. In order to cater to the varied demands of the users, they have to rise to the occasion. Though re-designing and re-engineering is not a panacea, it is proved that it can solve many of the problems faced by the libraries in a better way.

As part of the re-engineering, major functions of the libraries have to be re-defined in order to suit the modern ICT oriented operations. Ramesh C. Gaur proposed a re-engineering plan for selected management libraries in India (Gaur, 2003). In order to re-engineer the university libraries in the context of present Information and Communication Technologies, one may follow the re-engineering framework as suggested below:

4.37 RE-ENGINEERING PROCESS

As any management process should primarily be based on planning, re-engineering and re-defining of libraries also should start with proper planning. The plan should carefully consider each operation of the library. It includes detailed information regarding the service objectives, resources available, approaches, methodologies, tools and techniques, etc. of the library. It should be able to provide a clear understanding of each function to be re-defined and step by step procedure of each activity to be re-engineered. The following steps or processes may be adopted by the libraries for framing the methodologies for re-engineering and re-defining:

i. Identification of functions to be re-defined

ii. Identification of the process/activity to be re-engineered

iii. Selection of the re-engineering team with proper division of activity and mechanism for proper coordination

iv. Understanding the current process
v. Developing a vision for the new improved process
vi. Planning for detailed actions for implementation with specified time frame for completion
vii. Budgeting
viii. Identifying manpower, ICT facilities and other resources
ix. Training and orientation for the improved process planned
x. Implementation of actions planned
xi. Evaluation of change on re-engineering and re-defining
xii. Managing change
xiii. Review of the results
xiv. Feedback and fine tuning
xv. Reporting to the top management
xvi. Incentives or encouragement for efficient implementation
xvii. Sustaining the re-engineering process with continuous learning, process improvement, feed back and fine tuning

4.38 MANAGING CHANGE

According to Lawrence (1992), the real problem is not technical change, but the human changes that often accompany technical innovations. One of the most baffling and recalcitrant of the problems which business executives face is employee resistance to change. Such resistance may take a number of forms – persistent reduction in output, increase in number of "quits" and requests for transfer, chronic quarrels, sullen hospitality, wildcat or slowdown strikes and of course, the expression of a lot of pseudological reasons why the change will not work. Even the pretty forms of this resistance can be troublesome. He suggests to gets the people involved to "participate" in making change. It is also essential to understand the true nature of resistance. Resistance is usually created of certain blind spots and attitudes. The management can take concrete steps to deal constructively with these staff attitudes. The steps include emphasizing new standards of performance for staff specialists and encouraging them to think in different ways, as well as making use of the fact that signs of resistance can serve as practical warning signal in directing and timing technological changes.

Change management can take many forms and include many change environments. The most common usage to the term refers to organisational change management. It is the process of developing a planned approach to change in an organization. Typically the objective is to maximize the collective benefits for all people involved in the change and minimize the risk of failure of implementing the change. The discipline of change management deals primarily with the human aspect of change, and is therefore related to pure and industrial psychology. Technical disciplines like Information and Communication Technology also have developed similar approaches to formally control the process of making changes to environments.

Change management can be either 'reactive', in which case management is responding to changes in the macro environment (that is, the source of the change is external), or proactive, in which case management is initiating the change in order to achieve a desired goal (that is, the source of the change is internal). Change management can be conducted on a continuous basis, on a regular schedule (such as an annual review), or when deemed necessary on a program-by-program basis. Change management can be approached from a number of angles and applied to numerous organizational processes. It's most common uses are in the management of ICTs, strategic management, and process management. To be effective, change management should be multi-disciplinary, touching all aspects of the organization. However, at its core, implementing new procedures, technologies, and overcoming resistance to change are fundamentally human resource management issues.

Change management encompasses the requesting, determining attainability, planning, implementing and evaluation of changes to a *system*. It has two main goals: supporting the processing of changes – which is mainly discussed here – and enabling traceability of changes, which should be possible through proper execution of the process described here (Crnkovic, Asklund & Persson-Dahlqvist, 2003). *Change management* is an important process, because it can deliver vast benefits (by improving the system and thereby satisfying customer needs), but also enormous problems (by ruining the system and/or mixing up the change administration). Furthermore, at least for the Information Technology domain, more funds and work are put into system maintenance (which involves change management) than to the initial creation of a system (Dennis, Wixom & Tegarden, 2002). Consumer-oriented approach in libraries is being advocated by experts and to be able to shift to this new approach from a traditional one, we need to have sound knowledge of factors playing important role in change management (Pandya, 2002).

As the process of re-engineering and re-defining the library and information services involves drastic changes in the in-house operations and service set up, proper adoption of change management principles also become part of it. The modern ICT environment necessitated such an approach.

Though computer and other ICTs have been using, most of the library operations were performed in ad-hoc manner without proper integration of user, staff, information resources and systems. Some positive re-structuring has happened in libraries due to computerization and automation which indirectly increased job satisfaction and job status of the professionals. Participatory decision making and implementation of programmes can combat the evil issues arising on the way of managing change. Re-engineering and re-defining is a very powerful management tool that can produce wonderful results. Proper implementation and sustainability of the re-engineering process is an important aspect of this management approach. Hence, it is important to ensure that the re-defined functions and re-engineered processes must be effectively used and sustained. Since the ultimate objectives of this process are enhanced value addition in information services, maximization of user satisfaction and professional enrichment, the effectiveness of it has be measured in this angle.

5

Management of ICTs: A Comparison

The re-engineering and re-defining provide tools and techniques to identify the strengths and weaknesses in the application of modern ICTs in libraries and points out scientific and most suitable methods to re-define the service setup. In the application of ICTs, differences in different environments could be seen due to the changes happened in the variables such as time, technology, social, cultural and political situation, management style adopted, etc. Efforts to underline the unexploited areas of modern ICTs by the university libraries are possible by re-engineering.

The prevalence of red-tape procedure observed by Ongaro on Italian one-stop shops is exists in the management process of the universities in India. Proper coordination and single window procedure in services and management of the libraries will help to increase user satisfaction, service quality, greater organisational flexibility, etc.

The findings of Sue Beer in Shetland and the Western Isles of Scotland revealed that access to better telecommunications, ideally broadband or high speed Internet, is crucial to effective information access and this plays a vital role in providing effective information access and services in the libraries in India also. The role of National Knowledge Network is a major steps towards this direction.

The results of a re-engineering process at the Bayerische Staatsbibliothek (Bavarian State *Library*) in Munich, Germany indicated that the introduction of digital resources had considerable impact on the in-house activities of the libraries and it was also helped to bridge the gap between traditional and new material. In order to cope up with the new situation, the library utilized the **principles** of re-engineering **and change management.** Academic libraries in India need re-engineering and change management to get best results in the environment warranted by the modern ICTs.

Most of the findings of the study on 67 academic libraries in Taiwan, reported by Chen regarding the perceptions of library professionals in adopting innovative ideas and information technologies, were found relevant in the Indian context also. In order to provide an effective pathway to library organizational change, need for professional development, increased management leadership, culture of learning organization, etc. are inevitable.

Lynne Brindley, based on case study experience of the British Library established the need and relevance for re-defining libraries in the present context. The pointed stressed such as Knowing and meeting the requirements of the library users properly, integration of marketing principles, continuous improvement in quality and productivity, stress for digitization and web based services, consortial and other partnership approaches, etc. are also relevant to the University Libraries in India.

Some experiments and findings revealed by Childerhouse et al. and several other researchers related to the BPR in supply chain management are applicable to the library and information systems also. The identified cultural, organizational, technological and financial barriers to improve the performance of an organization are pertinent and valid in the context of university libraries in India.

The disadvantages of the practice of disintegrated approach highlighted by Lunin and D'Elia are prevailing in the university libraries. These disintegrated system resulted in fragmentation and duplication of resources and services, which caused confusion, especially when the users' needs were for integrated and/or cross media information services. So, it is advocated to establish an integrated information service unit to streamline the administration and implementation of technologies into more efficient and effective ways and also to satisfy the needs of information users as done by the University of Wisconsin at Parkside, University of Montana, Lehigh University, University of Minnesota, University of North Carolina, Rice University, University of Maryland, University of Iowa, etc. It is underlined the need for integration of activities within the library and also complementary role between external departments and institutions.

The want for convergence of LIS and IT as disclosed by Pinfield et al., is also justified in the context of Library and Information System in India. Convergence and subsequent hybridization to form digital libraries and web based services warranted such a change. This was already supported by Wilson and Halpin based on the case study done in British Universities. The phenomenal growth and rate of change in ICT and electronic information services witnessed the advent of many converged services, and the subsequent financial implications and impacts upon management, resources and staff training and development. Such changes in the deployment of staff resources, and the changing role and duties of academic library staff, have encouraged a new professional philosophy. Essential and desirable skills have become more diverse and demanding. Such a transformation is also justified here. The prediction of Dr. Kalam in this line is also applicable to the Indian library situation and this was indirectly supported by Gopinath and Sreenivasulu. Though Allan Foster reported that many universities in UK and USA were in the line of integrating libraries and computer services, such integration may not be workable here because of entirely different technological, administrative and political environment prevailing in the country. But, the level of convergence suitable to Indian context has to be identified with more in-depth studies.

Information Literacy is an important area that needs to be re-engineered in the libraries in the country. The IFLA/UNESCO Guidelines and ACRL Guidelines undoubtedly support this need. The faculty and student users strongly desired to have provision for enough ILP with stress on modern ICTs. The library professionals also felt the urgent need for this. As the information literacy is crucial in deciding the life long learning skill of individuals, these are critical to the creation of an equitable global *'Information Society'*. The observations of Hussain and Raza; Ali and Hassan; and Colaric revealed that many users were unaware of many facilities and resources, available in the library, including the options in OPAC, and the user education and ILP are the inevitable necessity to augment the services and optimization of its efficacy. OCLC; Valentine; Malone and Videon; Lombardo and Miree; Biradar and Sampath Kumar; and Oladokun have reported similar findings on the use of search engines; electronic information resources, etc. Indian library situation is synchronized with the above observations and justified that the user education and ILP has to be integrated into the curriculum and reinforced both within and outside of the educational setting. The provision for distance delivery of ILP through Library Websites to the outstation users are also essentail as done by many of the university libraries in western countries. The NAAC considers the ILP System of KAU as one of the best practice prevailing in the country. But, it needs to be extended to all courses in KAU and also to other universities in India.

Many studies like McGillis and Toms; Crowley et al; Spivey; Wright; OCLC; etc. have reiterated that library's Web page is the most common vehicle for the delivery of instruction and information. Most of the university libraries in developed nations could exploit this possibility to the maximum. Though few university libraries in India have done some progress in this direction and library professionals and users stressed the need for Library Websites, it is a fact that many university libraries in India did not made any significant contribution in this line. It may be due to financial, technological and management reasons. Delay in adopting the modern ICTs has also its own role. Re-engineering and re-defining mayt be a best solution to tap the potential of ICTs and Web based services.

The process of Re-engineering and Re-defining has been evaluated by Hammel, Kuettner and Phelps; Badiger; Whithhead; Liang; Chia; Khong and Richardson; Jeal; Eden and Bierman; Smith, etc. and reported the results. With more or less similar stress, all have declared that the re-engineering has helped to increase customer satisfaction, reduce cost of production or service, increase efficiency and effectiveness, improve motivation and morale of staff, increase in the credibility of the institution, etc. The principles of re-engineering and re-defining can be applied to university libraries in India with due advantage. But as reported by many researchers, the success of BPR and its sustainability is based on many factors such as having a visionary leadership; managing change effectively; effective management of risk; participation in decision-making; impact on the target organization; accurate utilization technology, especially the ICTs; creating a culture for organizational learning; providing time for adapting to the new situation; working on strategic alliances; consortia and resource sharing; making every effort to achieve concrete results; respecting human factors; responding proactively to organizational politics; establishing a solid infrastructure for future development and continuous improvement, etc.

The proper management of change process has been observed by Badiger and Whithhead as one of the key factors in persuading the workforce for adapting to the ICT environment and the consequent success of BPR. Al-Mashari, Irani and Zairi support change management, TQM and benchmarking as important tools for BPR. The experience of University of Salford, UK puts stress on users or customers. The skills and development of staff as well as users were proved to be a major success factor in the proper application of ICTs in the university libraries. Re-structuring of LIS courses, continuous professional development through in-service programmes, Web based awareness and education, etc. are required.

Real integration of information activities and information services, with re-engineering and re-defining the activities and procedures of conventional divisions of the library was the target of Yuan Ze University, Taiwan. The National Library Board of Singapore also implemented an integrated project on libraries by leveraging on four building blocks - content, services, people and infrastructure. The study reports of Eden and Bierman; and Smith also established the need for major departmental re-organization. Such actions in this line are avowed for reaping the benefits of ICTs.

Regarding the human resource utilization, the university libraries need thorough re-structuring. The findings of study by Vijayakumar are worth considering here. While there was more manpower in the Sections concerned with behind the screen operations like Acquisition, Technical Processing, Documentation, Periodicals and IT, the staff provided in service points, especially Reference Section was less and hence he strongly suggested redeployment. His study concluded that the libraries were having more number of staff in professional category and at the same time the semi-professionals and para-professionals were short than needed. This calculation was based on the then existing activites and programmes of the libraries. At the same time, it is to be noted that the libraries were mainly concentrated on conventional activities and services. From the users' perspective, several other programmes and services are also to be undertaken by the libraries in the modern ICT environment. Towards this goal, not only re-deployment of staff but also providing additional staff, both in professional as well as non or para professional level is advocated. Rigourous ICT based information literacy and user education programmes, web based digital document delivery, online information services to remote users, activities related to the development of digital library and institutional reposities, documentation and IPR activities, digital reference service, etc. are very much needed in the present context. It is stressed that training and development of the professionals as one of the measures to boost up the job satisfaction. Concerted efforts on the part of all stakeholders such as the universities, individual libraries, professionals, central and state governments, UGC, library schools, and Professional associations highlighted to overhaul the university library system.

The users of the university libraries are facing shortage of information resources available in print as well as in digital format. Though the users have natural inclination to avail special types of documents such as online journals, digital databases, electronic theses, multimedia documents, etc., the libraries are not able to meet many of their needs. As compared to the users' requirements, the libraries are having poor ICT facilities in terms of quantity and configuration of computer systems, LAN and Internet Servers, CD and other database servers, printers, high speed scanners, UPS systems, powerful and viable computer networks, wireless accessibility of resources, multimedia display systems and projection facilities, speed of Internet connectivity, etc. Since working hours of most of the university libraries could not be extended to round the clock, the available ICT facilities itself were underutilized. The number of ibraries providing digital services round the clock at least by establishing wireless accessibility is limited.

The Universal Bibliographical Control is the ideal situation in which the libraries would be able to provide effective information services. But, it is fact that the services of most of the university libraries are not targeting to achieve the UBC. The Inter Library Services are neither provided by the libraries nor utilized by the users at an extensive level. Effective partnerships between libraries, institutions and agencies within the state, country or outside country towards such services are almost absent. Even for meeting the information requirements for research purposes, the users are either settling with the available or accessible resources within these libraries or finding their own ways to satisfy their needs at least to the minimum extend possible. Of course, it is true that the libraries could considerably strengthen the service area of online journals and databases. But, this is too far below from the service set up of good university libraries of international or national repute.

All the libraries have adopted modern ICTs for their operations and services. But, they are highly lagging in exploiting these technologies, especially the latest Web technologies. It is true that several activities have been improved with computerization. But, manual operations could not be reduced to that extend. Integrated automation of all operations of the libraries was not even planned by most of the libraries. The websites or web pages of the libraries were maintained only for name sake and only limited provisions are available for the users to interact with the libraries. The OPAC and WebOPAC are also functioning in a more or less similar manner. Libraries could not effectively extend the services to the outstation campuses of the same university or to the affiliated institutions or colleges either through Websites, Intranet or Extranet. The main campus networks itself not strengthened with WiFi or WiMax solutions. As RFID system was not adopted extensively, issue system and security desk of most libraries are semi-automated with barcode technology. Even that itself was not fully utilized for stock verification also.

At the user level, inadequate provisions exist for information literacy and user education. Regular ILPs are not available both for student and faculty users. Only some universities have the provision for curriculum based ILP for their students. The ILP system is mainly depend on many factors such as the available facilities, cooperation, leadership, dynamism of the individual professional, etc. but not mandatory. Many users did not have enough knowledge on the availability on the information resources and how to use these resources effectively. In order to solve the issues of information overload, the users are not fully equipped with effective search technologies and strategies. There is no a state or national level standard or regulations or benchmarking for providing ILP.

In-adequacy of fund, facilities, manpower and management are the major problems faced by the libraries in improving the efficiency and service effectiveness of the libraries. As proved to be effective in many service organizations, including the libraries, radical re-structuring or re-engineering has been advocated to re-define the management process of the university libraries in India. As the university libraries are functioning as an integral part of the university system of the country, nationwide standards, rules and regulations are essential to properly take off the university library system. Since the higher education system is sandwiched to the school education and lifelong education systems, scientific organization of school and public library systems are also critical for the growth and development of the university library system.

6

Restructuring Libraries through Re-engineering and Redefining

Re-engineering and Re-defining provides tools to refine the management process and service set up of University Libraries in the modern context of Information and Communication Technologies.

6.1 MAJOR AREAS OF RE-ENGINEERING AND RE-DEFINING

1. Digital revolution and the recent advancements in ICTs have made tremendous changes in the functioning and management process of the university libraries.
2. As a universal phenomenon, no library in the world was able to be self reliant in itself and it is becoming more and more complicated to acquire all the information resources in print medium, digital medium was found to be an effective solution to provide best access to the users by way of online journals, databases, digital library, etc. This in turn

was found suitable to fill the gap created by the digital divide.

3. In the above context, in order to serve the clientele better, all libraries need to exploit the possibilities of modern ICTs by acquiring ICT systems in the form of hardware, software and power systems, general, technical and matching professional competencies and management skill.
4. Though the university libraries have automated many of their operations, all need to move further in order to establish an integrated, fully computerized and automated system.
5. The libraries could exploit only a very few possibilities of ICTs and hence they could not achieve Universal Bibliographic Control and desired efficiency and effectiveness in services. Because of this, the users as well as professionals were found dissatisfied.
6. Functional effectiveness in acquisition, access and process of information resources in various formats, development and maintenance of OPAC and WebOPAC, digital document delivery to remote users, Web based clearing of library counter services and resources, development of full-text databases, digital libraries and institutional repositories, consortia based operations for e-journals and databases, user education and information literacy, professional development with stress on ICTs, network administration and website maintenance, marketing of information, etc. were major areas need special attention to improve the situation.
7. Finance, knowledge level on ICTs among library staff, professional dynamism and leadership, vision and support of the administrators and policy makers,

prevailing educational set up and social environment in the state, etc. were some of the major hurdles in reaping maximum possibilities of ICTs by the university libraries.

8. Regular training and professional development programmes with stress on modern ICTs are essential not only for the library staff in the UGC-Cadre but also for the staff in the Non-UGC Cadre. The training need for theoretical as well as practical aspects on general aspects like communication, public relations, psychology, management, etc. are also required.
9. Almost all operations and services of the university libraries need to be re-defined to suit the present circumstances.
10. The principles of Business Process Re-engineering are suitable to effectively apply to re-define and re-structure the operations and service system of the libraries.
11. Most of the conventional departments or divisions prevailing in the university libraries are functioning as watertight compartments and their existing system of workflow and management pattern was more rigid to adopt the principles of change management. In the light of the ICT based operations, many activities of some of the divisions are not at all needed as such and some have to be merged with other divisions. In order to ensure an integrated and continuous flow of work and also to reap maximum economy and service efficiency, a flexible pattern of management divisions is suitable.
12. The pooling and sharing of information resources and facilities and inter library loan between the libraries in India or with other libraries outside the country

is an important area yet to be exploited by the libraries for meeting the users' needs. Lack of leadership, staff and facilities, failure in identifying the needs of the users for information resources, hurdles in the existing government rules, etc. are some of the major reasons attributed towards this situation.

13. Partnerships, consortia based activities and pooling and sharing of information resources is another area the libraries have to be vigorously taken up to meet the varied needs of the users. Though the ICTs offer unlimited potential in this regard, integrated and coordinated projects are yet to be planned and implemented in this direction.
14. The system of student centred education demands for the adoption of library oriented teaching-learning process and student evaluation system and hence the existing system in the universities also needs drastic reformation. Since the teaching programmes and evaluation system of most of the courses run by the universities and their evaluation methods could not be able to brought the students from the conventional text book oriented learning, it is an urgent requisite to design the courses and their evaluation system in the line of IITs, IIMs, IISc, NITs, IRMA, ISI, etc., where library and self learning stand in the pivotal position.
15. Some university libraries are facing the problem of lack of sanction for enough number of professional positions and in all libraries many sanctioned posts, including the post of University Librarian, are lying vacant for several years. This situation retard the growth and development of the libraries to a great extend.

16. A uniform staff policy is essential for all libraries in the universities in India. Though the libraries implemented the UGC-Scheme, many litigation and court cases on appointment, seniority, and promotion, other staff management aspects, etc. are arised because of lack of uniform and proper statutes and rules in this regard. Improper or non-implementation of UGC Career Advancement Scheme such as quality improvement and assessment based promotion, retirement age, academic and faculty status for the librarians, lack of scientific promotion scheme for the professionals in the Non-UGC cadre, etc. are also the personnel aspects to be rectified as part of the re-engineering of the libraries.
17. While the educational and research institutions like central and many of the state universities, IITs, IIMs, IISc, research institutions under DRDO, CSIR, ISRO, DAE, State Governments, etc. have classified the library professionals as faculty and/or scientists, in many universities they have been grouped as non-teaching and non-academic staff.
18. While digital preservation poses several challenges such as short media life, obsolete hardware and software, etc. in the life long or permanent preservation, it is high time to frame policies and working plan at national level and also at the university or institution level to preserve our knowledge resources for the posterity.
19. The university libraries could not be able to provide attention for the documentation and development of bibliographical as well as full-text databases of the local content available.
20. Management of databases in multi-lingual formats is a major problem faced by the libraries. The

libraries either adopted transliteration for cataloguing the documents available in non- English language or left out such documents from cataloguing.

21. Availability of good and cheap Library Management Software is an urgent necessity. Most of the libraries are facing problems in the network administration, software updation and maintenance, multilingual issues, etc.
22. In all libraries, the management of modern ICTs is vested with few professionals and other staff member have either not shown enough interest in these aspects or they have been automatically sidelined because of lack of training and confidence in handling such systems.
23. While the demand for in-house training and continuous Professional Development Programmes (PDP) is high, most of the libraries are not able to rise to the requirements. The infrastructural facilities and expert manpower available in the libraries for such training programmes are also poor. Even though the required facilities like computers, multimedia laboratory, LCD projector, high speed Internet, separate space, etc. can be commonly used both for PDP and ILP, the authorities have failed to arrange good facilities towards this purpose.
24. Though the quality of teaching-learning process in schools is a basic determinant of quality of higher education system, school libraries, especially that in state government controlled schools, are facing utter neglect. Most of the libraries in such schools are confined to book stock in few shelves. No minimum essential facilities and library hours for students to read and use the library and the available information resources. Moreover, most of the

libraries in state government controlled schools are manned by teachers in other subjects as compulsory additional charge and they are neither interested in library work nor trained or professionally capable. Lack of facilities and reading environment of this type causes separation and moving of creamy layer of comparatively good students to CBSE and ICSE controlled schools which in turn reduce the chances for competitive learning in state controlled schools. This phenomenon severely affects the quality of education of students, especially those from rural and backward families and regions. This situation not only affects the reading skills and quality of education of the students in schools but also in colleges and universities. Some CBSE/ICSE schools in the many states run the libraries only for name sake as a demo peace to meet the requirements of the controlling agencies. There are cases also where management insists the librarians to have BEd qualification also along with BLISc. This is mainly targeted to use these 'demo librarians' for handling classes in other subjects. In some cases, the management is utilizing the 'demo librarians' for office work. There are also cases of qualified librarians only in records. Since most of parents are not capable to evaluate the real quality of education that gets to their wards, they are satisfying with the 'window dressing' and 'demo education' and also with the high marks, grade cards and certificates. Of course, the parents financially and mentally capable to arrange libraries and reading rooms in their houses could help to excel their children.

25. Lack of proper Policies, Rules, Regulations, Guidelines, etc., regarding the establishment and maintenance of library and information systems and

services highly affected the sector. The prevailing involvement in this direction by the Union and State Governments, UGC and other Regulatory Bodies in Education, etc. are not effective to obtain best results.

6.2 RE-ENGINEERING AND RE-DEFINING PROCESS

As stressed by the National Knowledge Commission, the library and information system in the country has a vital role in transforming the country into a Knowledge Society. The university system in a country has to be viewed as an integral part of the society. And hence, actions and happenings in many other sectors have direct bearing and impact on this system. Since several operators are playing in the university system in India, all of them could be controlling agencies and patrons of it. Hence, the process of re-engineering and re0defining has to be addressed with the patronage of Government of India, University Grants Commission, State Governments, concerned Universities, University Libraries, Library Professionals, Library Schools and finally the Users of the Libraries.

6.2.1 Role of Government of India

1. As a constitutional commitment to their citizens, the Government of India should ensure by Act the establishment and efficient functioning of an Integrated National Library and Information System (INLIS) which should comprise of school libraries, college libraries, university libraries, research libraries and public libraries because interlinked services from all these libraries are basically needed for the integrated development of a citizen in different stages of his life. There should be a permanent statutory national commission to control INLS.

2. Instead of functioning in isolation, all the above mentioned constituent library systems should work in active partnership and complementary role. Hence, a National Policy and Plan of Action on Library and Information Services should be framed to achieve the above target within a phased period of not more than ten years.
3. Functional arrangements at national level for effective library co-operation and pooling and sharing of information resources between Public, Academic, Research and Special Libraries should be made.
4. As education is a life long process, legislation for Integrated Public Library System in India should be made by which 24 hours functioning of the National Library, minimum 12 hours working of State and District libraries in all states and districts and minimum six hours (2-8 pm compulsory) working of Local / Panchayath libraries should be ensured. The public library service should be made available free of charge to all citizens of the country and the fund for the development and maintenance of the library system should be mobilized through Library Cess.
5. As regulatory and accreditation mechanism on Library and Information Science Education and Research, the Library Council of India (LCI) should be constituted by central legislation.
6. The Delivery of Books and Publications Act should be amended to include information content in all formats and the collection and registration of all information documents should be legally entrusted to the District Libraries coming under the INLIS. It should be obligatory with penal clauses on the part of all content generators and publishers to deposit

and register the documents through their respective district libraries. The District Librarians should issue Registration Certificates after including the document in the Indian National Bibliography (INB). The INB may be developed and maintained as a distributed system in the model followed by OCLC for the development of World Catalogue. It is ideal to establish distributed district level fulltext repositories of these information documents.

7. The major hurdle in pooling and sharing of information resources in India is the lack of union catalogues under the respective library systems. Effective mechanism should be made by the Government of India to develop and maintain Union Catalogues by each library systems in the country such as Public Libraries, University and College Libraries, School Libraries and each group of Research Libraries under ICAR, CSIR, DRDO, ISRO, DAE, ICMR, ICSSR, etc. Since almost all expenditure for the development and maintenance of academic, research and public libraries in India is met from the public exchequer, the government should ensure the development of the system on scientific lines with maximum efficiency at minimum cost.

8. Another area in which strict directions and effective implementation needed is the national level Library Consortia for e-journals. In the present world of inter disciplinary nature of education and research, students, teachers and scientists need all types of documents irrespective of subject restrictions. So, it is ideal to form a single Indian Library Consortium for Higher Education and Research. Since this involves cumbersome process in implementation and

maintenance, it is essential to establish at least separate national e-journals consortia for Public Libraries; University and College Libraries; School Libraries; and Research Libraries with full coverage and compulsory participation of all institutions under each category. The government should provide enough budget allocation to the Inflibnet for extending the e-journals consortia to all universities and colleges in the country.

9. Coordinated efforts and action plan should be made for the development and maintenance of local and indigenous content in electronic format for research reports, theses, patents, standards, government orders, judicial records, etc. The efforts like National Programme on Technology Enhanced Learning (NPTEL) should be strengthened and this should be extended to other sectors also. Legislation for Open Archiving of these documents may be made.

10. Support for development and training on open source or free software for Library Management; Open Archiving; Digital Library Development, etc. may be done in collaboration with agencies like UNESCO, universities and research institutions, Inflibnet, Library Associations, etc.

11. In order to clear the prevailing confusion regarding the designations of different categories of librarians, the Central Pay Commission or the Government of India should consider the implementation of uniform and distinctive pattern of designation for the Library and Information Science Professionals in the country.

12. Since the quality of teaching-learning process in schools is a basic determinant of quality in higher education system, the Government of India should ensure functional libraries of required standard in

all schools in the country.

13. While digital preservation poses several challenges such as short media life, obsolete hardware and software, etc. in the life long or permanent preservation, it is essential to frame policies and working plan at national level and also at the university or institution level to preserve our knowledge resources for the posterity. Traditional proven or well known media such as paper, micro fiche, micro film, etc. may be considered for the permanent preservation of at least one copy of our information resources.

6.2.2 Role of UGC or Controlling Agencies in Education

1. Mandatory clauses should be included in the UGC Regulations for the establishment, development and maintenance of libraries with the required minimum infrastructure and other standard facilities in terms of documents, services, staff, fund, etc. in all universities, deemed universities, colleges and similar institutions of higher education in the country, including those in medicine and allied sciences, veterinary science, agriculture, engineering, technology, education, management, law, etc. Penal clauses should also be there to enforce this by way of fine, withdrawal of affiliation/ approval/ accredidation, etc.
2. As part of the Regulation, UGC should prepare and notify the standard norms for university/deemed university, college and department libraries which should specify the required provisions and facilities such as space, furniture, ICT facilities, connectivity, staff, proportion of budget and library fees on total

budget and total fees, minimum working hours, services, etc. Evaluation of the universities/ deemed universities, colleges, departments and courses should be done by the accreditation agencies like NAAC, NCTE, AICTE, IMC, VCI, etc. based on these regulations also. There should be effective mechanism to revise the norms at least once in five years.

3. Insist standardization and benchmarking for university and college libraries and their services with regular audit and penalty; linked with grant, grading, recognition, etc.
4. The UGC E-Journals Consortium should be extended to all universities in the country, including the agricultural universities with maximum access provision. At the same time, it should be mandatory and obligatory on the university libraries to provide journal article service free of charge through e-mail to all students, teachers and scientists under the university and its affiliated colleges and institutions. In order to provide effective service, websites should be hosted by all university libraries with provision for electronic acceptance and clearing of requests by the users. In order to ensure proper implementation of the system, automatic electronic audit mechanism may be insisted in the websites by the UGC.
5. The UGC E-Journals Consortium should be extended to all universities/ deemed universities, colleges in the country, including the agricultural colleges and research stations with minimum access provision. Essential journals and other documents like encyclopedia, dictionary, etc. which are need frequently by all the students, teachers and scientists may be identified and included in this service.
6. As a means to adopt student centred teaching-

learning process, guidelines should be given to the universities to introduce library oriented teaching, learning and evaluation methods.

7. User education and Information Literacy Programmes; with stress on modern ICTs, national and international library and information systems, digital libraries, online databases and other web resources, information retrieval software, tools and techniques, etc.; should be included as a compulsory course in the syllabus of first semester for all under graduate, post graduate and research courses of the universities and deemed universities. This course should have enough practical sessions to train students in the use of classification scheme and catalogues, retrieval of information in different formats, evaluation of accessed information, etc.
8. The College Libraries should be re-named as the Department of Library and Information Services and made them as Statutory Teaching Departments and required number of staff in the UGC and Non-UGC cadres should be ensured.
9. The designations of the library positions in UGC Cadre should be changed as follows:
   i. Assistant Professor & College Librarian / Assistant Librarian;
   ii. Associate Professor & College Librarian / Deputy Librarian;
   iii. Professor & University Librarian
10. In the context that large number of post of University Librarian are vacant and this situation is prevailing for long period all over the country, the UGC should issue strict directions to fill up these posts immediately.
11. Since the experience criteria fixed by UGC for the

recruitment of University Librarian was 18 or 15 years experience in the post of college librarian or deputy librarian respectively, this is leading to dearth of enough qualified and competent candidates. Hence, these norms should be amended as 18 years in any professional or semi-professional cadre in university or research libraries of equivalent status and the candidate applying for the post should be in the UGC Cadre of Deputy Librarian or higher. PhD should be made as the compulsory qualification for the post of Associate Professor & Deputy Librarian and also for Professor & University Librarian.

12. Refresher courses for the teachers in library science/ librarians should give more stress on modern ICT topics like library automation and networking, hardware and software, WiFi and WiMax technologies, development of digital libraries and institutional repositories, website construction, web hosting and maintenance, web server and security aspects, knowledge classification, retrieval and management in web environment, etc. Weightage should be given for practical sessions and hands on learning rather than the theoretical presentations. It will be ideal if good libraries with all modern facilities and technologies have been identified for such courses.
13. Exchanging of teachers/librarians between countries for training and visit has to be enhanced and more number of scholarships may be instituted for such programmes.
14. As the library professionals in the Non-UGC Cadre are actively involved in the academic activities of the library, professional development of these people are equally important for the efficient and effective

functioning of the libraries. In order to catch and train them in the beginning, the UGC may introduce compulsory refresher courses of minimum one week duration in each promotion period for them.

15. It may be better to consider the implementation of Flexible Complementing Scheme of Career Advancement as prevailing in DRDO, CSIR, etc.; with suitable modification to avoid the personal influence on assessment process; for the Semi-Professionals employed in the libraries of the universities and colleges.
16. The UGC should insist by Regulation all research students and project coordinators for the compulsory deposit of one copy of their theses/dissertations or research reports in electronic format to the Theses and Report Repository to be maintained by the UGC. By this regulation, it should be obligatory on the part of all the universities to create Academic and Research Regulations to this effect and permitting the access and use the information content of the document through network or web to any student or researcher or scientist for his academic non-profit research programmes with due citation and acknowledgement for the author and the concerned university in the cited document. A unique Repository Document Number may be issued for successful online filing of the theses or report to be made either by the Registrar or University Librarian on behalf of the student or scientist. It should be made obligatory on the part of the universities to insist this Repository Document Number for accepting the theses and research reports from the students or scientists.

6.2.3 Role of State Governments and Universities

1. As library is an important facility which determines the quality of education and research, the government should earmark a separate fund for the establishment and maintenance of university and college librariaes with the required standard, ICT facilities, information resources in print and non-print, qualified and competent staff, etc.
2. As part of the government set up and as an advisory body of the government, the State Higher Education Councils shall effectively interfere in the formulation and implementation of standard, effective and uniform policies, regulations and guidelines for the establishment and maintenance of libraries in colleges and universities.
3. The University Regulation should have a provision to constitute University Library Committee, College Library Committee and Department Library Committee in the universities, colleges (including affiliated colleges) and postgraduate departments of the university respectively. The committee shall be chaired by the Vice Chancellor or Principal/Dean or Head of the Department of the concerned university, college or department and the Member-Secretary shall be the professional head of the concerned library. The members of the committee shall include representatives of the teachers and students from each faculty or course with due weightage. The committee shall have the authority to frame policies, guidelines, procedures for growth, development and general management of the concerned library.
4. The College Libraries shall be re-named as the Department of Library and Information Services and made them as the Statutory Teaching Departments and required number of staff in the UGC, Non-UGC

Semi-Professional and Non-Professional cadres should be ensured.

5. A uniform staff policy is essential for all university and college. Even after the implementation of UGC Scheme in India, lot of drawbacks exists in the implementation of the UGC-Scheme. Many litigation and court cases on appointment, seniority, and promotion, other staff management aspects, etc. are created because of lack of proper statutes and rules in this regard. Improper or non-implementation of UGC Career Advancement Scheme with regard to quality improvement and assessment based promotion, retirement age, academic and faculty status for librarians; lack of scientific promotion scheme for the professionals in the Non-UGC cadre, etc. are the personnel aspects need immediate attention of the State Higher Education Councils in order to revamp the university libraries. While the educational and research institutions like central and many state universities, IITs, IIMs, IISc, research institutions under DRDO, CSIR, ISRO, DAE, Government of Kerala, etc. have classified the library professionals as faculty and/or scientists, universities in some states grouped them as non-teaching and non-academic staff. Since this has demoralizing effect among the professionals, orders are required to classify the library professionals as academic and teaching faculty with equal designations and status. In order to avoid confusion prevailing among different categories and cadres of librarians in the state, the re-designation of all categories of library professionals, semi-professionals and non-professionals is necessary as given earlier.
6. The government should implement the UGC or

equivalent Central Government Scheme in strict sense for the librarians in all universities and colleges, including medical and engineering colleges and poly techniques, etc. There should be minimum one professional in the faculty cadre to head the libraries of all (i) constituent/affiliated colleges; (ii) university teaching teaching departments; and (iii) all divisions/departments of the university libraries.

7. All recommendations of the V.P. Joy Committee may be implemented on priority basis.
8. In order to settle the problems of UGC qualified librarians in the Non-UGC Cadre, limited departmental selection similar to that in DRDO, CSIR, etc. may be implemented in universities. By which candidates with 5 years' of service may be considred for promotion to the UGC Cadre. Universities shall introduce Professional Development Courses of minimum one week duration for them in each promotion period. Since the modern ICTs have a critical role in the functioning of the libraries and many professional are in need of development of practical and in-dept competencies in ICTs.
9. As a means to adopt student centred teaching-learning process, the State Higher Education Councils may persuade the universities to introduce library oriented teaching, learning and evaluation methods. Towards this, User education and Information Literacy Programmes; with stress on modern ICTs, may be included as a compulsory course in the syllabus of first semester of all under graduate, post graduate and research courses of the universities.
10. Since all the state universities are governed under

the strict control by the state government, in order to sanction staff positions to the libraries, government sanction is essential. As some university libraries are running with extreme shortage of sanctioned staff, the libraries are not able to extend their working hours for effective utilization of resources. Hence, it is necessary to study the situation by the concered State Higher Education Councils and the government may give necessary sanction for the optimum number of staff in the libraries.

11. In order to ensure smooth acquisition, access and management of documents in electronic form, the purchase and audit rules need to be revised by the governments. Since many foreign publishers and vendors insist on electronic payment for books and journals, such amendments are inevitable.
12. As school education is the feeder system to the colleges and universities, it is an immediate necessity to revamp the school libraries by ensuring standard facilities like space, documents, qualified librarians, ICT systems, etc. The reading skills of the pupil have to be inculcated in the primary level which will be fostered in the secondary and higher secondary levels. Minimum one period in a week should be allotted for library based learning. It is also needed to ensure LIS trained post graduates in higher secondary schools and LIS trained graduates in Secondary/Primary schools along with necessary supporting staff. Otherwise, the information and knowledge will be residing only in the documents and government orders.

6.2.4 Management Refinement by University Libraries

1. The functions of the University Libraries shall be re-defined and re-engineered to take up the challenges posed by the modern ICTs. The principles of BPR, Total Quality Management and Change Management should be targeted to achieve maximum efficiency in the changed environment and provide better services to the clientele with the available resources.
2. Re-structuring the conventional divisions of the university library is inevitable in order to enable smooth flow of work under the fully automated environment. Divisions divisions of the library should be defined with flexible assembly of functions and operations.
3. Provision of adequate orientation, education and training for all categories of staff in libraries is extremely important now. Hence, continuous professional development programmes with enough practical and stress on modern ICTs should be arranged within and outside the library.
4. Library Consortia has been proved to be more economical and efficient and hence the libraries may be resorted to consortia based operations for activities and services like acquisition, classification, cataloguing, e-journals, digital document delivery, etc. As far as possible, it is better to go for national level consortia and if not possible, may form regional or state or university level consortia.
5. Pooling and sharing of information resources, technical knowledge, management expertise, etc. are another area which needs special consideration by the libraries. Proper understanding and tie ups for resources sharing and Inter Library Services are essential to provide maximum service to the users.

6. As OPAC and WEBOPAC are the basic tools to know the users about the availability or accessibility of documents in the libraries, all libraries should develop these tools within a time frame.
7. All University Libraries need websites with Content Management System and the websites should hosts WEBOPAC of all documents available and accessible in the library. Any remote user should be able to access these tools and avail the facilities and services either free of change or on payment as the case may be. Members should be able to reserve and renew books, clear dues through online payment, etc. through the website. The library websites should be transformed as clearing centres for Information Exchange, Document Delivery Services (DDS) and Information Literacy Programmes.
8. The libraries should develop digital libraries, full text databases and institutional repositories of theses, dissertations, reports, articles, course materials, and other general documents.
9. It is necessary to adopt the principle of advertising and marketing of information resources and services which will automatically work as a quality improvement mechanism to a great extend.

6.2.5 Continuous Professional Development

1. As affirmed by Dr. S.R. Ranganathan, the users are kings and queens, the professionals should be able to serve the clientele with all sorts of sincerity, knowledge, enthusiasm, leadership, resources, technology, etc.
2. Though the profession of library and information science is a dynamic and challenging profession, in

order to succeed in this role, the professionals should be able to acquire and practice the latest technologies, especially the ICTs, associated with this. Continuous Professional Development is the only way to improve the skills and techniques involved in the profession.

3. In order to excel in the profession, over and above the professional competencies, the librarians should acquire several other general competencies such as diplomacy, language, communication and presentation skills, project management, personnel management, financial management, purchase management, public relation, research methodology, etc.
4. Educating the public, effective public relation is another major role the library professionals have to undertake because here the profession of librarian is filled with several classes and categories of people with diverse qualifications and different tasks and objectives. Most of the common people are unaware of the library profession and the real role they have to perform in the society. Moreover, vast majority of "Librarians", are non-qualified and non-trained and they are serving the field as librarians in public libraries. Moreover, in some states several posts of "Library Assistants" have been created in the colleges and few universities by re-designating the posts of Library Attenders and similar posts of Class IV. The interest, approach, and management style, etc. of these librarians or library assistants are totally different from the professional librarians. But, the public opinion and understanding about the profession is more associated with the style and

acations of the first group. So, in order to move against this social set up, a continuous and unified professional approach should be adopted by the individuals and associations to educate the common man, politicians, administrators, educators, etc.

6.2.6 Re-structuring of LIS Education

1. As the basic strength of a library professional is largely depend on the competencies imparted through the library and information science courses. In the era of ICTs, modern librarian requires several specialized skills associated with this. But, it was observed that there is a wide gap between the needed competencies and those imparted through the courses. Most of the library professionals were not fully equipped to efficiently undertake the challenges posed by the modern ICTs in information management. So, LIS courses should be restructured to imbibe enough technical competencies among the professionals by including more ICT based modules such as hardware and software, network administration, communication technologies, web programming, web designing, web serving and hosting, digital libraries, etc. General modules such as education psychology, communication and presentation skills, public relations, project management, technology management, etc. are also needed by the modern librarians.
2. The process of review of curriculum should take place on a regular basis, preferably once in two years. The review also should take into account the needs and opinion of the employers, practitioners, professional associations, library users, etc.
3. As the modern courses on library education calls for more weightage on information, knowledge, ICTs,

technology management, etc., most of the papers and modules of LIS and Documentation courses are having pure science or applied science orientation. Moreover, a modern librarian should have in-depth knowledge in subjects like computer science, ICT, digital libraries, mathematics, statistics, management, psychology, etc., it may be idel to offer the courses under the faculty of science or technology. Re-designing the LIS courses and change of name of the course from MLISc into MSc/MTech in LIS or Documentation is to be finalized after wider discussion under various forums.

4. Inclusion of project work and internship of minimum 1-3 months duration as compulsory modules in the LIS undergraduate and postgraduate courses will help to imbibe enough practical knowledge.
5. As there is no effective mechanism in vogue to fix, measure and control the standard of LIS courses offered in India, constituting a statutory body, named, Library Council of India (LCI), may be established to look after such matters. Since this is an urgent need, the work of standardization and accreditation of LIS courses may be entrusted immediately to the AICTE or NCTE till the establishment of Library Council of India.

6.2.7 User Empowerment for Knowledge Management

1. Effective management of universal knowledge is an important and fundamental process that leads the individual or institution or societies to real success. Hence, the acquisition and management of more and more nascent knowledge becomes a life long need. At the same time, the knowledge management will become complicated according to the speed in the

process of knowledge generation. Hence, the users can play a complementary role with the librarians or knowledge intermediaries in the process of knowledge dissemination and management.

2. Since the role of users in a library is that of patrons, they can do a lot for the growth and development of the library by the process of mutual enrichment. Utilizing the existing the resources and demanding for maximum and quality services is the approach they can adopt for mutual benefit.
3. Proper awareness of the users on other successful library information systems within and outside the country will help to identify the rights and raise the demands by the users clearly.
4. The common behaviour of the users to settle with the available information resources will lead to the reduction of quality of education and research in which they are involved. Missing a single piece of relevant information may lead to duplication of research and development efforts and prolong the completion of projects. Hence, control over all relevant information resources and its accessibility is a basic necessity for all research programmes. The users should be able to raise their demands effectively and persuade the library professionals to make available the required resources either through internal sources or through inter library loan.
5. Since the User Education and Information Literacy is an important aspect, the users should actively participate in such programmes. The users should be able to identify the needed training areas and topics and request for their arrangement by the library.

References

Abrahamson, E. (1996). Managerial fashion. Academy of Management Review. 21(1), 254-285.

ACRL (Association of College and Research Libraries) (2000). Information literacy competency standards for higher education. Chicago: Association of College and Research Libraries. http://www.ala.org/acrl/ilcomstan.html. (Accessed on 25-12-2006).

ACRL (Association of College and Research Libraries) (2004). *Guidelines for Distance Learning Library Services*. Chicago: Association of College and Research Libraries. http:// www.ala.org/ ala/ acrl/ acrlstandards/ guidelinesdistancelearning.htm. (Accessed on 14-08-2005).

Ahmed, N.U. and Montagno, R.V. (1996). Operations strategy and organizational performance: an empirical study. International Journal of Operations & Production Management. 16(5), 41-53.

ALA (American Library Association) (1989), Presidential Committee on Information Literacy. *Final report*. American Library Association, Chicago, IL. http://www.ala.org/acrl/nili/ilit1st.html\. (Accessed on 20-12-2006).

ALA (American Library Association (2000). The

Information Literacy Competency Standards for Higher Education http://www.ala.org/ ala/acrl/ acrlstandards/standards.pdf.

Ali, Naushad P.M. and Hassan, Md Eshan (2003). The use of electronic services at IIT Library Delhi: a study of users' opinion. IASLIC Bulletin. 48(2), 71-82.

All India Council for Technical Education (AICTE). http://www.aicte.ernet. in/AboutAICTE.htm. (Accessed on 15-03-2006)

Allweyer, T. (1998). "Modellbasiertes Wissensmanagement", IM Information Management and Consulting. 13(1), 37-45.

Al-Mashari, M. and Zairi, M. (2000). Revisiting BPR: a holistic review of practice and development. Business Process Management. 6(1), 10-42.

Al-Mashari, M., Irani, Z. and Zairi, M. (2001), Business process reengineering: a survey of international experience. Business Process Management Journal. 7(5), 437-455.

ALPS (The Association of Learned and Professional Society Publishers) (2006). http://www.alpsp.org/ default.htm. News release: http://www.alpsp.org/ publications/SPP2press.pdf. Executive summary: http://www.alpsp.org/ publications/ SPP2summary.pdf> Report description: http:// www.alpsp.org/ publications/ pub13.htm. (Accessed on 04-07-2006).

Ameen, Kanwal (2006). Collection Management Policy (CMP): a Framework to achieve library goals. Pakistan Journal of Library & Information Science, 2006(7), 69-86.

Andhra Pradesh (2003). Government Order. G.O.Ms.No.35 dated 16-06-2003.

Andraski, J.C. (1994). Foundations for successful continuous replenishment programs. International Journal of Logistics Management. 5(1), 1-8.

André, Pamela, Q.J. and Pisa, Maria G. (1994). Managing National Resources in a Time of Change: the National Agricultural Library Perspective. Library Management. 15(7), 16-22.

Antony J. and Banuelas, R. (2001). Six sigma: a business strategy for manufacturing organisations. Manufacturing engineering. 80(3), 119-121.

Antony J. and Banuelas, R. (2002). Design for six sigma: a breakthrough improvement strategy for achieve competitive advantage. Manufacturing engineering. 81(1), 24-26.

Arunachalam, Subbiah, (2006). LIS-Forum News. *lis-forum@ ncsi.iisc. ernet.in*. (Accessed on Sept. 08, 2006).

Association for Automatic Identification and Mobility (2007). http:// www. aimglobal. org/technologies/rfid/ what_is_rfid.asp. (Accessed on 10-08-07).

Association of Indian Universitites (2010). Universities handbook 2010. 2 volumes.

Badiger, S. (2001). Reengineering Ramnarain Ruia College Library: a transition phase between old expectations and new opportunities. SRELS Journal of Information Management. 38(4), 295-300.

Bar Council of India. http://barcouncilofindia. nic.in/. (Accessed on 16-02-2006).

Bargellini, Maria Laura and Bordoni, Luciana (2001). The role of the library in a new learning scenario. Electronic Library. 19(3), 153-157.

Bavakutty, M., Abdul Majeed, K.C. and Nasirudheen T.P.O. (2008). Future librarianship in knowledge society. New Delhi: Ess ess Publications. 480p.

Beer, Sue. (2004). Information Flow and Peripherality in Remote Island Areas of Scotland. Libri. 54(3), 148–157.

Bertot, John Carlo, McClure, Charles R. and Ryan, Joe (2000). Statistics and Performance Measures for Public Library Networked Services. Chicago, London: American Library Association. ISBN-13: 978-0-8389-0796-2, 102p.

Billington, James H. (2006). UNESCO and US Library of Congress meeting on World Digital Library Project. (01-12-2006, Paris). http://www.loc.gov/about/welcome/ speeches/wdl/wdl_6-6-05.html (Accessed on 05-12-2006).

Biradar, B.S. and Sampath Kumar, B.T. (2005). Use of Internet by physicists in universities of Karnataka State: a comparative study. ILA Bulletin. 41(4), 25-40.

Biswas, Bidhan Chandra, Jalal, Samir Kumar and Ghosh, Bhabani Kumar (2003). Application of Total Quality Management (TQM) in Library and Information Services: an overview. IASLIC Bulletin 48(3). 167-177.

Bostick, Sharon L. (2001). Academic Library Consortia in the United States: An Introduction. Liber Quarterly. ??11(1), 6-13.

Bowers, M., Debeau-Melting, L., DeVries, J. and Schellinger, M. (1996). Organizational restructuring in academic libraries: a case study. Journal of Library Administration. 22(2/3), 133-44. DOI: 10.1300/J111v22n02_10.

Branin, J.J., D'Elia, G. and Lund, D. (1993). Integrated information services in an academic setting: the organizational and technical challenge. Library Hi

Tech. 44(4), 75-83.

Breaux, Ann-Marie and Dawson, Laura (2006). Striking thirteen: librarians, publishers, and book vendors better have their eyes wide open for the changes to come with the new ISBN-13. http://www.abreaux@ybp.com. (Accessed on March 01, 2006).

Brindley, Lynne (2006). Re-defining the library. Library Hi Tech.24(4),484–495.

Budapest Open Access Initiative (2002). http://www.soros.org/ openaccess/ read.shtml. (Accessed on 20-12-2007).

Byres, Fred R. (2003). Care and handling of CDs and DVDs: a guide for librarians and archivists. Washington: Council on Library and Information Resources, National Institute of Standards and Technology, USA, 42 p.

Cakar, Figen; Bititci, Umit S. and MacBryde, Jillian. (2003). A business process approach to human resource management. Business Process Management Journal 9(2), 190-207. http://www.emeraldinsight.com. DOI: 10.1108/14637150310468. (Accessed on 24-07-2006).

Campbell, Stephen and Kleiner, Brian H. (2001). New developments in re-engineering organisations. Management Research News. 24(3/4), 5-8.

Carpinetti, L.C.R., Buosi, T. and GeroÂlamo, M.C., (2003). Quality management and improvement: a framework and a business-process reference model Business-process reference model. Business Process Management Journal. 9(4), 543-554.

Casey, Michael E. and Savastinuk, Laura C. (2006). Library 2.0: Service for the next-generation library. Library Journal. 9/1/2006. http://www.

libraryjournal.com/article/CA6365200.html (Accessed on 17-06-2006).

Caudle, Sharon L. (1995). Reengineering for Results: Keys to Success from Government Experience. Washington: National Academy of Public Administration. 128p.

Central Council of Homeopathy (CCH). http://www.cchindia. com/ central_act.htm. (Accessed on 12-12-2006).

Central Council of Indian Medicine (CCIM). http://www.ccimindia.org/. (Accessed on 22-02-2007).

Chaudhry, Abdus Sattar (2006). Role of libraries in promoting E-learning: a review of Singapore initiatives. Pakistan Journal of Library & Information Science, 7 (2006), 57-67.

Chen, Kuan-Nien (2006). Library evaluation and organizational learning: a questionnaire study. Journal of Librarianship and Information Science, 38 (2), 93–104.

Chen, Derek H.C. and Dahlman, Carl J. (2004). Knowledge and Development: a cross-section approach, Washington: World Bank, 88p. http://www-wds.worldbank.org/servlet/WDSContentServer/WDSP/ IB/2004/08/31/ 000009486_20040831091103/Rendered/ PDF/wps3366knowledge.pdf (Accessed on 20-10-2006).

Chen, Derek H.C. and Kee, Hiau Looi (2005). A Model on Knowledge and Endogenous Growth. World Bank Policy Research Working Paper No. 3539. Washington: World Bank. http://www-wds.worldbank.org/external/default/WDSContentServer/IW3P/IB/2005/03/17/000112742_20050317091850/Rendered/INDEX/wps3539.txt (Accessed on 20-06-2007).

Chia, Christopher (2001). Transformation of libraries in Singapore. Library Review. 50(7/8), 343-348.

Chikate, Anil N. and Gadge-Chikate, Sharmila (2007). Internship: a study of the programme at DLISc of RTM Nagpur University, Nagpur. ILA Bulletin. 43(1), 19-27.

Childerhouse, P., Towill, D.R. and Disney, S.M. (2001), Industrial evaluation of a toolkit for engineering smooth material flow in supply chains. In *International Symposium on Logistics, Salzburg, pp. 157-164.*

Childerhouse P. et al. (2003). Information flow in automotive supply chains - identifying and learning to overcome barriersto change. Industrial Managemcnt & Data Systems. 103/7, 491-502.

Clark, T.M. and Hammond, J.H. (1997). Re-engineering re-ordering processes to improve total supply chain performance. Production and Operations Management. 7(3), 248-65.

Cleeve, Marigold (1995). The library is for turning: human resource management and re-engineering. Library Management. 16(4), 37-41.

Colaric, Susan M. (2003). Instruction for Web Searching: an empirical study. College & Research Libraries. March 2003, 111-122.

Comings, John, Garner, Barbara and Smith, Cristine, ed. (2007). Review of Adult Learning and Literacy: Connecting Research, Policy, and Practice, Volume 7: connecting research, policy and practice. Oxford: Routledge. 363p.

CONSER (2007). Cooperative ONline SERials. http:// www.loc.gov/ acq/conser/ aboutcn1.html (Accessed on 02-01-2007).

Corcoran (Janet) (2006). Writing and editing for the library website. FreePint Newsletter. 211(August 10, 2006). http://www. freepint. com/issues/ 100806.htm. (Accessed on 17-06-2006).

Cornel University Library (2007). http:// www.library.cornell.edu/ olinuris/ref/ research/ webeval.html (Acccessd on 04-04-2007).

Council of Architecture (COA). http://www.coa-india.org/ home/ home.htm (Accessed on 11-07-2007).

Council on Library and Information Resources (2005). Library as place: rethinking roles, rethinking space. Washington, D.C.: CLIR, 81p. http:// www.clir.org/ pubs/abstract/pub129abst.html. (Accessed on 18-04-2006).

Creth, S.D. (1993), Creating a virtual information organization: collaborative relationships between libraries and computing centers. Journal of Library Administration. 19(3-4), 111-132.

Crowley, Gwyneth H.; Leffel, Rob; Ramirez, Diana; Hart, Judith L. and Armstrong, Tommy S. (2002). User Perceptions of the Library's Web Pages: a Focus Group study at Texas A&M University. Journal of Academic Librarianship 28(July 2002), 205–210.

Crnkovic I., Asklund, U. and Persson-Dahlqvist, A. (2003). Implementing and Integrating Product Data Management and Software Configuration Management. ISBN:1-58053-498-8. London: Book Artech House Publisher.

CSIC, 2008a. Webometrics Ranking World Universities. http://www. webometrics.info/ (Accessed on 29-05-2008).

CSIC, 2008b. Ranking Web of World Repositories. http:// repositories. webometrics.info/top300_rep.asp (Accessed on 29-05-2008).

D'Angelo, Ed (2004). Barbarians at the Gates of the Library. http:// webjunction.org/do/ DisplayContent?id=8563. (Accessed on 27-09-2006).

Davenport, T.H. (1993). Process Innovation: Reengineering Work through Information.ISBN 0875843662. Boston, MA: Harvard Business School Press. 352p.

Davenport, T.H. and Short, J.E. (1990). The new industrial engineering: information technology and business process redesign. Sloan Management Review. 17(Summer), 11-27.

Demas, Sam (2005). From the Ashes of Alexandria: what's happening in the College Library?. In Library as Place: Rethinking Roles, Rethinking Space. Council on Library and Information Resources Washington, D.C., 25-40 p. (available at http://www.clir.org/ pubs/ abstract/ pub129abst.html) (Accessed on 17-08-2007).

Dennis, A., Wixom, B.H. and Tegarden, D. (2002). System Analysis & Design: an Object-Oriented approach with UML. ISBN 0471413879. Hoboken, New York: John Wiley & Sons, Inc. 544p.

Dental Council of India. http://www.dciindia.org/. (Accessed on 17-12-2006).

Dew, S.H. (2001). Knowing your users and what they want: surveying off-campus students about library services. Journal of library administration. 31(3/4), 177-193.

Distance Education Council (DEC). http://www.dec.ac.in/ powers_ funct.htm.

Doyle, Christina S. (1994). Outcome Measures for Information Literacy within the National Education Goals of 1990. Final Report to National Forum on Information Literacy. Summary of Findings. 84p. http://books.google. com/books?id= Z1IJ6A97WnsC& printsec= frontcover&dq=Doyle,+ C.S.+ (1992).+

Outcome+Measures+ for+ Information+Literacy+ within+the+ National+Education+Goals+of+1990.+ Final+Report+to+National+Forum+on+ Information+Literacy.+ Summary+of+Findings &ie=ISO-8859-1&output=html (Accessed on 20-12-2006).

Drucker, Peter F. (1994). Knowledge Work and Knowledge Society: the social transformations of this century. The 1994 Edwin L. Godkin Lecture. Harvard University's John F. Kennedy School of Government on May 4, 1994. http://books.google.com/ books?id= kDuEFn2hSw4C&pg=PA146&lpg= PA124&dq=Drucker+(1994).+ Knowledge+Work+ and+Knowledge+Society:+the+social+ transformations+of+this+century.+ The+1994+ Edwin+L.+Godkin+Lecture&ie= ISO-8859-1& output=html&sig= iyjZllZrAUK AwxwZbopc8c2S6lc (Accessed on 15-05-2006).

Dubey, Yogendra P. (2003). New challenges in information management and e-learning in the age of globalization: issues and opportunities. Library Herald. 41(2), 81-89.

Dubois, H.F.W. (2002). Harmonization of the European vaccination policy and the role TQM and re-engineering could play. Quality Management in Health Care 10(2), 47-57.

Economist Intelligence Unit (2006). The 2006 e-readiness rankings: a white paper from the Economist Intelligence Unit, written in co-operation with the IBM Institute for Business Value. London: Economic Intelligence Unit. http://a330.g.akamai.net/7/330/ 2540/ 20060424215053/ graphics.eiu. com/ files/ ad_pdfs/2006 Ereadiness_ Ranking_WP.pdf. (Accessed on 12-07-2007).

Economist Intelligence Unit (2008). E-readiness rankings 2008 maintaining momentum: a white paper from the Economist Intelligence Unit, written in co-operation with the IBM Institute for Business Value. London: Economic Intelligence Unit. http:// a330.g.akamai.net/ 7/330/25828/ 20080331202303/ graphics.eiu.com/upload/ibm_ ereadiness_2008.pdf (Accessed on 11-05-2008).

Eden, B. and Bierman, K.J. (2002). Knowledge Access Management at Lied Library: cataloguing and Web site re-engineering. Library HiTech. 20(1), 90-103.

Encyclopaedia Britanica (2007). http:// www.britannica.com/. (Accessed on 12-01-2007).

Federal Research Public Access Act of 2006 (2006). http:/ /cornyn. senate.gov/doc_archive/05-02-2006_COE06461_xml. pdf. (Accessed on 19-08-2007).

Field, C.D. (2001). Theory and Practice: Reflections on Convergence in United Kingdom Universities, Liber Quarterly. 11(3), 267–89. http://webdoc. gwdg.de/ edoc/aw/liber/lq-3-01/liber_quarterly_jg-11-2001-heft3.pdf. (Accessed on 12-10-2006).

Follett Committee Report (1993). http://www.ukoln.ac.uk/ services/papers/ follett/report. (Accessed on 10-19-2006).

Foster, Allan (2006). Convergence Counselling: Integration of IT Departments and Libraries. http:// www.freepint.com/issues/ 211206.htm. (Accessed on 22-12-2006).

Francis, A.T. (1993). COCHINET- a draft proposal for Cochin Library Network, In *Seminar on Library Networks in India, Bangalore, 12-13 August 1993,* edited by IK Ravichandra Rao. Paper/page K. Bangalore: DRTC-INSDOC, 1993.

Francis, A.T. (1997a). Regional Information Networks: necessary thrust area for INFLIBNET to establish integrated information system in India. In *"Information Technology Applications in Academic Libraries"* edited by Murthy & Mangala. P. 102-6. Ahmedbad: INFLIBNET/ UGC, 1997.

Francis, AT. (1997b). Personnel management in high-tech environment. In Sustainable University Library development by R. Raman Nair. New Delhi: Ess Ess Pub., 53-63.

Francis, A.T. (1998a). Integrated Agricultural and Rural Information System (IARIS): an evaluation of the existing Information System in Kerala. In *Towards the new Information Society of Tomorrow: Innovations, Challenges and Impact*. Ed by Malwad et al. P. III-153. New Delhi: FID – International Federation for Information and Documentation, 1998.

Francis, A.T. (1998b). Software problems of library automation in India. In *Information management in academic and research libraries*, edited by Mahapatra et al. Ahmedbad: INFLIBNET/UGC, 60-64.

Francis, A.T. (2005). Library consortia model for country wide access of electronic journals and databases. In *Multilingual computing and information management in networked digital environment, Third International Convention on Automation of Libraries in Education and Research Institutions (CALIBER), Kochi, February 2-4, 2005, Proceedings, edited by T.A.V. Murthy et al*. Ahmedabad: Inflibnet Centre/UGC, 497-504.

Francis, A.T. and Kabir, Humayoon S. (2008a). Re-engineering the Management of Human Resources in University Libraries. In *National Conference on Re-engineering Library and Information Services 1-2 February, 2008, Coimbatore, India.*

Francis, A.T. and Kabir, Humayoon S. (2008b). Re-defining Information Services through Library Websites: a study with special reference to the University Libraries in Kerala, India. (Paper submitted to the DESIDOC Journal of Library and Information Technology).

Francis, A.T., Razak, Abdul C. and Kabir, Humayoon S. (2006). Role of Information Professionals as Teachers and Trainers in Agricultural Education: an experience of the Kerala Agricultural University, India. In *Preparing Information Professionals for Leadership in the New Age: Asia-Pacific Conference on Library and Information Education and Practice (A-LIEP), Singapore, April 3-6, 2006, Proceedings, edited by C. Khoo, D. Singh and A.S. Chaudhry.* Singapore: School of Communication & Information, Nanyang Technological University, 642-644.

Francis, A.T., Sushama Devi, C.K. and Razak, Abdul C. (2007). Content Management for Digital Delivery of Agricultural Information: Redefining need of libraries in the context of digitization of theses and research reports. In *International Conference on Semantic Web and Digital Libraries (ICSD)*: Conference papers. Edited by ARD Prasad and Devika P. Madalli. Bangalore: Documentation Research and Training Centre/Indian Statistical Institute, 554.

Freeman, Geoffrey T. (2005). The Library as Place: changes in learning patterns, collections, technology, and use. In. *Library as Place: Rethinking Roles, Rethinking Space. Council on Library and Information Resources Washington, D.C.* pp. 1-9. http://www.clir.org/pubs/

abstract/ pub129abst.html. (Accessed on 13-11-2006).

Furey, T.R., Diorio, S.G. (1994). Making reengineering strategic. Planning Review. 22(4), 6-11.

Gadre, Asha and Satalkar, Vasudha (1997). Transactional Analysis (TA) and Library Profession: Egogram of an ideal librarian. ILA Bulletin. 32(3-4), 14-17.

Gaur, Ramesh C. (2002). Re-engineering library and information services: study of management libraries in India with special reference to Delhi, Gurgaon, Faridabad, Noida and Ghaziabad. Phd Thesis. Agra: B.R. Ambedkar University.

Gaur, Ramesh C. (2003). Re-engineering library and information services. Mumbai: Allied Publishers. 304 p.

Gosh, SB and Das, Anup Kumar (2006). Open access and institutional repositories – a developing country perspective: a case study of India. World Library and Information Congress: 72nd IFLA General Conference and Council, 20-24 August 2006, Seoul, Korea. http://www.ifla.org/IV/ ifla72/index.htm. (Accessed on 19-05-2007).

Gopinath, M.A. (1996), Education for digital information system: a courseware. In *Digital Libraries: Dynamic Storehouse of Digital Information, Papers presented at the SIS 1996; 15th Annual Convention and Conference, Bangalore, January 18-20 1996, edited by N.M. Malwad, N.M., T.B. Rajasekahr, I.K. Ravichandra, and N.V. Satyanarayana, N.V.* New Delhi: New Age International Publishers, 210-215.

Grassian, E.S. (2004). Information Literacy: Building on Bibliographic Instruction. American Libraries. 35(9), 51-53.

Grassian, E.S. and Kaplowitz, J.R. (2001). Information Literacy Instruction: theory and practice. ISBN 1-

555-70406-9. New York: Neal-Schuman Publishers, Inc. 468p.

Grimshaw, A. (1995). **BPR: the never ending process.** Information Management & Technology. 28(1), 26-27.

Grover, V., Jeong, S.R., Kettinger, W.J. and Teng, J. (1995). The implementation of business process engineering. Journal of Management Information Systems. 12(Summer), 109-144.

Gupta, Sangita (2007). Digital preservation: challenges and strategies. ILA Bulletin 2007, 42(4), 24-27.

Gupta, Sangita, Singh, Gurudev and Gopal, Krishan (2006). Blog: a recent online tool of information sharing and dissemination. ILA Bulletin 2006, 42(2), 5-9.

Habib, M. (2006). Conceptual model for academic library 2.0. *Michael Habib's weblog on library and information science*. http:// mchabib.blogspot.com/2006/06/conceptual-model-for-academic-library.html. (Accessed on 10-06-2006).

Hamel, Gary and Prahalad, C.K. (1993). Strategy as stretch and leverage. Harvard Business Review. 1993(March-April), 75-84.

Hammel, Todd, Kuettner, Dorothea and Phelps, Tom (2002). The re-engineering of Hewlett-Packard's CD-RW supply chain. Supply Chain Management: an International journal. 7(3), 113-118.

Hammer, M. (1990). Re-engineering work: don't automate, obliterate, Harvard Business Review. 1990(July-August), 104-112.

Hammer, *Michael and* Champy, *James A.* (1993). Reengineering the Corporation: a manifesto for business revolution. New York: Harper Business Books, *ISBN* 0887306403. viii, 231p.

Harnad, Stevan (2006). Peter Suber's Open Access News. *http:// www.earlham.edu/~peters/fos/2006_09_03_ fosblogarchive.html#115765784787267505* (Accessed on 08-09-2006).

Hendriks, Boyd and Wooler, Ian (2006). Establishing the return on investment for information and knowledge services: a practical approach to show added value for information and knowledge centres, corporate libraries and documentation centres. Business Information Review. 23(1), 13–25.

Higa, Mori Lou et al. (2005). Re-designing a library's organizational structure. College and Research Libraries. 66(1), 41-58.

Hosein, Sharida (2006). Teaching Information Literacy at the University of the West Indies in Trinidad. Information Development. 22(2), 110-115.

Hussain, Akhtar and Raza, Masoom M. (2002). Online Public Access Catalogue: its development, utility and limitations. IASLIC Bulletin 47(4), 204-209.

Hyde, A.C. (1995). A primer on process reengineering. The Public Manager, 1995(Spring), 55-68.

ICAR. Indo-American Agricultural Library Survey and Study Team, Final Report (1969). New Delhi: ICAR, 49-60.

I-Cube, IAMAI and IMRB International (2006). Press Release. http://www.iamai.in/ section.php3?secid=15&press_id= 1357& mon=11 (Accessed on 12-07-2007).

I-Cube, IAMAI and IMRB International (2007). Internet in India. http://www.iamai.in/Upload/Research/I-Cube-2007-Summary-Report-final.pdf (Accessed on 12-06-2008).

IFLA/FAIFE (2005). Libraries, National Security, Freedom

of Information Laws and Social Responsibilities, IFLA/ FAIFE World Report 2005, World Report Series Vol. V. Edited by Susanne Seidelin and Stuart Hamilton. Copenhagens: IFLA/FAIFE Office. http:// www.ifla.org/faife/report/ FAIFE-WorldReport2005. pdf. 406p. (Accessed on 10-05-2006).

IFLA/FAIFE (2007). Access to libraries and information: towards a fairer world. IFLA/FAIFE, IFLA/ FAIFE World Report 2007, World Report Series Vol. VII. Edited by Theo J.D. Bothma. Hague: IFLA. http:// www.ifla.org/ faife/report/ifla-faife_ world_report_ series_ VII.pdf. 480p. (Accessed on 30-05-2008).

IFLA/UNESCO (2006). IFLA/UNESCO Internet Manifesto Guidelines: September 2006. http://www.ifla.org/ faife/ policy/ iflastat/Internet-ManifestoGuidelines. pdf. (Accessed on 11-07-2007).

India, Advisory Committee Report (1959). Ministry of Education and Youth Services, Advisory Committee for Libraries. Chairman: K P Sinha. Report 1959. New Delhi, Govt of India, 1959.

India. Department of Higher Education. (2006). http:// education.nic.in/higedu.asp (Accessed on 10-05-2006).

India. Ministry of Food and Agriculture. Agricultural Universities in India. Report of the Cummings Committee (Chairman: R.W. Cummings), 1960-62. New Delhi, 1962, 28 p.

India. University Education Commission, 1948-49. Report. Delhi, Manager of Publications, 1949, 2 Vol. (Chairman: S. Radhakrishnan), 110.

India, Education Commission, 1964-66, Chairman: D.S. Kothari. Report. New Delhi, Government Press.

India. National Knowledge Commission, (2006). Report to the nation 2006.http:// knowledgecommission. gov.in/

downloads/ report2006/ eng/ NKC% 20Report% 20to% 20the%20Nation% 202006.pdf (Accessed on 26-09-2007).

Indian Academic Library Association (2008). Faculty status for academic library professionals: a concept document on the provision of faculty status to the library professionals in universities and colleges. Submitted to Pay Review Committee, UGC. Bangalore: IALA. 25p.

Indian Council for Agriculture Research. http:// www.icar.org.in/. (Accessed on 16-02-2006).

Indian Nursing Council. http:// www.indiannursingcouncil. org/. (Accessed on 11-12-2006).

International Engineering Consortium (2007). http:// www.iec.org/ online/ tutorials/ broadband_ media/.

Irani, Z., Hlupic, V. and Giaglis, G. (2000), Business process re-engineering. International Journal of Flexible Manufacturing Systems. 12(4), 247-52.

ITU (2005). http://www.itu.int/ ITU-D/ict/statistics/ at_glance/ top20_ broad_2005.html. (Accessed on 12-07-2007).

ITU (2006). Promoting Global Cybersecurity: ITU announces results of global survey and launches cybersecurity gateway on World Telecommunication Day 2006. Press Release. Geneva: International Telecommunication Union. www.itu.int/ newsarchive/ press_releases/2006/09.html. (Accessed on 12-07-2007).

ITU and UNCTAD (International Telecommunication Union and United Nations Conference on Trade and Development) (2007). World Information Society Report 2007. Geneva: ITU. 207p. http://www.itu.int/ wisr. (Accessed on 12-07-2007).

Jadav, Pralhad (2007). Building a Library Web Site on the Pillars of Web 2.0. http://www.infotoday.com/ (Accessed on 15-01-2007 through nmlis@yahoogroups.com).

Jaswal, Bushra Almas (2006). Impact of Digital Technology on Library Resource Sharing: revisiting LABELNET in the Digital age. Pakistan Journal of Library & Information Science. 2006(7), 87-104.

Jeal, Yvette (2005). Re-Engineering customer services: University of Salford Information Services Division. New Library World; 2005. 106(7/8), 352-362.

Jebaraj and Devadoss (2004). Library and Information Networks in India. Library Philosophy and Practice. 6(2) Spring 2004, 1-8.

Johnson, Ian M., Reid, Peter H. and Newton, Robert (2002). Guidelines for e-reference library services for distance learners and other remote users. Aberdeen: The Robert Gordon University. 120p. http://portal.unesco. org/ci/ en/files/17486/ 11000932541Guidelines_ for_e-reference_library_ services_ for_distance_ learners.doc/ Guidelines+ for+e-reference+ library+ services+for+ distance+ learners.doc. (Accessed on 20-10-2007).

Joint Steering Committee (JSC) for Revision of AACR, (2007). Resource Description and Access. http://www. collectionscanada.ca/ jsc/ rda.html (Accessed on 16-08-2007).

Kalam, A.P.J. Abdul (2006). World Knowledge Platform: a speech, at the IBM Investors Meet at Bangalore on June 2006. http://www.ciol.com/ content/ developer/ newsmakers/2006/106060701.asp?nl= 3_181844_Jun8. (Accessed on 12-06-2006).

Kaloo, U. and Towill, D.R. (1978), Productivity drift in extended learning curves. OMEGA, Vol. 6, 295-304.

Kahle, Brewster (2005). Towards universal access to all knowledge—Internet Archive. Journal of Zhejiang University Science. 6A(11), 1193-1194.

Karnataka State College Librarian's Association (KSCLA) (2006). http://geo.yahoo.com/serv?s=97490479& amp;grpId= 13132242& amp; grpspId=1600079640& amp;msgId= 669& amp;stime= 1153825321 (Accessed on 16-08-2006).

Kaur, Amritpal (2000). Five Laws: their relevance in Information Technology environment. ILA Bulletin. 2000(1), 24-27.

Kerala Agricultural University, Report of the Expert Committee on Staff Pattern for KAULIS (1999). (Convener: R. Raman Nair). Thrissur: KAU, 78p.

Kerala, Expert Committee on College Libraries (1994), Convener: V.P. Joy. Report. Trivandrum, 1994.

Kerala (1999). Government Order No. G.O.(P). 82/99, dated 02-08-1999. Trivandrum.

Kerala (2006). Government Order No. G.O.(P). 125/06, dated 17-03-2006. Thiruvananthapuram.

Kerala (2008). Government Order No. G.O.(MS). 50/08/ H.Edn, dated 09-05-2008. Thiruvananthapuram.

Khare, Anand (1976). Innovation success and creative thinking. Bangalore: Bablu Books Company. 157p.

Khong, K.W. and Richardson, S. (2003). Business process re-engineering in Malaysian banks and finance companies. Managing Service Quality Volume 13(1), pp. 54-71.

Kini, Srinivasa Narasimsha (2002). Information discovery in distributed systems: a novel concept based on modelling of information elements. PhD Thesis. Cochin: Department of Computer Science, Cochin University of Science and Technology. 176p.

Kock, N. (2003). Communication-focused business process redesign: assessing a communication flow optimization model through an action research study at a defense contractor. IEEE Transactions on Professional Communication. 46(1), 35 – 54. DOI: 10.1109/TPC.2002.808350.

Konnur, P.V. and Bhandi, M.K. (2004). Academic Libraries for the 21st Century. 2nd International *Convention on Automation of Libraries in Education and Research Institutions (CALIBER),* New Delhi, February 11-13, 2004, Ahmedabad: INFLIBNET Centre/UGC.

Kotler, Philip (1999). Marketing management: analysis, planning, implementation, and control. 9th revised ed. Indianapolis: Prentice Hall 832p.

Krishan Kumar (2000). Library Manual, New Delhi: Vikas Publishing House, 386p.

Kumbar, Mallinath and Raju, Vasantha N. (2007). ILA Bulletin. 43(1), 13-18.

Kuny, Terry and Cleveland, Gary (1998). The Digital Library: myths and challenges. IFLA Journal. 24(2), 107-113. DOI: 10.1177/ 034003529802400205.

Lawrence, Paul R. (1992). How to deal with resistance to change. In *People: managing your most important asset.* Boston: Harward Business Review, 36-44.

Lazarus, K. (1979). In *March of Library Science,* edited by V. Venkatappaiah. New Delhi: Vikas Publishing House Pvt. Ltd., 540-547.

Lebowitz (G) (1997). Library services to distant students: an equity issue. Journal of Academic Librarianship. 23(4), 302-308.

Lee, Sang M. and Asllani, Arben (1997). TQM and BPR: symbiosis and a new approach for integration.

Management Decision. 35(6), 1997, 409–416.

Lee, Kyong-Ho, Oliver Slattery, Richang Lu, Xiao Tang, and Victor McCrary (2002). The State of the Art and Practice in Digital Preservation. Journal of Research of the National Institute of Standards and Technology. 107 (1), 93–106. http://nvl.nist.gov/ pub/ nistpubs/jres/107/1/j71lee.pdf. (Accessed on 19-08-2005).

Lee, In (2004). Evaluating business process-integrated information technology investment. Business Process Management Journal. 10(2), 214-233.

Liang, C.C. and Yin, R.L. (1996). The infrastructure for academic information kaleidoscope: a comparison study of integrated information services in the University campuses in Taiwan and the United States. Paper presented at the Association for Educational Communication and Technology National Convention, Indianapolis, Indiana, February 14-18, 1996.

Liang, Chaucer Chaoyun (1999). Critical success factors for reinventing the academic library. Reference Services Review. 27(2), 127–133.

Lihitkar, Shalini and Rajyalakshmi, D. (2005). Computerization of Nagpur University Library and users' perception: a study. ILA Bulletin 2005. 41(4), 5-14.

Lombardo, Shawn V. and Miree, Cynthia E. (2003). Caught in the Web: the impact of Library Instruction on business students' perceptions and use of print and online resources. College & Research Libraries. 64(1), 6-21. http:// www.ala.org/ala/ acrl/acrlpubs/ crljournal/ back issues2003b/january031/ lombardo.pdf (Accessed on 20-10-2006).

Longue, Susan (2003). The Changing Role of Libraries in

Instructional Support. Information Technology and Libraries. 22(2). http://www.lita.org/ ala/lita/ litapublications/ital/2202editorial.cfm (Accessed on 18-03-2007).

Loughman, T.P., Fleck, R.A. and Snipes, R. (2000). A cross-disciplinary model for improved information systems analysis. Industrial Management & Data Systems. 100(8), 359-369.

Lumande, Edward, Ojedokun, Ayo and Fidzani, Babakisi (2006). Information Literacy Skills Course delivery through WebCT: The University of Botswana Library experience. International Journal of Education and Development using ICT. 2(1). http:// ijedict.dec.uwi.edu/viewarticle. php?id=96&layout= html (Accessed on 10-02-2007).

Lunin, L.F. and Ball, M.J. (1994). Redesign/reengineering of an information services division in a major health sciences institution: lessons learned at the University of Maryland at Baltimore. Journal of the American Society for Information Science. 45(5), 319-344.

Lunin, L.F. and D'Elia, G. (1991). Perspectives on integrated information centers within academic environments. Journal of the American Society for Information Science. 42(2), 116-151.

Maharana, B. et al (2004). Open Archives Initiative (OAI): Pros And Cons. In UGC Refresher Course on Information Technology for Librarians: proceedings, Mumbai, September 6-21, 2004. Mumbai: Tata Institute of Social Sciences.

Majka, D.R. (2000). The "great exchange": the economic promise and peril of the digital library. The bottom line: managing library finances. 13(2), 68-73.

Malone, Debbie and Videon, Carol (1997). Assessing Undergraduate use of electronic resources: a quantitative analysis of works cited. Research Strategies. 15 (43), 151-158.

Maness, Jack M. (2006). Library 2.0 Theory: Web 2.0 and its implications for Libraries. Webology. 3(2), June, 2006. http:// www.webology.ir/2006/ v3n2/a25.html. (Accessed on 28-08-2006).

Martey, AK (2002). Management issues in library networking: focus on a pilot library networking project in Ghana. Library Management. 23(4/5), 239-251.

McClure, Charles R. et al. (2002). Statistics, Measures, and Quality Standards for Assessing Digital Reference Library Services: guidelines and procedures. Information Institute of Syracuse, New York and Studies Syracuse University Information Use Management and Policy Institute, Florida. P. 104.

McGahan, A.M. (2004). How industries change. Harvard Business Review. 82(10), 87-94.

McGillis, Louise and Toms, Elaine, G. (2001). Usability of the Academic Library Web Site: implications for design. College & Research Libraries. 62 (July 2001), 355–367. http://www.ala.org/ala/ acrl/acrlpubs/ crljournal/ backissues2001b/july01/mcgillis.pdf (Accessed on 13-07-2006).

McGuinness, Claire (2007). Exploring strategies for integrated information literacy: from "academic champions" to institution-wide change. Communications in Information Literacy. 1(1), 26-38.

Meachen, E. (1997). Positioning the library for the future. College & Undergraduate Libraries. 4(1), 1-13.

Medical Council of India. http://www.mciindia.org/. (Accessed on 11-10-2006).

Mittal, Savitha (2005). Digital library resources. New Delhi: Ess Ess Publications. 282p.

Morgan, Steve (2001). Change in university libraries: don't forget the people.' Library Management. 22(1/2). 2001. pp. 58-60.

Moran, Barbara B. (2001). Restructuring the university library: a North American perspective. Journal of Documentation. 57(1), 100-114.

Moyo, Lesley Mutinta and Cahoy, Ellysa Stern (2003). Meeting the needs of remote library users. Library Management. 24(6/7), 281-290.

Murdock, Jeanne (1995). *Re-engineering* bibliographic instruction: the real task of information literacy. Bulletin of the American Society for Information Science & Technology. 21(3), 26-27.

Murphy, Marcy (1991). "Preface." In *Special Libraries Association. Future Competencies of the Information Professional*. Washington, DC: SLA. (SLA Occasional Paper Series, Number One), v-vi.

NAAC (National Assessment and Accreditation Council), India (2006). Library and information services: case presentations. Best Practice Series. Bangalore: NAAC. 79p.

Nandi, Atin and Panigrahi, Pijushkanti (2005). Library services in the Dot Com era: its protection against cyber crimes. IASLIC Bulletin, 50(2), 116-124.

National Agricultural Library (2008). National Agricultural Library: Advancing access to global information for agriculture. NAL Discussion Paper Blue print for success: the National Agricultural Library 2008-2012. 37p.http://www.nal. usda.gov/ about/reports/ nal_report_ web_041808.pdf (Accessed on 30-05-2008).

National Council for Teacher Education. http://www.ncte-in.org/ index.asp. (Accessed on 12-09-2006).

NCLIS (2006). http://www.nclis.gov/digitization/ Mass Digitization Symposium- Report.pdf. (Accessed on 12-06-2007).

Neelameghan, A. (1993). International and Regional Information Systems and Networks: examples of recent experiences in developing countries. In *Seminar on Library Networks in India, Bangalore, 12-13 August 1993,* edited by IK Ravichandra Rao. Paper/page A. Bangalore: DRTC-INSDOC, 1993.

Netcraft (2007). Survey of websites. http:// news.netcraft.com/archives/ 2007/ 04/02/april_2007_ web_ server_survey.html. (Accessed on 19-08-2007).

Netcraft (2008). Survey of websites http:// news.netcraft.com/ archives/ 2008/08/29/ august_2008_web_server_survey.html (Accessed on 04-09-2008).

NISO (National Information Standards Organization) (2008). RFID in US libraries. NISO RP-6-2008. www.niso.org/standards/ resources/ RP-6-2008.pdf. (Accessed on 12-02-2008).

Nissen, Mark E. (2001). Beyond electronic disintermediation through multi-agent systems. Logistics Information Management. 14(4), 256-275.

Nozero, Victoria A. and Vaughan, Jason, (2000). Ultilization of Process Improvement to Manage Change in an Academic Library. Journal of Academic Librarianship. 26(6), 416-421.

NPTEL (National Programme on Technology Enhanced Learning) (2006), India: Joint venture of IITs and IISc to provide study materials in engineering sciences and technology. http://nptel.iitm.ac.in/. (Accessed on 22-09-2006).

OCLC (2002). How academic librarians can influence students' Web-based information choices. OCLC White Paper on the Information Habits of College Students. OCLC Online Computer Library Center, Inc., June 2002, 12p.

OCLC (2006). Students' Perceptions of Libraries and Information Resources: a Report to the OCLC Membership. A companion piece to perceptions of libraries and information resources. http:// www.oclc.org/ reports/ 2005perceptions.htm (Accessed on 18-12-2006).

Ojedokun, A.A. and Lumande, E. (2005). The integration of information literacy skills into a credit-earning programme at the University of Botswana. African Journal of Library, Archive and Information Science. 15(2), 117–124.

Oladokun, Olugbade Samuel (2006). The Networked World of Lifelong Learning and the Challenging Role of the Library. Information Development. 22(2), 102-109.

Ongaro, E. (2004). Process management in the public sector: the experience of one-stop shops in Italy. The International Journal of Public Sector Management. 17(1), 81-107.

OPAL (2008). Online Programmes for All Libraries. http:/ /www.opal-online.org/ (accessed on 12-02-2008).

Open University Library (2001). SAFARI: Skills in Accessing, Finding and Reviewing Information. Open University Library, Milton Keynes, UK. http:// ltssolweb1.open.ac.uk/ safari/ signpostframe. htm. (Accessed on 15-04-2007).

Osmania University (2006). MLISc Syllabus. Revised Syllabus from the academic year 2006-2007. (Accessed through NMLIS Group on 01-08-2006).

Palmatier, G.E. (1988). Reducing uncertainties in demand.

APICS Conference Proceedings, pp. 102-107.

Pandya, Shweta N. (2002). Change management in libraries. ILA Bulletin 2002, 38(2), 32-35.

Papavassiliou, Giorgos and Mentzas, Gregoris (2003). Knowledge modelling in weakly - structured business processes. Journal of knowledge management. 7(2), 18-33.

Parekh, Harsha (2003). The digital movement: challenges and opportunities for librarians. ISALIC Bulletin 48 (1), 2003, 46-52.

Parvathamma, N. (2001). Digital divide in India: need for correcting urban bias. In *Digital Libraries: dynamic landscapes for knowledge creation, access and management. The Fourth International Conference of Asian Digital Libraries (ICADL), Bangalore, December 10-12, 2001, Conference Papers, edited by Shalini R. Urs, T.B. Rajashekar and K.S. Raghavan.* Bangalore: University of Mysore and Indian Institute of Technology, 448-449.

Peppard, J. and Rowland, P. (1995), Business Process Re-engineering, Prentice Hall, London.

Pharmacy Council of India. http://pci.nic.in/. (Accessed on 25-12-2006).

Pinfield, S. et al. (1998). Realizing the Hybrid Library. D-Lib Magazine, October 1998, http://www.dlib.org/dlib/october1998/10pinfield. html. (Accessed on 29-10-2005).

Polarose (2008). www.polarose.com (Accessed on 11-01-2008).

Ponzi, L. and Koenig, M. (2002). Knowledge management: another management fad?. Information Research. 8(1), Paper no. 145 (Available at http://InformationR.net/ir/8-1/paper145.html).

Prasad, A.R.D. (2007). Semantic Web technologies for meaningful information mapping and retrieval. IASLIC Bulletin 2007. 52(1), 25-34.

Prasad, V.S. (2006). Increase access to library resources. Hindu Report. Coimbatore. http://www.thehindu.com/2006/06/12/stories/2006061215770500.htm (Accessed on 12-06-2006).

Prasher, R.G. (1991). Managing university libraries. New Delhi: Today and Tomorrow's Printers & Publishers. 351p.

Probst, G., Raub, S. & Romhardt, K. (2000). Managing knowledge: building blocks for success. Chichester: John Wiley & Sons, Ltd.

Raina, Roshan Lal (2004). Conducting Continuing Professional Development Programmes (CPDPs) for LIS professionals in the area of quality management: an approach at IIML. ILA Bulletin 2004, 40(4), 5-8.

Rajyalakshmi, D. (2004). Information professionals – knowledge skills, for information management. ILA Bulletin 2004, 40(3), 5-12.

Raman Nair, R. (2006). Agricultural information service for the farmers and the public: a study. ILA Bulletin 2006, 42(3), 5-12.

Ramesh Babu, B. and Gopalakrishnan, S. (1998). Internet: a survey of its use in Chennai. In *Towards the new Information Society of Tomorrow: innovations, challenges and impact,* Papers presented at the 49th FID (International Federation for Information and Documentation) Conference and Congress, New Delhi, October 11-17, 1998, edited by NM Malwad et al. New Delhi: Indian National Scientific Documentation Centre, III-9-13.

Ranganathan, S.R. (1940). Reference service and bibliography, v. 1, Madras, Madras Library

Association, 1940, 25p. (Source: Library manual; Krishan Kumar. Vikas Publications).

Ranganathan, S.R. (1956). Mechanisation of library service. IASLIC Bulletin, 1(2), 12-17.

Ranganathan, S.R. (1957a). Five laws of Library Science, 2nd ed. Reprint in 1988. Bangalore: Sarada Ranganathan Endowment for Library Science, 449p.

Ranganathan, S.R. (1957b). Information service and imported confusion number one. IASLIC Bulletin. 2(1-2), (Reproduced in IASLIC Bulletin 49 (3), 2004, 131-139.

Ranganathan, S.R. (1968). Philosophy of 'Free Book Service for All'. Library Science with a Slant to Documentation and Information Studies. 29(3), 119-126. (Reprinted from: Free Book Service for All – an international survey, edition 1, 1968).

Rause, A. and Watson, D. (1994). Some Classic Theories of Organizations-Change, and their Implications for Business Process Innovation and Reengineering. Computer Science and Technology. 54, 513-523.

Ray, P. and Fry, M. (1993). Integrated management: Emerging trends and future challenges, *Eighth International Joint Workshop on Computer Communication (JWCC-8), Taipei, December 1993.*

Reddi, Usha Vyasulu (2006). Role of ICTs in Education and Development: Potential, Pitfalls and Challenges. In "Learning package on participatory adult learning, documentation and information networking (PALDIN): Participatory lifelong learning and information and communication technologies". New Delhi: Jawaharlal Nehru University, 173-186. (http://www.unesco.org/education/aladin/ paldin/pdf/course_02.pdf (Accessed on 30-08-2007).

Rehabilitation Council of India (RCI). http://www.rehabcouncil.nic.in/index.htm.

Rema Devi, T. (2005). Building up digital resources for effective E-Learning Programmes. In *Multilingual computing and information management in networked digital environment, Third International Convention on Automation of Libraries in Education and Research Institutions (CALIBER), Kochi, February 2-4, 2005, Proceedings, edited by T.A.V. Murthy et al.* Ahmedabad: Inflibnet Centre/UGC, 606-611.

Rodden, T. (1996). Populating the application: a model of awareness for cooperative applications. Proceedings of the International Conference on Computer Supported Cooperative Work (CSCW 1996), Boston, Massachusetts, 1996. pp. 87-96.

Romer, P. (1990). Endogenous technological change. Journal of Political Economy. 98(5), S71–102.

Romer, P. (1993). Economic Growth. In *The Fortune Encyclopedia of Economics*, edited by David R. Henderson. New York: Time Warner Books.

Saha, Karuna (1998). Interpersonal relations in Indian organizations and strategy and improving human responses: a study based on library organization. ILA Bulletin. 34(1-2), 15-19.

Salih, Muhammed T.K. (2004). Computerisation of university libraries in Kerala. PhD Thesis. Tenhipalam: Department of Library and Information Science, University of Calicut.

SALIS (2006). SALIS 2006 National Conference on *Initiatives in Library and Information Centres in the Digital Era*, Coimbatore, June 8-9, 2006, Recommendations. (Accessed as E-Mail on 09-07-2006 from: Arunachalam Hariharan, President,

SALIS <hariharan_ah@ yahoo.com> Message-ID: <20060710063204. 63361.qmail@ web39613.mail. mud.yahoo.com.

Sathyanarayana (2006). LIS-Forum News. *lis-forum@ ncsi.iisc. ernet.in* (Accessed on May 23, 2006).

Saxena, K.B.C. and Amal, A. (1995). Information technology support for reengineering public administration: a conceptual framework. International Journal of Information Management. 15(4), 271-293.

Sayers, Richard (2006). Principles of awareness-raising: Information literacy, a case study. Bangkok: UNESCO, 2006. 124 p. ISBN 92-9223-082-4.

Schafer, Jay and Thornton, Glenda A. (1999). From ownership to access: Re-engineering library services. Reference Librarian. 30(63), 25-40. DOI: 10.1300/ J120v30n63_02.

Schäffler, H. (2004). How to organise the digital library: reengineering and change management in the Bayerische Staatsbibliothek, Munich. Library Hi Tech. 22 (4), 340 – 346.

Schniederjans, Marc J. and Kim, Gyu C. (2003). Implementing enterprise resource planning systems with total quality control and business process reengineering Survey results. International Journal of Operations & Production Management. 23(4), 418-429.

Shah, P.C. (2005). Towards self-sufficiency through information marketing. IASLIC Bulletin 50(4), 2005, 195-200.

Shahid, *Syed Md.* (2005). Use of RFID Technology in Libraries: a New Approach to Circulation, Tracking, Inventorying, and Security of Library Materials.

Library Philosophy and Practice. 8(1) (Fall 2005). http:// www.webpages.uidaho. edu/~mbolin/ shahid.pdf. (Accessed on 09-08-2006).

Sharma, J.S. (1978). Library organization. New Delhi: Vikas Publishing House Pvt. Ltd. 196p. (Pp. 165-166).

Sharrow, M.J. (1995). Library and IT collaboration projects: nine challenges. Cause/Effect. 18(Winter), 55-56.

Shaw, Ralph R. and Krishna Rao D.B. (1957). Report on Library and Bibliographical Services for Agricultural Teaching and Research in India. New Delhi: ICAR, 59p.

Sherman (2006). Thirty three reasons why libraries and librarians are still extremely important. http:// www.degreetutor.com/library/adult-continued-education/ librarians-needed (Accessed on 04-05-2006).

Siddiqui, Asif Fareed (2002). Use of library collection in the Jawaharlal Nehru University Library, New Delhi. IASLIC Bulletin. 47(3), 149-161.

SLA (Special Libraries Association) (2003). Competencies for Information Professionals of the 21st Century Revised edition, June 2003. http://www.sla.org/PDFs/ Competencies2003_revised.pdf. (Accessed on 10-10-2006).

Smith, G. (2001). Aiming for continuous improvement: performance measurement in re-engineered technical services. Library collections, acquisitions, and technical services. 25(1) Spring, 81-92.

Somanathan Nair, K.P. (1997). A study of the attitude of the librarians in Kerala towards the use of Information Technology and information activities:

PhD Thesis. Trivandrum: Department of Library and Information Science, University of Kerala. 396p.

Somanathan Nair, K.P. (1998). SATTIT: a scale to measure professional librarians' attitude towards Information Technology. IASLIC Bulletin.43(2).1998, 59-66.

Sornam, Ally A. and Nagarajan (2004). Personality patterns of college librarians: a study. ILA Bulletin. 40(2), 5-10.

Soundararajan, K.R. (1979). Standards for library staff in college libraries. *In XXV All India Library Conference, Trivandrum, 14-18 May 1979, Working Papers. Symposium I: Formulation of necessary standards for different types of libraries in India, Paper 12, 8 p.* Trivandrum: Indian Library Association.

Spivey, Mark (2000). The Vocabulary of Library Home Pages: An Influence on diverse and remote end-users. *Information Technology and Libraries.* 19 (3), 151–56.

Sreekumar, M.G. (2005). Role of Internet in enhancing the resource sharing and enriching the information resources in the special libraries in India: an investigation. PhD Thesis. Tenhipalam: Department of Library and Information Science, University of Calicut.

Sreenivasulu, V. (2000). The role of a digital librarian in the management of Digital Information Systems (DIS). The Electronic Library Volume 18(1), 12-20.

Srinivasulu, B. (2006). Why can't we change MLISc degree to MSc degree. Accessed through LIS Forum, lis-forum@ncsi.iisc.ernet.in <2006060807 2033.0BAE4 E5BC7@ws7-2.us4.outblaze.com>. (Accessed on 08-06-2006).

Srivastava, Ranjana (2002). Information use pattern of

researchers in chemistry: a citation study. IASLIC Bulletin. 47(4), 185-192.

Suber, Peter (2002). Open access to the scientific journal literature. Journal of Biology. 1(1), 1-3.

Sullivan, Maureen (2004). Organization Development in Libraries. Library Administration & Management. 18(4), 179-183.

Tadasad, P.G. and Maheswarappa, B.S. (2001). Cataloguing practices among college libraries in Karnataka State. ILA Bulletin. 37(3), 92-100.

Towill, D.R. (1991). Engineering change, or is it change engineering? A personal perspective. Proceedings IEE, Part A. 4(4), 11-32.

TRAI (Telecom Regulatory Authority of India) (2007). Press Release – No. 35/2007. 17th April, 2007. http://www.trai.gov.in/trai/upload/ PressReleases/ 449/ pr17apr07no35.pdf. (Accessed on 12-07-2007).

TRAI (Telecom Regulatory Authority of India) (2008). Press Release – No. 27/2008. 24th March, 2008. http://www.trai.gov.in/trai/ upload/ PressReleases/549/ pr24mar08no27.pdf (Accessed on 02-05-2008).

UGC (1959). Report of the Library Committee, 1959. New Delhi: UGC, 228 p.

UGC (2006). http://www.ugc.ac.in/new_initiatives/ infonet.html. (Accessed on 22-09-2006).

UGC (2007). UGC Infonet Digital Library Consortia. Press Release. http://www.ugc.ac.in/notices/ press_release_inflibnet.PDF. (Accessed on 07-08-2007).

UIUC (2008). The Library of the University of Illinois at Urbana-Champaign. http://oai.grainger.uiuc.edu/ (Accessed on 22-09-2006).

UNESCO (2005). A manual on how to create a website.

New Delhi: UNESCO. http://portal.unesco.org/ci/ en/ files/ 20938/ 11401731359 How_Create_ Website. pdf/ How_Create_Website.pdf. (2006). (Accessed on 23-09-2006).

UNESCO (2008). Towards Information Literacy Indicators: conceptual framework prepared by Ralph Catts and Jesus Lau with a list of potential international indicators for information supply, access and supporting skills by UNESCO Institute of Statistics. Paris: UNESCO. 44p. http:// unesdoc.unesco.org/ images/0015/001587/ 158723e.pdf (Accessed on 30-05-2008).

UNESCO Institute for Statistics (2006). Education counts Benchmarking Progress in 19 WEI countries: World Education Indicators – 2006. Montreal: UNESCO Institute for Statistics. 143p.

UN-GIAD (2006). The Global Alliance for Information and Communication Technologies (ICT) and Development. (The programme was launched on 19 June, 2006 in Kuala Lumpur Malaysia). http:// www.un-gaid.org/. (Accessed on 22-06-2006).

University Grants Committee, Great Britain (1967), Committee on Libraries, Report, London: HMSO, 65p.

Valentine, Barbara (1993). Undergraduate Research Behavior: Using Focus Groups to Generate Theory. Journal of Academic Librarianship. 19(Nov. 1993), 300-304.

Varalakshmi, R.S.R. (2006). What is missing in LIS curriculum of India? Ideas for its transformation. Paper presented at the XXIII IATLIS (Indian Association of Teachers in Library and Information Science) National Conference on Building Curriculum with a Difference: A Vision for LIS

Education in the 21st Century, 23-25 November, 2006, Punjabi University, Patiala: Conference Report.

Veeran, M.C. (2004). A survey of organization, administration and utilization of university libraries in Kerala with special reference to Calicut Univeristy Library. PhD Thesis. Tenhipalam: Department of Library and Information Science, University of Calicut.

Veerankutty, Chelatayakkot and Jalaja, V. (2005). Effectiveness of name searching in Web OPAC: from Authority Control to Access Control. In *Multilingual computing and information management in networked digital environment, Third International Convention on Automation of Libraries in Education and Research Institutions (CALIBER), Kochi, February 2-4, 2005, Proceedings, edited by T.A.V. Murthy et al.* Ahmedabad: Inflibnet Centre/UGC, 348-357.

Venkatraman, N. (1994), IT enabled business transformation: from automation to business scope redefinition. Sloan Management Review. 1994 (Winter), 73-87.

Veterinary Council of India (VCI). http:// www.vci.nic.in/ index2.asp (Accessed on 11-07-2007).

Vijayakumar, J. K. and Vijayakumar, Manju (2002) E-journals in a networked environment: its impact on academic libraries in the digital millennium. In *Proceedings National Seminar on Library Co-operation in a Networked World* edited by Bavakutty M., Veeran, M.C.K. and Muhammed Sali T.K., Kozhikode, 75-82.

Vijayakumar, K. P. (2007). Manpower utilization in the University Libraries of Kerala: an evaluation. PhD

Thesis. Thriruvananthapuram: Department of Library and Information Science, University of Kerala.

VuFind (2007). The Library OPAC that meets Web 2.0. Villanova: Villanova University. http://www.vufind.org/ (Accessed on 20-09-2007).

WebJunction (2006). Trends in E-learning for Library Staff: a Summary of research findings. http://data.webjunction.org/wj/ documents/ 14077.pdf. (Accessed on 10-07-2007).

White, Sonya and Creaser, Claire (2007). Trends in scholarly journal prices 2000-2006: LISU Occasional Paper no. 37. Leicester shire: Loughborough University. 142p. http://www.lboro.ac.uk/departments/dis/lisu/pages/ publications/oup2.html. (Accessed on 12-09-2007).

Widén-Wulff, G. (2001). Informationskulturen som drivkraft iföretagsorganisationen (Åbo Akademi University Press, Åbo, 2001). (Adopted from Widén-Wulff and Ginman (2004). Journal of Information Science, 30(5), 448–458, Original not consulted).

Widén-Wulff, Gunilla and Ginman, Mariam (2004). Explaining knowledge sharing in organizations through the dimensions of social capital. Journal of Information Science. 30(5), 448–458. DOI: 10.1177/0165551504046997.

Whithead, R. (2001). Workflow and business process re-engineering: making the right journey and measuring and implementing change en route. Information management and technology. 34(6), 267-269.

Wiig, K.M. (1995), Knowledge Management Methods: practical approaches to Managing Knowledge, vol. 3. Arlington: Schema Press, 490p.

Wikipedia, 2007. Institutional Repository. http://en.wikipedia.org/ wiki/Institutional_Repository. (Accessed on 10-04-2006).

Willard, Terri and Andjelković, Maja (2005). A Developing Connection: bridging the policy gap between the Information Society and Sustainable Development. 2005 Manitoba: International Institute for Sustainable Development (IISD). ISBN 1-895536-77-4. 220p. http://www.iisd.org/ pdf/2005/ networks_dev_connection.pdf. (Accessed on 13-08-2006).

Wilson, T.D. (1998). Redesigning the university library in the digital age. Journal of Documentation, Vol. 54(1), 15-27. DOI: 10.1108/EUM0000000007159.

Wilson, Kerry M. and Halpin, Eddie (2006). Convergence and professional identity in the academic library. Journal of Librarianship and Information Science. 38(2), 79-91.

Williams, Helene and Zald, Anne (1997). Redefining roles: librarians as partners in information literacy education. *Information Research.* **3**(1). http://informationr.net/ir/3-1/paper24.html. (Accessed on 20-02-2006).

Wilson, Louis Round and Tauber, Maurice F. (1956). University Library, 2nd ed. New York: Columbia University Press, 25p.

Witten, Ian H. (2001). Visions of the Digital Library. In *Digital Libraries: dynamic landscapes for knowledge creation, access and management. The Fourth International Conference of Asian Digital Libraries (ICADL), Bangalore, December 10-12, 2001, Conference Papers, edited by Shalini R. Urs, T.B. Rajashekar and K.S. Raghavan.* Bangalore: University of Mysore and Indian Institute of Technology, 3-15.

Wright, Carol A. (2004). The Academic Library as a Gateway to the Internet: an analysis of the extent and nature of Search Engine Access from academic library home Pages. College & Research Librarier 65(4), 276-286.

WSIS (2005). World Summit on the Information Society: Outcome Documents Geneva 2003 – Tunis 2005. Geneva: International Telecommunication Union (ITU). 95p.

Xiaoyin-Zhang and Haslam, Michaelyn (2005). Movement toward a predominantly electronic journal collection. Library Hi Tech.23(1), 82-89.

Young, Doyle W., Pieters, Gerald R. and Cherin, David A. (1994). Building Centers for Learning. Human Resources Professional. 7 (July/August), 10-14.

YouTube (2008). www.YouTube.com

Zecubes (2008). www.zeecube.com

Zhuang, Yue-ting (2005). Digital libraries: a test bed for multimedia technology. Journal of Zhejiang University Science. 6A(11), 1201-1203.